I'll Be Back **Right After** This

I'll Be Back **Right After** This

My Memoir

Pat O'Brien

ST. MARTIN'S PRESS
NEW YORK

www.stmartins.com

The Library of Congress Cataloging-in-Publication Data is available upon request.

ISBN 978-0-312-56437-7 (hardcover)
ISBN 978-1-250-02123-6 (e-book)

St. Martin's Press books may be purchased for educational, business, or promotional use. For information on bulk purchases, please contact Macmillan Corporate and Premium Sales Department at 1-800-221-7945, extension 5442, or write specialmarkets@ macmillan.com.

First Edition: August 2014

10 9 8 7 6 5 4 3 2 1

To Sean,
this is who your daddy is

Contents

Toto, I've a feeling we're not in Kansas anymore.

—The Wizard of Oz

When alcoholics do drink, most eventually become intoxicated, and it is this recurrent intoxication that eventually brings their lives down in ruins. Friends are lost, health deteriorates, marriages are broken, children are abused, and jobs terminated. Yet despite these consequences the alcoholic continues to drink. Many undergo a "change in personality." Previously upstanding individuals may find themselves lying, cheating, stealing, and engaging in all manner of deceit to protect or cover up their drinking. Shame and remorse the morning after may be intense; many alcoholics progressively isolate themselves to drink undisturbed. An alcoholic may hole up in a motel for days or a week, drinking continuously. Most alcoholics become more irritable; they have a heightened sensitivity to anything vaguely critical. Many alcoholics appear quite grandiose, yet on closer inspection one sees that their self-esteem has slipped away from them.

—from *The Handbook of Medical Psychiatry* by David Moore

Preface

"Pat, There's This Tape"

On the morning of St. Patrick's Day, March 17, 2005, I woke up fully dressed, my shiny Louis Vuitton shoes still on my feet, two empty bottles of 1972 Silver Oak cabernet on my antique marble bed stand. I had no idea where I was or how I got there.

At the bottom of the bed stood a cluster of people, all of them watching me grimly. I blinked at them in a daze. What was going on? Through the familiar fog of another red-wine morning, I heard one of them speak as if from a mile away: "Pat, there's this tape."

I stared at him uncomprehendingly until his features came into focus. It was Ernie Del, my loyal attorney. Gathered round him stood the president of CBS Paramount; the executive producer of my show, *The Insider*; and several other suits I had no desire to see in my bedroom early in the morning. Between them, they had enough personal problems to commit most of them to a rehab, to an asylum, or to long-term marriage counseling. But, in this case, I was going somewhere. Indeed, I was waking up to an intervention. Me! Pat O'Brien.

The night before I had gone to bed on top of the world, the host of a hit entertainment show, proud father of a loving son, with a trophy girlfriend, an ex-wife whom I still spoke with, and a twenty-four-karat Hollywood lifestyle right down to the vintage sports cars in my garage. More than that, I was a household name not just for my interviews with the biggest names in showbiz but my years in sports, reporting and hosting the Olympics, the US Open Tennis Championships, the NFL (including four Super Bowls), the NBA on CBS, the World Series, and the Final Four. You name it and I had been there either on the sidelines or sitting in the hallowed hosting chair. I was at that moment, indeed, the "man." Or so I was told over and over in arenas and stadiums and on red carpets all over the world. I had worked hard to get here.

Within minutes I learned that all those years of work meant nothing. I went from hero to zero: one moment the center of my own star-studded universe, the next a blackout alcoholic in the midst of a sex scandal. I had left endless drunken voice mails with a woman I didn't even know telling her I wanted to, well, "fuck her"—and regrettably much more. Never mind that I didn't remember making the call or even know what a blackout was, but that was my famous voice, all right. The voice mails had been released to the media (details on that later) and had gone viral, replayed endlessly virtually everywhere but notably on shows like Howard Stern's. Hence the intervention—with a different twist—not to save me, but more important to this group, to save the show. One of them, Terry Wood, the Paramount executive in charge of programming, was screaming, "We have to save the franchise. We have to save the franchise." The problem was, although I was the franchise, nobody was asking me about my condition. There was no way out on this one. For the next few years I ricocheted from rehab to rehab, my fall precipitous, painful, and certainly not pretty.

What a fall it was.

I was the guy who numbered among his friends and acquaintances Magic Johnson, Paul McCartney, Ringo Starr, Jack Welch, Bill Clinton, Arnold Schwarzenegger, the Kennedys, the Eagles, Oprah Winfrey—actually she suggested I write my memoir—Dr. J, Michael Jordan, Bill Walton, Andre Agassi, Heidi Klum, Michael J. Fox, Gregory Hines, Diddy, Justin Timberlake, and Wilt Chamberlain. My career had so far spanned more than forty years, from the Vietnam War, four presidents, Watergate, and the Patty Hearst saga. The

Richard J. Daley years in Chicago and the Chicago riots, lunches with Johnny Carson and in a chapel alone with Pope John Paul II. Presidential conventions and inaugurations and a history book of news stories. Then there were the indelible sports stories, such as the rivalry between Magic Johnson and Larry Bird, Tonya Harding and Nancy Kerrigan, and John McEnroe and Bjorn Borg. I had discussed life with Arthur Ashe and consoled Muhammad Ali after his final fight in the Bahamas. I partied with Vitas Gerulaitis and got drunk with Mickey Mantle and, on the other side, was the first person to play golf with him after he got sober. Then there were the stars of Hollywood I had come to know, on and off dozens and dozens of red carpets. During my life in broadcasting I had ended up drinking with Madonna, singing with the Isley Brothers and the Temptations, swimming with Mark Spitz, dancing onstage with James Brown, chain-smoking with Charlie Sheen and with Catherine Zeta-Jones. There were Kevin Costner and Tiger Woods and jamming with B.B. King and Little Richard, Brian Wilson of the Beach Boys, and Ringo Starr. This all incredibly happened to me, a poor kid from Sioux Falls, South Dakota, who tap-danced to help his mom put food on the table.

Of course, after the fall the test is how you pick yourself back up. As George Clooney said, "Nobody goes undefeated." Mine is a story of daydreams and fulfilled and unfulfilled ambitions, of the craving for love from strangers and for belonging at the table, of failure and of redemption. Throughout my life I have enjoyed the luck of the Irish, rubbing shoulders with a who's who of the rich, famous, and infamous, and cursed by, perhaps, the Irish DNA as I searched for my soul in the bottom of a bottle. It's been a roller-coaster ride, and, boy, did I have fun on the way. It is a journey that began nearly seventy years ago in a downtrodden neighborhood near the railroad tracks. I've had the best seat in the house and the worst seat in the house. This is my story. My life story, inside and out.

I'll Be Back **Right After** This

1

Send in the Clowns

Looking back on all of it now, there isn't much I would change. I definitely would not have let my son down. I most certainly wouldn't have made such a quick, foolish, almost spur-of-the-moment exit from my family. I wouldn't have put a giant diamond ring on a woman who I actually allowed to treat our relationship as a revolving credit card. I probably wouldn't have smoked . . . and maybe that fourth rehab wasn't all that necessary. But the rest, along with the aforementioned, were all things I could have controlled and didn't. Still, all that emotional suicide is what got me here, and I'm pretty happy with my life today. I subscribe to the John Steinbeck theory that the certain way to be wrong is to think you can control things. So I'm guessing all this unfolded for a reason, and if that is, indeed, the case, I am supremely grateful.

Trying to piece together my childhood has never been easy. I have so many unanswered questions, and too many things weren't written down or documented—some simple, some quite complex. For example, on her deathbed, literally, my mother told me there was no apostrophe in our name. I'm like, "Really, Mom? Now?" To this day my sister insists that I had a form of polio that was corrected when Jonas Salk introduced the polio vaccine when I was seven years old. I was always told, "You were on your way to an iron lung." The only symptom I had was crooked legs with a big bone protruding on each side . . . but there's nothing to confirm this one.

Even so, when I met Dr. Salk, I thanked him for saving my life. Whatever, I would not have done well in an iron lung. Although, given what I've been through, I think I would have figured it out.

Pinpointing my fears growing up, they were over belonging and not having a dad to belong with. It seemed I was the only person without a dad, so, growing up, I felt a little out of the normal kids' conversation. Nobody to go fishing with, nobody to go hunting with, no father-son banquets, no playing catch and all that stuff I only saw on TV. I've spent decades looking deep inside, and that's what I've come up with.

But outside of that, life growing up in a dysfunctional family was, honestly, not as bad as it reads because mostly I never had a chance to know better. I do know that I wasn't molested, beaten, or afraid to be who I thought I was. And who was I anyway?

My young adult world revolved around school, music, and lots of church.

My mother was Lutheran, and we were paid-in-full members of the First Lutheran Church right in the middle of Sioux Falls. I went to every church event, sang in the choir, was an altar boy, usher, attended Bible school in the summertime, and buried my parents there. I even gave a sermon from the pulpit once when I was about sixteen, and I called it "Dare to Be Different." I took my sermon to heart. An inviting social life surrounded the Lutherans, especially a summer outing called Camp Teepeetonka, which was part Lutheran and part YMCA. In the fellowship hall, below the church, all the kids would gather after the services before we marched across the street to Shultz's Soda Shop. It was all right out of the Ron Howard movie *American Graffiti*.

The first house I lived in was on South Main Street in Sioux Falls, South Dakota. We lived humbly on the top floor of a broken-down wooden house that was five houses from the railroad tracks. No lawn. No trees. Just a house with a broken, cracked sidewalk leading to it that somehow never got repaired. It was the poor side of town and I always wondered where those railroad tracks led. I would find out, but I spent days and nights alone in one of the ditches on either side of the tracks, wondering where the people on the trains were going. I wanted to go with them.

Our neighborhood was highly blighted and neglected, but it was near the center of town and thus the city fathers designated it as the staging area for every parade that was scheduled in this Midwestern city. Back then, they had circus parades and Shriners' parades . . . and homecoming parades and Christmas parades and usually a short one on St. Patrick's Day. So I grew up watching all these people and things and freaks assemble for the parades. It was awesome. Shriners on horses and motorcycles, big scary clowns running around smoking cigarettes, baton twirlers, high school bands waiting for the whistle to blow, and midgets. Yes, when the circus came to town, along with the animals and the trapeze artists, usually a good number of midgets hung out in my front "yard" smoking big cigars and drinking beer. The little people were always laughing, as if they knew something the rest of us didn't. I figured they had arrived somehow by those tracks. More important, it was my first look at show business.

Show business has always been in my blood. From the very beginning, I wanted to be loved, and being born on February 14, Valentine's Day, was a great beginning. The long-running Pat O'Brien Show debuted at McKennan Hospital in Sioux Falls, South Dakota. My mother and father promptly named me after their favorite actor: Pat O'Brien. In postwar America, Pat (whom I got to know later in my life) was one of the biggest movie stars, always playing the tough Irishman, as in *Angels with Dirty Faces,* or holding his own with Tony Curtis and Marilyn Monroe in *Some Like It Hot,* or as the legendary Knute Rockne alongside Ronald Reagan. So, right away, just by having his name, I was instantly famous. Later, when I was famous, Pat saw me in a crowd in a Chicago theater and called me backstage, and we had a long friendship. In fact, when I went on the air in Los Angeles, I had to get his permission from AFTRA to use that name. My first day on television in LA, he called and reminded me, "Kid, in this town I'm the real Pat O'Brien."

My father, the great Joe O'Brien, was a navy veteran turned electrician and local union organizer. Once a local Golden Gloves boxer, he was a strapping fella complete with mustache and Clark Gable hat, suit, and the kind of handsome looks that usually takes you places. His looks and personality took him to every local bar he could find, and in the end that was his destiny and downfall. He was a hopeless alcoholic who probably never heard of a way out. My mother, Vera, was actually in show business. She was in one of the first all-girl bands after the Big War. They called themselves the Jive Bombers, and after that, she was everybody's favorite pianist. She played with Gene Krupa, Nelson Riddle, and pretty much every big band that swung through the Midwest. She was prematurely gray and, unlike most Norwegians, had a keen sense of humor. She had her eyes on the big time, but never made it. I became my mom's big-time moment. And so began my life on the stage.

My mom's drummer in her band and best friend was the talented Lila Lee Christy, who was also a skilled tap dancer. She turned her basement into a dance studio and called it Tanglefoot Dance Studios. I was her first customer. With my mom on the piano and Lila's tutelage, at the age of about four I was transformed into a first-class tapper . . . ending up as a bit of a local celebrity. I appeared at the town's biggest event, the Farm Show, and at summer band concerts under the stars. There were recitals and local appearances and state fairs—any place that had a crowd and a stage and a piano, there we were. I was not even five years old and I was on the road.

Now, when you are five and in a little tuxedo, you are cute. But when you are five and in a tuxedo and tap-dancing and people pay attention, then you're a cute asset. The money I earned—sometimes as much as $20 a show—was duly handed over to my mom to help with rent, food, and, well, costumes. As the years went on, I was onstage as much as Lila and my mom could manage: All dressed up in tuxes, sequins, hats, and whatever brought attention. An early *Dancing with the Stars*.

Apart from broadcasting, it is that unusual skill I am proud of.

As a kid growing up with an indefinable, inarticulate feeling of being somehow different, an uneasy outsider, I got a sense of self-worth from tap dancing. I kept it up until the sixties arrived, when it was just "too cute" for me to be tap-dancing in public with makeup and funny costumes, but the skills took hold. Years later, Sammy Davis Jr. told me that I was the "second-best white tap dancer" that he ever saw (Tommy Tune being number one). Well into my forties I got to dance with the legendary Gregory Hines in his Hollywood studio. He, too, told me, "For a white boy . . ." I got entry into all-African-American hoofers' clubs in LA and even danced once with the famed Step Brothers. I met Sammy Slide and all the greats in those dark rooms. It was like the movie *Tap* with a white guy. I still have a pair of green tap shoes Gregory gave me, and, as we'll learn later, I have another famous Gregory putting me in tap shape and, well, who knows? That talent has always surprised and amazed friends through the years, and yet it's the one thing about me that is not on the Internet. A healthy secret.

Yet, with all the triumphs in my life, as with most people the humiliating moments are the ones that come to the fore. My first public interview, for example. I was about eight or nine years old and was onstage tap-dancing for about two thousand people at the Farm Show in Sioux Falls. When I finished to much applause, the local celebrity radio host and master of ceremonies, Ray Loftesness, knelt down next to me and asked if I was a Democrat or a Republican. My innocent reply, to the amusement of all, was "I'm a Lutheran." Indeed, I was a Lutheran, despite my Irish Catholic name . . . but only on Sunday mornings, when my mother would proudly show me off to the other parishioners. As the local tap-dancing "celebrity," I was not only the apple of her eye, but in many ways an ornament, her thwarted showbiz ambitions now channeled through me. The perfect child. The special one. This O'Brien was going places. It worked both ways, though, as I was proud to be with Vera, who always made people laugh and feel good, and later in my high school days she became "the cool mom" who frowned at nothing. I remember that every time she saw me, to the day she died, the look on her face changed. It was the look of motherhood, proud and enthralled by her son. If that look had a smell, it would be the wondrous odor of French toast and bacon on a South Dakota morning. I loved my mom very, very much.

But there was, as I said, something missing: a dad.

Joe O'Brien. Is there a better name for the guy at the end of the bar? The guy who knew all the jokes? The guy who seemed to know everybody. The problem was that I didn't know him and he didn't know me. By the time I was three, my mother got tired of his drunken antics and threw him out of the house. So everything I knew about my dad was handed to me from a sad, alcoholic handbook. "Your dad was the greatest guy ever," my mom used to say, "until he started drinking." The problem was he never stopped drinking. When my mother was carrying me, he got drunk and tried to throw her off a balcony. He beat her. He was abusive. It got to be too much. He literally disappeared from our lives. After he died, I found a letter . . . the only one . . . that he had written to me: "Dear Pat, Boy are you getting to be a good looking fellow. I sure enjoyed getting your picture. Sure is good. Grandma couldn't hardly wait until I got home to open my package. I hear you are a real good dancer. I will be up some time soon and you can dance for me. From your Daddy."

Sadly, I never got to dance for him . . . but about the time I turned seven, I was old enough to travel 320 miles to Knoxville, Iowa, to see him every summer. Now, imagine this: I'm seven years old, and with one suitcase in hand my mom takes me to the train station in Sioux Falls. The Milwaukee Road was a strong and vital travel source back in the fifties, and so there I was, hopping on the old Hiawatha for the journey. In those days, it was as easy as having the conductor keep an eye on me. The train stopped in Des Moines, and for the remaining few miles, I had to transfer to a bus. To this day, I remember getting off the train and walking to the Greyhound bus station and boarding the bus to Knoxville. I would usually not have more than a dollar in my pocket and a couple of dimes to call home, collect, if anything went wrong. Remarkably, nothing ever did. Can you imagine sending your seven-year-old alone on a trip like this today? No. Unthinkable.

I would always look forward to my dad's waiting with arms open to pick me up—just like in the movies or on television, but more often than not it was his new wife, Dorothy. Dorothy was a loud-mouthed, unattractive, heavyset woman who fit all the horrible stereotypes of the bad stepmom. Her idea of hospitality was to take me shopping.

Typically, if my dad picked me up, we would drive directly to the State Fair, where I could be babysat by the attractions. On one occasion, he put me on that parachute ride where they strap you in and raise you about two hundred feet in the air and then drop you. I was afraid of heights, and as I was ascending and screaming, "Daddy" . . . I would look down and there was Joe at the beer kiosk hanging out with his buddies. Joe was a hopeless drunk whose saving virtue was his ability to keep a bar enthralled with his tall tales and jokes. At the time I thought it was cool.

In my imagination, he was a larger-than-life character who was my guide, supporter, best buddy, and the dad who would tell me there wasn't really a bogeyman in the closet. In reality, he provided none of these comforting skills. I remember one time when I was about ten, he took me with him to a bar in Albia, Iowa, and while he sat in a big booth drinking tall Budweisers and shots, I sat against the wall drinking what was then known as chocolate pop. My dad had everyone at his booth laughing and carrying on; then suddenly he looked over at me and excused himself. He walked up to me and said the words I will never forget: "Pat, this is who your daddy is."

I wanted my dad to be John Wayne, the guy who would put me on his shoulders, the dad I could bring to school and show off. Didn't happen. Joe O'Brien was a card-carrying member of the CIA: Catholic, Irish, and Alcoholic. He was a dapper fella, larger-than-life in many ways, but his simple solution to seemingly every problem that came up was "You're an O'Brien; figure it out." In one memorable "superman" moment, we were at a farm in Iowa and he decided to jump, bareback, on a wild horse. While all the farmhands were screaming, "Joe! Don't do it!" . . . my dad calmly brought the horse to its senses and, holding on to its ears, rode it around the pen for a couple laps, then jumped off. He winked at me and said, "That'll show those sons' a bitches." Later, in one of my rehabs, we did what is called horse therapy . . . where we were asked to "relate" to a strange horse. The theory was that horses have quick judgment on personalities. Like my dad, I was good at that, too. The horses liked me. My dad's other words of advice, out of nowhere, were "Learn to love basketball and always vote Democratic." I followed that advice, ironically, to the max.

Joe was a good electrician but could never hold on to a job long enough to make it worth it. He did work on the big Oahe Dam project near Pierre, South Dakota, and was the main electrician for the big courthouse and federal buildings in Sioux Falls. Years later when the grid finally went out, they went up to the attic to see what had happened. They found hundreds of tin whiskey-bottle caps that the rats had moved around enough to short out the entire building. During the war, my dad was a Seabee, but was sidelined after he drunkenly tried to outrun a tank. The tank won and my father sat out World War II in a full body cast. But it was a good story. To an Irishman, worth it.

They say that to find his equal an Irishman is forced to talk to God. My father was that kind of Irishman. Or as John Lennon once wrote, "If you had the luck of the Irish, you'd wish you were dead." As a dad and a provider, not much happening. The only Christmas present he ever presented to me as a young child was a Lionel electric train set he won in a raffle on Christmas Eve in a bar. On a whim, he bought a ticket for a dime and, after settling his bar tab, came home with the train.

It was about the only thing he ever bought me or my sister, Kathleen. He never paid alimony or helped out with the rent. As a result, we moved from one dingy apartment or house to another, my bedroom normally the living-room sofa. As a kid growing up, I would often ask my friends' parents to drop me off in a leafier part of town so they would think I lived in a bigger, nicer house. Then I would walk the rest of the way home.

Meantime, my mom, Vera, picked up the slack and went to work. A tall, stately woman with a sense of humor, she was welcome in what was, in the 1950s, a man's world. She worked in the men's department of Montgomery Ward, one of this country's most popular retail stores. She was the only woman in the store. So with that, along with her piano gigs and my dancing money, we never went without much. It was a simple life, but in that simple world, we never felt as poor as we actually were. Vera provided clothes, meals, and a roof over our heads. And she never, ever, said, "Turn the music down." Now, that's a good mom.

When I was a kid, my world was, pretty ordinary, I thought. But shit happens. For example, during my first week in first grade at Irving School, my teacher, Miss Walters, hauled off and slapped me right in front of the class. I don't remember what I was doing, but I do remember the slap, and I do know that this might have set the stage for my attitude toward authority. Now, in the 1950s, there was no day care, so because my mom worked, my sister and I were placed in the care of the local orphanage or a center called United Way. Technically, we were orphans with one catch. We got to go home at night. One time, though, they treated us kids to an afternoon movie, *House of Wax,* about a scary man (Vincent Price) who captured and killed women and dipped them in . . . wait for it . . . wax. Phyllis Kirk played one of the victims. The movie so horrified me that my mom had to leave work early and come and get me. Later in life, Phyllis and I became colleagues at KNXT/CBS in Los Angeles, and the first time I saw her, my skin crawled and my heart started beating fast. When I first interviewed Price, I told him the story and his laugh reminded me of that horrific matinee, and once again my skin crawled and my heart started beating fast. The images of youth are not planted in you; they are stamped to your soul.

Nothing compared, however, to the stigma that came with being a child of divorce in the fifties. Everybody kind of heard of it. Nobody ever talked about it. If as a kid you had divorced parents, you were automatically different. One time in gym class in junior high school, I was trying to climb those horrible ropes to the top of the gym. While all my classmates sat below me, I pulled and pulled and just couldn't get my skinny, little body to the top. As I looked down at everyone giggling and judging, my gym teacher, Mr. Bauer, yelled out, "You know why O'Brien can't make it to the top? Because his parents are divorced." There I hung, wondering if anything would ever, ever top this humiliating moment.

2

One Night Only

In the late fifties and early sixties, the world was literally divided in East vs. West. The Soviet Union vs. us capitalists in the West. During this Cold War period, the hot topic was that pretty much at any moment we would all die in a nuclear holocaust. In school, we had drills in hiding under our desks and covering our faces, as if that would save us from an atom-splitting nuclear event. The British Empire was falling apart, and a new state was smack-dab in the middle of the Arab world, Israel. TV shows seemed to run forever, and if you had a TV, you would enjoy *The Ed Sullivan Show, The Lone Ranger, Lassie, Rawhide, The Twilight Zone,* and, everybody's favorite, *I Love Lucy.* A new house cost about $8,000 . . . a new car would run you $1,500 . . . and you could fill it up for about twenty cents a gallon. The best suit you could buy was about $30, and depending on where you worked, you made about $3,500 a year. The national sports hero was a New York Yankee named Mickey Mantle. Where we lived, it was inconceivable that we'd ever see a baseball game, let alone New York. Nobody was complaining all that much.

But things were changing. Irving Berlin and Frank Sinatra and Bing Crosby were getting upstaged by a kid out of Tupelo, Mississippi, with the laughable name of Elvis. I can remember that we had to sneak over to a neighbor's house and go into the basement to listen to Elvis Presley, because he certainly wasn't getting any airplay

11

in South Dakota. My mom loved him . . . while few moms would tolerate this kind of revolution. My favorite time of the day was after the sun went down when I could get these mammoth fifty-thousand-watt radio stations on my dial. Through KOMA in Oklahoma City and WLS in Chicago I learned of the "outside world." Little did I know that just a couple hundred miles away in Hibbing, Minnesota, a guy named Robert Zimmerman was doing the same thing. Part of what made him Bob Dylan was that late-night searching on the radio and finding out that those railroad tracks that went through our towns went somewhere exciting.

It was also a time when everything was black or white: literally and figuratively.

Sioux Falls measured success by the side of town you lived in. South was good; north was bad. People, such as us, who lived on the north side of town, northenders, were sons and daughters of working people. That usually meant they worked at John Morrell and Company, a meatpacking plant that employed thousands and thousands of locals and was located, you guessed it, on the north side of town. Morrell's was not only the largest building in Sioux Falls, but the smelliest. Meatpacking left behind a lot of waste, notably manure . . . so our neighborhood always smelled like shit. My grandmother worked her entire life at Morrell's, and now we had become an official part of the family. Shortly after my father abandoned us, Vera hooked up with a tenant in the house we lived in and promptly married him. Al Moss. My stepdad. He brought with him four kids . . . Chuck, Sonny, Rick, and Karen, and they were all juvenile delinquents. They were abusive and mean to my mother and mean to me. But Al was a trouper and a great substitute father. He worked at Morrell's, like just about everybody else in my world, and I can still smell his clothes, drenched in odors of pork and smoked meat. He didn't talk much; in fact, he didn't talk at all. His passion was tinkering with used cars and smoking Winston cigarettes. Two memorable moments, though: One day a horrific car crash occurred outside our little house, and when we ran out, a guy was trapped under a 1965 Mustang. Without a second's thought, Al ran over and lifted the car high enough for the poor guy to slide out. Al was never shy about coming to my rescue either. One day he marched into the principal's office at Washington High School after I was banned from attending school for letting my hair grow like that of my heroes: John, Paul, George, and Ringo. They told me to "go home and cut it." And here was this laborer, bashful and struggling for words, standing up to these "educated men" who sat in judgment on me. In his reticent, inarticulate way, Al made his point and I was allowed back in school, thinking, *Wow, this is a real dad.*

So there I was . . . a northender with divorced parents . . . a step-dad who made about $80 a week . . . and to make things even more complicated, we were living in what was simply called "the black neighborhood" . . . not because it was mostly populated with African-Americans, but because roughly three or four black families lived there. Two of my best friends were black: one the son of a veterinarian and the other a big, fat loser who played in the drum-and-bugle corps, George Miles. He spent a good amount of time in and out of reform schools. He was in so much trouble and in and out of so many courtrooms, a judge once ordered him out of the state. I remember his packing up and my strolling over to say good-bye and asking him what he was going to do. His answer? "I'm going to California and get in a band." Another of those places where the tracks took people. Big, fat George turned out to be Buddy Miles, the great singer and drummer who, after forming the Buddy Miles Express, played with a cat named Jimi Hendrix. The next time I saw George, he was putting a heroin needle in his arm backstage at one of his concerts in the 1980s. He died when I was in my third rehab. Life has its remarkable moments of serendipity.

Junior high school is a blur to me. Because of the part of town I lived in, I was forced to attend the famed Axtell Park Junior High School, which was set up for grades seven through nine. It was known then as the "tough school," where the guys wore their hair in ducktails, the girls were ugly, and the teachers could still physically beat you up. I remember Mr. Meerdink (yup!), who threw me up against a locker one day for an offense I can't remember. I also remember him as the guy serving food in the basement of First Lutheran Church after my mother's funeral. And I remember Don Grebin, who was one of those teachers you always remember; he took a personal interest in trying to get me to focus on life after junior high, but try as he did, I never got focused. Mr. Grebin particularly enjoyed the dynamic of me and my best friend, Ron Matchett, who was black, hanging out together in this black-vs.-white environment. Ron and I spent most of our time getting kicked out of soda shops and stores because of his color. At the time, I couldn't figure that out . . . but as the years rolled by, Ron and I remained good friends. In the 9/11 era, he changed his name to Muhammed Abdulla.

By the time I got to high school, things were changing. A guy named John F. Kennedy was elected president and suddenly there was something we could all focus on: the New Frontier. The boring and lackluster Eisenhower days were over, and now it was all about this handsome, hip president who was speaking, it seemed, directly to us. And just when we were all getting to know him, on November 22, 1963, he was murdered in Dallas. I remember this day as if it were yesterday. I was sitting in homeroom daydreaming and looking out the window. I noticed that this guy on the roof of the building across the street was lowering the flag. Our homeroom teacher came in and she was crying. She gave us the news . . . school was let out . . . and we all went home, where our parents were crying as well.

The thousand days that were the Kennedy administration and the surrounding echoes of Camelot piqued my lifelong interest in politics. Even way out there in South Dakota, and without the benefit of the Internet and "instant news" . . . people my age were energized by the prospect of the New Frontier and perhaps how to keep the flame alive. It's amazing how later in life all these faraway stories and names in the headlines would come right back at me in a big way. I later worked on the Bobby Kennedy 1968 campaign before he was murdered, and through my career I became close to the Kennedy family.

Meantime, in my teenage years, my world started to expand. I was still making that trip to Iowa every summer to visit my father, Joe . . . who was somewhat of a local Golden Gloves standout in the forties. So Joe would always tell me about the sweet science. Looking back, I'm guessing a lot of his bravado was the Irish whiskey talking, but after all the translations, I came to know the names of Rocky Marciano, Jersey Joe Walcott, Sonny Liston, Floyd Patterson, Jack Dempsey, and a young upstart named Cassius Clay. Also, boxing was about the only sport that was regularly on one of the two television channels we got in the Midwest.

Now, outside of traveling through Des Moines, Iowa, every year to see my father . . . I'd never been anywhere . . . so it was time to get out and "see the world." A good buddy of mine . . . also from the dreaded divorced family . . . would regularly go see his mother, who lived in Denver. So one summer I decided to travel on a Greyhound bus and tag along. Neither of us had ever been in such a big city, so our eyes were wide-open to the strange sights and sounds of big-city life. Even though I lived in a severely depressed neighborhood near a meatpacking plant and a penitentiary . . . I was convinced there had to be worse neighborhoods out there, so we went exploring. We ended up down on Larimer Street. Today, Larimer Street is famous for its shops and restaurants and historic buildings . . . but back then it was the closest thing to a ghetto I had ever seen. I was scared to death.

It was nightfall and here we were, strolling up and down Fourteenth Street as if we owned it. We noticed an old tavern, the kind you see in old Western movies where the double doors swung open and kept swinging after a gunslinger walked through them. We walked through them, and there, at the end of the bar, was the largest person I had ever seen in my life. He was hunched over a beer. While we plucked up the courage to enter the bar, once inside its gloomy interior, we got cold feet and ran out. Outside the bar two punks with switchblades came out of nowhere and demanded our wallets. I never felt so white in my life. All of a sudden, like a bolt of thunder, the huge black guy at the end of the bar came barreling outside and just beat the hell out of the switchbladers, who dropped their weapons and ran. Before I could catch my breath or settle my heart down, the bartender came out and said, "I don't want you kids to tell anyone about what just happened! Do you know who that is? That's Sonny Liston, the world heavyweight champion, and he just saved your lives." Well, it was the great Sonny Liston, who had just famously beat Floyd Patterson and who was going through some severe personal struggles, among them Mob ties and alcoholism. He had moved to Denver to dry out and seek spiritual guidance . . . but on that night, God was on our side. We walked away unscathed with a story we were even afraid to tell. I always thought that if I ever wrote a book, I'd call it *Sonny Liston Saved My Life*.

For many teenagers, that run-in with Sonny Liston would have been a life-defining story. Not me. Mine was and is the night of February 9, 1964. That was the night four lads from Liverpool appeared on *The Ed Sullivan Show* from New York City. Along with 78 million other Americans, I was glued to my television to hear Mr. Sullivan introduce me to the rest of my life when he said, "Ladies and gentlemen, the Beatles!" As I told *TV Guide* many years later on the twenty-fifth anniversary of that night, "I left Washington High School that Friday as Elvis Presley and came back on Monday as John Lennon." I had never seen anything as cool as these guys and, from that moment on, became an obsessed "Beatlemaniac." (Two weeks later, they showed up in Miami for a publicity stunt with that guy Cassius Clay, who was training for a fight against the guy who saved my life, Sonny Liston.) My life was taking shape. I wanted to look like them, walk like them, dress like them, sing like them, and I would have made a deal with the devil to be like them. And you know what? I got pretty damn close.

The next year, 1965, I was sitting in the cafeteria of Washington

High School when a classmate, Ken Mills, interrupted my sloppy-joe-and-milk lunch with this request: "Would you like to become a member of Dale Gregory and the Shouters?" I didn't give it much thought. I said yes and then wondered what I had just gotten myself into. First of all, I didn't play any instrument, other than a few chords my piano-playing mom had taught me at home. I wasn't the greatest singer. And perhaps the most important element, I didn't have anything to play. Well, the Shouters needed a keyboard player, so a couple days later I marched into Williams Piano Company and, on a payment plan, bought a Wurlitzer electric piano. The music had begun. The outsider had suddenly become an insider, and with my long hair, sharkskin suit, "Beatle boots," a song list, and a little stage presence, I was off and running. Life at that moment could not have been better.

The boys in the band were an unlikely quintet. Dale Gregory arrived via a surf guitar band; Greg Blomberg, who remains my best friend, was a rhythm guitar player who sounded like Mick Jagger; Ted Christy, whose mom, Lila, taught me to tap-dance, played drums; while Gary Tabbert was on bass. His father owned Tabbert Construction, a big company in Sioux Falls, and he backed us financially, built us a stage, and gave us a house to practice in. Thankfully, none of our parents ever said "turn the music down."

With all the attention being paid to the Beatles, you can imagine the kind of attention the Shouters received almost immediately. We didn't sound like the Beatles or look like them . . . but in Sioux Falls, South Dakota, we were the closest thing available. So our very first gig, at the Elmwood Hall outside of town, was sold-out and created a lot of excitement. Ironically, the first song I sang was "Boys," the one hit at the time sung by Ringo. Later I would actually play that song with him, but for now, it was all about the Shouters. We called our dances Shouter Shindigs and they were all quite the events. Here in the mid-1960s, a night out to see a live band was a highlight on everybody's calendar. The band soon became our lifestyle, and we were getting bookings by the dozens at all the memorable stops in the three-state area: Lake Okoboji in Iowa; Luverne in Minnesota; De Smet, Sioux City, Brookings, Aberdeen, and my personal favorite, Lane, in South Dakota. Lane was a dying farm town, but on band night it was jumping. At 8:00 p.m. maybe twenty people would be there. By 9:00 maybe two hundred. By 10:00 we would look out at five hundred, and by 10:30 and 11:00 there would be almost a thousand kids from all over who'd shown up at the Lane Ballroom. We could feel it: the Shouters had arrived.

Soon, we were backing up big, national groups such as the Animals. The legendary Eric Burdon casually handed me my first real drug: a yellow jacket, which was a little pill full of speed. I didn't sleep for three days.

Our greatest gigs, though, were in our hometown. We played at the first "Battle of the Bands," which drew roughly eight thousand kids. We played after big basketball games at the Sioux Falls Coliseum for crowds up to a thousand. The whole thing was controlled craziness. Our most memorable night was at the Coliseum when we opened for the Hollies, then one of the biggest bands of the British Invasion. Afterward, we invited the Hollies to Gary's house, which had a swimming pool inside. Our heroes were impressed. Later, Graham Nash remembered, "It was the first time I had been in a house with an indoor swimming pool. For a working-class boy from Salford in the north of England, that was quite something." Of course, we were equally starry-eyed; here was one of the world's biggest bands being served cookies and milk by our moms in a suburb of Sioux Falls. To this day, Graham and I remain friends, and I always remind him that "Our House" was loosely based on that summer night. He doesn't disagree.

While the Shouters were nowhere near the league of the Hollies, in our hometown we were always number one. We were inducted into the South Dakota Rock and Roll Hall of Fame in the first round in April of 2010. Our one and only single, "Did Ya Need to Know," which we recorded at the famed Dove Studios in Minneapolis, went to the top of the local charts and stayed there for a summer. To this day I still meet people who met their spouse at a Shouter Shindig.

We were rolling in cash, charging sixty cents to a dollar at the door, and with all the gigs, that money (all cash) piled up and eventually put me through college. And, yes, I did finally learn how to play the piano quite well and, through the years, have sat in with the likes of Booker T. & the M.G.'s, Wilson Pickett, Little Richard, my dear friend James Brown, and many other marquee groups including, yes, Ringo Starr & His All Starr Band. Again, life sometimes invites remarkable serendipity.

Perhaps the highlight of my entire high school years was seeing the Beatles on August 12, 1965, at the old Met Stadium in Minneapolis. The entire cast of the Shouters and a couple of other good friends paid $3.50 each to see the Beatles perform about a forty-minute set. I didn't hear one note over all the screaming, but to actually see my heroes was a life changer.

Years later, I found myself sitting in a New York club with Paul McCartney. He said to me, "Tell me about your band." So I did. When I finished, he said, "That's so cool that the Beatles were able to inspire that sort of thing." Well, just as the Beatles inspired a generation, the Shouters returned the favor and inspired Sioux Falls teenagers looking for something to do.

Indeed, life felt so good. I remember sitting with the other guys in the band in the second row of the majestic State Theater sometime in 1965 watching our idols, the Beatles, in their movie *Help!* From where I was sitting it seemed that they had everything I ever wanted: fame, fortune, girls—and they even got to smoke on-screen. They were rebels who were changing the world. Certainly they changed my life. When I watched Ringo with a lit cigarette in his mouth, George and Paul sharing a mike, and John standing on his own, I remember thinking, *Right now this is the coolest moment of my life.* I didn't want it to end.

In those days of the sixties, smoking was part of "looking cool" and so was getting the girl.

In matters of early romance, however, I was no Valentino or, for that matter, Lothario. My first girlfriend was the twelfth-grade prom queen, Val, who used to call me her Little Beatle. She was three years older than me and, because she didn't want to be seen out with a younger boyfriend, insisted I take her to the local drive-in movie theater. It was a tricky journey as my car, a 1961 Studebaker, could only make left turns because the steering column was broken. So to turn right I had to make three left turns. It didn't make dating Val any easier. On the night of the drive-in movie I thought I was being very grown-up and brought a bottle of cherry vodka hidden in a briefcase. After downing the bottle—I drank to give me Dutch courage—we started making out. The last thing I remember before I passed out was Val putting her hand down my trousers and saying, "Oh, you are a man." The next thing I know I had fallen out of the car. Val got a ride home with a friend. Not my finest hour. Next time I saw her, she was a flight attendant in the first-class cabin on one of my thousands of road trips in the friendly skies.

If my love life was tragic, my academic career looked equally doomed. Once you become famous a revisionist history arises about how you performed in school. It would be easy to say I was the smartest, funniest, and most popular kid in school. I wasn't; my sharp tongue and wisecracks made me as many enemies as they got me laughs. I always felt as if I was an outsider, that I never quite fitted in. Nor did I shine in the classroom, graduating with a paltry grade point average of 1.7. Hardly Harvard material, and unsurprisingly I only scraped into the school down the road, the University of South Dakota. My stepdad, Al, dutifully attended my high school graduation, but not my father, Joe. That just about said it all.

But Joe was not far away in my definition of celebrating, as the night of graduation I dove into a bottle of something and didn't come out. I got so drunk, I woke up the next morning on somebody's lawn with the sprinkler soaking me to the bone. Not terribly tragic for a high school graduate, but that very day the Shouters were making their first live television appearance on the local CBS station, KELO. Sick and tired and worn-out and hungover, I showed up on time with my "Beatles outfit"—shiny green silk and ruffled shirt and high boots—and there we were, live and in color. We were the hottest thing in the state, and we followed up this appearance with a long, long summer of gigs: fifty-two in a row. I kept thinking to myself, *This is great, but where does the million dollars and fame come in?* It took a while for all that . . . but in the meantime, I had other things to think about: college, another job to launch me to college, and a girl.

I found the girl right away. I was buying a 45 rpm Beatles record at Lewis Drug Store in Sioux Falls and ran into one of my best friend's old girlfriends, Linda Andersen. Linda was a cheerleader at the Catholic O'Gorman High School and was pretty much the cutest and nicest girl in town. I knew her well from the "streets," which in those days meant "cruising" up and down Minnesota Avenue with Greg Blomberg and Pat Garvey. We would spend endless amounts of time driving our muscle cars up and down the main drag and hanging out at the legendary Barrell Drive-in. The Barrell was a one-stop for burgers and fries and girls. Garvey and Blomberg and I had spent most all of our high school days at the Barrell. Weeknights, weekends . . . even Christmas Eve and Christmas night . . . our little crowd was there: Garvey, Blomberg, Opheim, Cloud, Cady, and me, watching the world go by. We collectively felt that showing up at the Barrell was imperative to life's moving forward. For me it was, because this is how I had known about Linda.

So there we were, Linda and I, buying records at Lewis Drug Store, and I suggested we "get together" soon. I later heard that she had a crush on me because I was not only in a band, but also a Democrat. Love at first sight. I having just been unceremoniously dumped by my high school girlfriend, Suzette, and Linda having broken up with one of my best friends, Ken Cloud, we were both available. And she was also on her way to the University of South Dakota. So that took care of the girl issue.

As for a job, between band gigs, I got a part-time job at, where else, Morrell's, shoveling hamburger meat. All I can say about this task is to imagine shoveling bubble gum, and there you go. I would come home every night so tired I could barely make it to the door. Then I would garner the energy and go cruise around town again. I quickly figured out that hard labor was not for me, and my stepdad agreed, saying, "You need to find a job where you don't have to lift anything."

Out of nowhere, I went to visit Mort Henkin. Now, Mort didn't seem as if he belonged in Sioux Falls. First of all, he was a Jew, and the only person of Jewish faith I had ever known was the son of the Horowitz family, who owned the local jewelry shop. He didn't have many friends. But Mort, he seemed big-time. Maybe a New York kind of guy, I didn't know, but what I did know was that he owned the big local radio station: KSOO. Mort knew me from my tap-dancing years and took a liking to me and promptly gave me a job as the summer relief late-late-night DJ. He paid me $20 a week. I was in heaven and was boasting to friends and, more important, to girls about my new status. I dutifully followed that night's playlist, gave the time and the temperature, and every now and then flicked the switch that brought in the national news from New York. Every time I turned that switch, I got more and more hooked on the idea that I had the power and means to bring people information they didn't have. It was the beginning of a long, loving relationship, and it never occurred to me that I would someday become one of this country's most famous and infamous broadcasters.

So, with a radio job, a new girlfriend, a few dollars in my pocket, and a black 1964 Chevy Impala, I set off to college—one lifetime behind me and many, many more ahead of me. I was eighteen years old and I was on my way.

3

Footprints on the Prairie

The fantasy, of course, never happens. I had always imagined my parents packing me up, a big going-away party, a big happy family all driving the first O'Brien to ever go to college right up to my new dormitory. That didn't happen. By now, my sister, Kathy, was in the navy and my half brother, David, was just entering high school . . . my mom and dad were both working hard and I was only moving sixty-seven miles away to Vermillion, South Dakota.

I worked my late shift at KSOO, signed off, and jumped into my car and drove myself to college. It was a lonely drive, but filled with excitement and anticipation of what might become of me. I had dreams of doing something . . . the problem was, I didn't have any goals to fulfill those dreams.

I arrived around midnight in this sleepy college town and unloaded all my belongings into a two-man dorm room. My roommate, some farm kid from Iowa, was sound asleep. Welcome to college, Pat! Yippee.

I sat there alone on my bed writing forlorn letters to the girlfriend who had unceremoniously dumped me while thinking about Linda Andersen and where she might be at this moment on campus.

During that first semester, I was a card-carrying loser. I let my hair grow to my shoulders, dressed like a vagabond, and failed to show up for class. I spent more time at the student union than I did in the library and kept pretty much to myself. Consequently, I was getting Ds and Fs in my chosen major, history. I had chosen that major because I had heard somewhere that it was the easy way out.

Then it happened.

I was strolling down the campus one night when a short, portly guy (old man, I thought at the time) approached me. He was wearing a hat and a two-string bolo tie. He marched right up to me and said, "You are Pat O'Brien, right?" He held his stubby, little hand out and said, "I'm Bill Farber."

William O. Farber was the legendary head of the political science department at the University of South Dakota and known as a political genius. Everybody knew Dr. Farber. Everybody.

After an exchange of pleasantries, he asked me over to his house the following evening to join him for a beer. Now, having a beer with the head of a department, let alone Dr. Farber himself, was a big deal, so I was intrigued. The next night, I duly arrived at 413 East Clark Street, right across from campus. It was known and still is known as Farber Hall.

That night changed my life forever; it still gives me goose bumps when I look back on it. He cracked open a couple of beers, and after we sat down in his living room, he got right to the point:

"Pat, I think you've got some skills you don't know about. I've watched you around campus and I believe you have some communication skills you are not using." During the first beer, I learned that he had watched me at the union with fellow students, and he could see that I could express myself in a way that kept an audience amused and intrigued. (Just like my dad, Joe.)

Then Dr. Farber cut to the chase: "This is what I propose: why don't you switch to the political science department and take some public affairs classes. If you do what I tell you, I will help you out."

I would later learn that this invitation was part of a routine. He would pick out students he thought had potential and take them under his wing. In the hippie days of turn on, tune in, and drop out, if a potential recruit actually turned up at the designated hour, that was quite an achievement in itself. Once under his wing, you were flying intellectually, having challenging conversations about politics, books, and current affairs. The weekly discussions in his sitting room were rarely frivolous; everything he said and did had a thought and purpose behind it. It was rather like going to worship. What made it so special was the feeling that someone actually cared about your well-being, and, yes, he quickly became a surrogate father, a mentor, guide, and counselor.

But, as I soon found out, I wasn't alone. An impressive group of former students were simply known as the Farber Boys. Under Doc's supervision, all of us started out slow and finished fast. Most notably, Tom Brokaw, a South Dakota native who, like most of us, drank too much, dated too much, didn't read too much, and didn't care that much. That is, until Doc arrived in our lives. He turned all of us into senators and congressmen, governors and federal judges, heads of corporations and professors, city planners and extremely successful businessmen. As Brokaw wrote in the foreword to Dr. Farber's book *Footprints on the Prairie*, "Doc Farber's influence reaches across decades, across partisan lines and school rivalries, into the centers of power, and in the lonely recesses of rural America."

I learned more in Dr. Farber's sitting room than in any classroom. Even after I left college, right up to his death in 2007 at the age of ninety-six, he would call and check in and always ask, "What are you reading?" Or even at the peak of my success: "What's next, Pat? My goodness, there's so much to do!"

One time I answered his book question by saying I was reading Martin Gilbert's weighty biography of Winston Churchill, but for Doc, that wasn't enough. He was keen that I should be reading more widely, soaking up the background of Churchill's aristocratic family, the Marlboroughs, who own Blenheim Palace in Oxfordshire, England. For Dr. Farber, the payoff for this intellectual involvement in the lives of his students was the creation of a cadre of young men—rarely any women—who placed public duty above personal greed and who would help other Farber Boys in their careers. His credo was simple: "I help you to help others." He had a high-minded vision of himself as a teacher creating a generation of public servants, guiding and cajoling young men of ability down the road that led to the greater good. "I feel like a playwright sitting in the balcony looking down onstage at my creations," he once told me. A playwright who arguably had more success in his day than Shakespeare.

The highlight of life as a Farber Boy was an invitation to join him on the modern-day equivalent of the grand tour, accompanying the academic around the great cities of Europe during the summer vacation. I had only flown on an airplane once—when Al took me on the seventeen-minute flight from Sioux Falls to Sioux City—let alone visited Britain and the rest of the Continent. Of course I couldn't afford to go, so Dr. Farber paid for everything. I just had to carry the bags, be ready to meet interesting people, and talk intelligently over dinner. So in August 1969 we set off on our great adventure. First stop was London, the capital of the greatest empire the world has ever seen. Within hours of landing he marched me to Trafalgar Square, pointing out Nelson's Column, the monument to the British admiral killed at the Battle of Trafalgar in 1805, the lofty stone façades of the South African embassy and the Canadian High Commission, and the imposing frontage of the National Gallery, home to one of the finest art collections in the world. That was my first lesson: the nature and formation of an empire. Dr. Farber was well connected, and through the good offices of South Dakota's conservative senator Karl Mundt, the State Department had sent advance telegrams to its delegations throughout Europe to inform them of our arrival. As a result we were given VIP treatment, in London, for example, treated to a private tour of the Houses of Parliament. Imagine what kind of impression that made on a boy from Sioux Falls. Those railway tracks really did lead to some impressive places.

From London we flew to Moscow, where we stayed at the hotel Hitler had earmarked for his personal use had the invasion in 1941 been a success. We then flew to Leningrad, now Saint Petersburg, where we spent two days wandering around the magnificent Hermitage Museum. At the Hermitage we were able to see the misnamed "public library," which no one ever saw, and were granted access to the library's hidden jewel: the library of French philosopher Voltaire, which Catherine the Great purchased from France.

Naturally I played second fiddle to the great man, carrying the bags while he dealt with local officials. I remember when he was buying tickets for the Bolshoi Ballet. "This is going to be tricky. I had better handle it," he muttered to me. As he couldn't speak Russian or French, he went through an elaborate pantomime of gestures indicating that we were American and wanted two tickets for the ballet. Finally the ticket agent said to him, in perfect English, "Sir, may I help you?"

For a sedentary, somewhat overweight academic he had great stamina, a reflection of his unbounded zest for life. At the end of a typical seventeen-hour day of high-minded pursuits, I remember sitting in the hotel bar at two thirty in the morning sipping a vodka when Doc leaned back in his armchair and said, "You know, Pat, a man measures his life by the adventures he experiences." I have never forgotten those words.

And adventures we had. After a tour of Stockholm in Sweden we made our way to Prague on the day that the Russians returned after their first invasion to quell the Prague Spring uprising the year before. Tanks rolled by the hotel before we made a hasty exit, heading to Paris and then Brussels. On the train to Brussels, Doc told me that I was scheduled to speak about disaffected American youth, the unrest roiling through campuses, and general adolescent turmoil—remember this was at the height of the Vietnam War—at a committee meeting of NATO (North Atlantic Treaty Organization). He gave me one word of caution—"don't use your talk to attack President Nixon."

I didn't have time to get nervous—which is why I suppose Doc sprang his little surprise on me only a day before I was to speak before this high-powered audience. Not that I had much of a clue who or what NATO was. Or what to say. I had never spoken in public before, but I had sung and played in a band and tap-danced since I was a kid. So audiences didn't faze me. What I said is something of a haze—it was along the lines that the unrest was caused by opposition to the Vietnam War—but if you are really interested, you can find a copy of my remarks in the Library of Congress. It gives me a kick just to write that.

Now, Dr. Farber was a resolutely old-style Republican, even though with a wink and a nod he would take some liberal postions. As for me, I heeded my father's early instructions and supported the Democrats. Most of my fellow students in the late sixties felt the same way, largely because we weren't all that excited about perhaps dying in Vietnam. Later in life, I grew up a little and was able to appreciate the service all those Vietnam veterans performed for our country. I became quite active in raising money for paralyzed and other veterans. But during these polarizing years in the sixties, I was selfish and just didn't want to go. So, at the time, one of my heroes was Tom Hayden, famous as one of the Chicago 8, who had been unceremoniously indicted and put on trial in front of the childish judge Julius Hoffman in Chicago. Tom, along with Abbie Hoffman, Jerry Rubin, and others, was charged with inciting the notorious riots at the 1968 Democratic National Convention in Chicago, a city ruled top to bottom and inside out by Mayor Richard J. Daley. More of my old friend the mayor later. So I read all of Tom's manifestos and attended a couple of New Left rallies to hear Tom speak about the conflict that was tearing our country apart. Tom later married Jane Fonda, infamously known as Hanoi Jane for her stern and public opposition to the Vietnam War. At one meeting in Iowa, I remember that we were all teargassed and chased to another building, where out of nowhere there appeared many photographers taking pictures of us. We assumed they were government agents filling up their files for Nixon's famous "enemies list" and were collecting info on anybody who said, "We won't go." Years later, Tom and I discussed those days and were thrilled with the public evidence that proved us right. They were spying on us and we weren't as paranoid as we thought back then. (Of course we were paranoid, but that was our problem, and that was part of the overall problem.) But out there in South Dakota, which seemed so far away from anything, we were very much on the fringes of political activity. Our long hair and our music and rampant drug use was our protest, and we were okay with that. We looked good, sounded good . . . and thought we felt good, right? It was a way to fulfill my overwhelming desire to simply belong.

Nowhere is this human impulse to belong tested more severely than in joining a college fraternity. I agreed to this excruciating and painful rite of passage out of a desperation to be part of the Delta Tau Delta fraternity. The Delts were the coolest, hippest, most liberal society on campus. To me they were the "studs," and to my surprise they were aggressively "rushing" me to join. It appealed to me that they made it sound as if I were the only pledge they wanted and they would do anything to get me with one caveat: I would do anything to be a Delt. We both honored that agreement.

As a long-haired smart-ass, a member of the state's most popular rock-and-roll band, a Farber Boy, and a native of the "big city" of Sioux Falls, I was singled out for special treatment.

To this day, I do not understand why I agreed to be abused and harassed and humiliated . . . but at the time it seemed like a grand idea to finally land that heralded Delt pin. Under today's standards of law and decency, none of this stuff would be allowed without a grand jury's involvement, but in my desperate effort to belong, here are some of the things I was "asked" to do:

Walk around campus with peanut butter under my arms and a gunnysack under my clothes.

Attach a string and a pencil to my penis and get autographs from various coeds.

Wear the worst-smelling perfume (I think it was called Hitler) head to toe and not shower during the final hell week.

Go blindfolded through the house and answer the question

"Would you eat shit to be a Delt?"—then be led to a toilet that smelled like shit, reach in and grab what felt like shit, and just as I was about to eat what I thought was shit, somebody would stop me. It was a banana.

And remember the scene in *The Social Network* in which the poor student had to carry a chicken around? Yes, that was me. I had to carry a live chicken around for a week—and keep it alive. I even had to take it to a basketball game between the university and our keenest rival, North Dakota. The chicken sat on my lap the entire game as mayhem erupted all around. Later, while covering the NBA, I was talking to legendary coach Bill Fitch about those days when he was the coach at North Dakota. We were talking about the rivalry and he said, "I remember some stupid motherfucker brought a chicken to the game!" The stupid motherfucker was yours truly.

Well, it got worse. One freezing South Dakota winter night my pledge class was forced to strip naked and run from the Delt house to the Vermillion River, about three miles round-trip. We did it.

Then, they put me alone and naked and with my chicken in the cold basement and poured cold water on us. I would have been better off in Vietnam, I thought. As I sat there shivering in the corner holding this poor, near-death chicken, I could hear the brothers partying upstairs to the Turtles' song "Happy Together." Ironically, all I wanted was to be happy and to belong. To this day, that song makes me cringe.

Finally, I cracked and said, "That's enough; I quit." My sponsor and lifelong friend, Terry Hendrick, came to my rescue, and as he cradled me in his arms, he said, "Just stick it out, OB. Just a little while longer."

Next thing I knew . . . one of the seniors announced that as soon as I killed the chicken, we'd all be Delts. I did, and there I was, the newest member of the coolest, hippest, and best fraternity. Right now, I'm laughing, too.

Later on in this glorious life, when I was hosting the Final Four, one of the security people approached my set and said I had a visitor. He was one of the guys who put me through the most hell. I said, sure, just tell him to stand down there in the hallway. He stood there through the entire game to say hi, and I never showed up. On another occasion, when I was hosting the World Series, I got a call from another guy I couldn't stand, wanting tickets. I told my secretary to put him on hold, and he held for just under an hour before I left the office and that blinking hold light. Another time, as I was in a suite in Seattle, the guest of then president Bill Clinton, another of those hell-week organizers was standing outside trying to get my attention. I just looked the other way. This guy used to paddle me relentlessly, so I was in no mood to give him the thrill of meeting the president. At the time, I thought revenge was a dish best served cold.

Outside of this childishness on both sides, being a member of Delta Tau Delta turned out to be everything I imagined and more. Socially, the fraternity was my launching pad. I became president of the Interfraternity Council, which oversaw all the fraternities. I became the house rush chairman and, ironically, the hell-week chairman. (And, yes, I ran a hell week just as mean, if not worse, as my own.) Academically, I was killing it, getting a GPA just short of a 4.0.

I also was the director and the lead character in what was called The Strollers Show. This *Glee*-like competition between paired-up fraternities and sororities was easily as good as any production you could see anywhere else. For three years in a row, Steve Manolis, Fritz Leigh, and I trained twenty-six young men and women with no musical backgrounds to get up onstage and dance and sing and act. Never has any group dominated this yearly ritual more than we did under my watch. Out there in the Midwest, it was like winning the Super Bowl. Suddenly, with all this going on in my life, I was the big man on campus. I was very comfortable with this.

And I got the girl. I was finally going steady with Linda Andersen, the O'Gorman cheerleader I met while buying a Beatles record.

She was and in many ways still is the girl of my dreams: smart, funny, good-looking, and the perfect woman to understand my cocky bravado and apparent lack of self-esteem. Linda made me feel good about myself.

Let's make something else perfectly clear. College in the sixties was, as you might imagine if you weren't there, a fucking blast. As the saying goes, if you do remember the sixties, you weren't there. The whole world was exploding. The Vietnam War was raging. Martin Luther King was murdered. And in June 1968, while I was working as a volunteer on his campaign throughout the state, another of my political heroes, Bobby Kennedy, was assassinated. On that night, I was upstate in Aberdeen, South Dakota, exploring the insurance business as a postcollege option and also going door-to-door for the Kennedy campaign. Linda was back in Sioux Falls stuffing envelopes at the Kennedy headquarters. We both watched on TV from the two cities until Bobby won the California and the South Dakota primaries and I went to bed feeling as if I had participated in my small way in sending him to Chicago for the Democratic National Convention and the nomination. At about midnight, television in South Dakota went blank with a test pattern. No cable. No Internet. No texting. No cell phones. At three in the morning, my phone rang in my cheap hotel room. It was Linda. "He's dead."

So as the world turned and found tears when there were barely any more, life went on as usual in Vermillion. We adjusted quickly and went back to our books and studies . . . our Beatles music . . . and drugs. Green hash seemed to be the favorite in my group. Lots of it. And endless nights and Saturday mornings at our favorite watering hole, Carey's, on Main Street, where we would routinely gather to watch *George of the Jungle* over tomato juice and beer. The musical highlight of college, besides trying to decipher the words to Beatles songs and trying to figure out if Paul was really dead, was the spring we hired an obscure Chicago band called the Big Thing to perform at the spring bash. We signed them for what we thought was an expensive $3,000. Between the time we booked them and the time of the concert, they changed their name and became the Chicago Transit Authority . . . and one of the biggest bands in the world. To our surprise, they honored the contract, and in return, on the day they showed up in our humble little community, hundreds of us went out and gathered enough purple violets to fill hundreds and hundreds of grocery sacks. When the curtain opened, we all threw the fragrant flowers onstage, and the band was both shocked and delighted. They played for three hours and would later say that night in South Dakota was their second-favorite concert to Wembley in London. Later, I got to be close friends with the members of Chicago, and they could never get over the South Dakota hospitality.

But through all the nights of drinking and smoking and late-night television and, of course, sex . . . one little thing was hanging over us all. We were eligible for the military draft. And the Selective Service System came up with a cute little idea to draft roughly a million soldiers: the very first draft lottery, which was held on December 1, 1969. Those with the first random 195 birthdays chosen were pretty much guaranteed to be shipped off to Vietnam. So there we all sat in the living room of the Delt house watching these idiots from the Selective Service youth advisory committees pull these little blue balls out of a barrel. If you got a number above 195, you were pretty much free. The lower your number, the higher your chances of being blown to bits in Vietnam. So we're all watching as September 14 was the first birthdate picked. We laughed. Three balls later some dork picked out a ball and shouted out, "February fourteenth!" I was number four. There was no way out . . . I was going to Vietnam. As I saw it, I had a couple of terrible options: move to Canada and be a genuine draft dodger, proclaim that I was gay, or join ROTC, the Reserve Officers' Training Corps, which allowed you to stay in school and train as a second lieutenant. I felt it might be better to go into the army as an officer, so I cut my hair and joined the ranks of the hated and laughed at ROTC. This sucked. But I made the best of it. ROTC provided me with $50 a month, which I used to pay rent and buy drugs and beer, and I would enter the army as a lieutenant. Sure enough, the moment I graduated with honors from the university, I was called up and promptly shipped in the heat of the war to the heat and humidity of boot camp in Fort Lee, Kansas.

Think about this for a moment. I'm the big man on campus, I have everything I want, I'm in love with Linda, I'm a Farber Boy with plans, and I'm going to fucking boot camp? As a patriot, there I went, and here was my tour of the army: a day to get in, a day to figure out how to get out, and a day to get out. There was nothing heroic about my tour. For one, with my long hair and smart-ass mouth and my general hatred of authority, I was not a standout soldier. I was there for two miserable, degrading days, and they announced that our unit would be suited up for Da Nang, Vietnam. We had one final group physical. They lined up three hundred of us in one big row. We were all naked. A charged-up, screaming sergeant asked if we were ready to serve in the U.S. Army and kill the enemy. I was not. Then he said, "If any of you faggots have a good reason why you can't serve your country, take one step forward. Okay, faggots, take three steps forward." Nobody moved. My mind was going a million miles an hour. I'm thinking, *This is kind of important* . . . so I dug deep for the courage—and with no real reason to not serve—took three steps forward. Nobody else did. Behind me, and remember we're all naked, my fellow recruits were yelling, "Queer," "Asshole," "Skinny fucker," "Faggot." The sergeant asked me what my problem was, and I said, "My knees are weak from my track-and-field days, Sergeant." So they dragged me out and called my family doctor. My family doctor was Robert Ogborn, who delivered me, delivered Linda, and kept my mom on lithium, and who was himself a well-known alcoholic. When he got the call, he thought I was in some kind of trouble, so whatever they said, he agreed: "Oh, sure, I'm looking at his files now, and I don't think Pat can march or walk too far with those knees." That was it. Four hours later, I was given an honorable discharge and $100 for my trouble and I was driving back to South Dakota. When I got home, I had a letter from

Richard Nixon, thanking me for my service and granting me the precious "honorable discharge." I was free.

With my military career effectively ended, I could focus on what I wanted to do. Except that I didn't know. I was very much in the thrall of Doc Farber. The idea of public service, working as a diplomat at the State Department or an economist, was uppermost in my mind, echoing what I thought was Doc's vision for my future. I had read him wrong. He subsequently told me that he always thought I should work in the communications industry, maybe television. He contacted another Farber Boy, Tom Brokaw, who was working local news in Los Angeles, and asked if he could find me a job. Meantime, during my final year at South Dakota, for the first time in my life, I hit my academic stride, graduating with an honors degree and a 3.9 grade point average. So, with Doc's encouragement, I applied for a master's degree course in international economics at the Paul H. Nitze School of Advanced International Studies (SAIS) at Johns Hopkins. To my astonishment I was one of the sixty or so admitted in the fall of 1970.

Doc Farber wasn't finished with me yet. Knowing that I needed to pay for tuition and living expenses, he wangled me a job with South Dakota's Democratic senator, George McGovern. Every senator has a dozen or so patronage jobs that he can give out to talented youngsters in his constituency. That year I was one of the lucky ones, working part-time in the Senate for the princely sum of $10,000 a year—enough to pay college fees.

On June 15, 1970, I said my farewells to friends and family and boarded an Ozark Air Lines flight to Washington. I had $200 in my pocket and two suitcases in my hands, about to start a new life in a strange city. So the adventure began. I was, once again, on my way.

4

"I Wanted to Get Laid, Not Jailed"

Most baby boomers like to brag that they "survived the sixties." In my case, the survival came later in life. There wasn't much to survive from in South Dakota other than some bad winters. Despite having no father to speak of, no money, sleeping on a couch my whole childhood, never having my own room, and despite many desperate attempts to "fit in" even when I was often the person people wanted to "fit in" with . . . I had a pretty good life, I thought. Now, in the summer of 1970, I was about to land in Washington, D.C.—with a job at the US Senate and a hard-earned ticket into one of the most prestigious graduate schools in the world. I can remember it as if it were yesterday my plane's touching down and my realizing that I didn't know one person in this new life I was about to begin.

When I got off the plane, the first thing that hit me was the weather. It was one of those terribly hot, humid seasons in the capital, and it was oppressively uncomfortable. I had a lead on housing through Johns Hopkins, so I made my way to my new digs on Whitehaven Parkway on the northern end of Georgetown. It was a nice house with forgettable roommates, and the good news was that I finally had my own room, which was smaller than my college dorm room, but I wasn't sharing it with a stranger and I was living in Georgetown, the city's most exclusive neighborhood. It was nighttime and too hot and humid to go outside, so I lay on my single bed and stared at the ceiling, that $200 burning a hole in my pocket but dreams of grandeur burning in my heart and mind.

That very week, I checked in with Senator George McGovern's Senate office to find out what menial office jobs I would be assigned to, but to my delight I discovered that I was going up in the world— literally. Senator McGovern had arranged for me to run the Senate private elevator, which could only be used by senators and their guests. So there I was, suddenly, thrust into the middle of the political discourse of the day. One by one they would get on and get off—the biggest names in politics from both sides of the aisle. In this particularly turbulent summer, Congress debated and repealed the Gulf of Tonkin Resolution. Passed in 1964, the resolution gave the president wide powers to continue the Vietnam War . . . and now in 1970, as the war grew more and more unpopular, the vote to repeal it was seen as a giant step toward peace in Southeast Asia. So every day, for three hours, as I ran the elevator up and down and up and down, my passengers were Strom Thurmond of South Carolina and Jessie Helms of North Carolina, Ted Kennedy, Robert Byrd, Mike Mansfield, Sam Ervin, Hubert Humphrey, William Fulbright, and all the political legends who would carry their debate with them in the elevator. It was fascinating . . . and about as inside as an outsider could get to the political climate of the day. More often than not, a senator would jump on and say, "Hello, Pat, let's go up," and then turn to a fellow senator and say, "Now, goddamn it, we've got to get rid of this fucking thing." The thing was repealed that summer . . . but the war raged on.

This ridiculously great job also came with a salary: $10,000 a year before taxes. So with one of my first paychecks, I hitchhiked out to a suburban-Maryland car dealer and asked him if there was anything for under $300. He said, "That thing over there if you have cash." And so, $250 later, I was the proud owner of a 1959 green Volkswagen. It had no radio, no heater, no windshield wipers, no gas pedal (I used a stick), and two big holes in the floor. When it rained, the car would fill up with water and I would freeze to death, but it got me around, famously.

Meantime, over at Johns Hopkins, I was now officially a student of the School of Advanced International Studies: SAIS. Even though, intellectually, I clearly didn't belong . . . it had a great international feel and, because the classes were so small and elite, a great feel of fraternity. I was pursuing my master's in international economics under scholastic circumstances I wasn't prepared for—but I was doing well.

Before long, however, Dr. Farber intervened in my life again. He said, "As long as you are there, you should be getting some communications work, somewhere." He dug into his book of former students and Farber Boys and pulled out the name of Tom Brokaw, who was a local NBC anchor at the time in Los Angeles. Brokaw, whom I had met once at the university when I won a political science excellence award, came to my rescue. Within a day he somehow got me a job at the local NBC station in Washington, WRC, as a copyboy for the local news. I showed up and was blown away that I was actually going to work in a big-time local newsroom. Little did I know what was next.

But first, let's go back a few years to the late 1950s when my stepfather proudly brought home our first television set. He and my stepbrothers carried this monster up the stairs to our apartment, and we all stood around as he plugged it in and turned it on. About ten minutes later, after he adjusted the rabbit-ears antennae, an image finally appeared. It was a news show and there he was, David Brinkley, one-half of the famed *Huntley-Brinkley Report*. He was the first thing I ever saw on our own television. From that moment on, like most Americans, we were Huntley-Brinkley fans for no other reason than habit, really. The anchor duo became my window on the world.

So now it's the summer of 1970 and I'm sitting in the WRC/NBC local newsroom using their "hotline" to call home free. I was chatting away and suddenly this familiar voice from behind me said, "And who are you?" I turned around and it was David Brinkley himself. I was stunned. I nervously introduced myself and he said, "Here's what's going on. My secretary's gone and Huntley's not doing the show today, and if I can arrange it, can you come back to the network side and answer the phones for a while?" I had been there less than forty-eight hours and had about as much seniority as summer cicadas. Still, I calmly said, "Of course, Mr. Brinkley," and simply abandoned my job. But not before I excitedly called my mom back to whisper, "You will not believe who I just met!"

I strolled back to Brinkley's office in the back of the building, not quite believing my good fortune to just spend a few minutes with him. Perhaps he wrote his own version of his Wikipedia biography when he titled his memoir *David Brinkley: 11 Presidents, 4 Wars, 22 Political Conventions, 1 Moon Landing, 3 Assassinations, 2,000 Weeks of News and Other Stuff on Television and 18 Years of Growing Up in North Carolina.*

Huntley and Brinkley were not only the first duo anchor team, but the first one to actually talk to each other on TV with their legendary sign-off: "Good night, Chet"—"Good night, David . . . and good night for NBC News." *The Huntley-Brinkley Report* was an American TV institution, loathed by most politicians—Brinkley was number one on President Nixon's infamous enemies list—but loved by the viewers. Chet was based in New York and David was anchored in Washington, D.C. . . . and each night, with his choppy, slow delivery, he just hammered the very town he lived in. He hated government, taxes, politicians, scam artists, con artists, teleprompters, producers, most correspondents, and people who tried to imitate his style. Virtually everybody was afraid of him. He was a lonely icon just sitting over his typewriter every day with a cigarette in his mouth and writing the news his way. If somebody else wrote it their way, he tossed it and rewrote it his way. For example, John F. Kennedy was not "assassinated"; he was "murdered." And so on. Brinkley got right to the point. One Thanksgiving Day he opened the news with this: "Good evening. While most of you out there enjoyed a glorious Thanksgiving feast today, here at NBC we ate cold pizza on a cold plate." I loved him.

On that first day, I answered the phones and made him coffee, and he sent me—Brinkley called me Buster presumably because he couldn't remember my name—for a pack of cigarettes. I brought him a pack, but it was not his brand—he smoked Winstons. He said to me, "Buster, I don't smoke those." So I replied, "Well, right now you are smoking these."

Now that could have gone one of two ways: he could have kicked me out on my smart-ass butt or he could have admired that I showed some balls. He laughed and told me to sit down. We chatted for a time, mainly about the Vietnam War, which was a constant and gnawing topic of conversation in those days.

While I wasn't a die-hard political activist—during my student days at South Dakota I was a campaign worker for Brinkley's great friend Robert Kennedy, who was "murdered" in 1968—given my time running the Senate elevator, my conversations with Dr. Farber, and my own interests, I was pretty well up on the issues of the day. I didn't realize it at the time, but that casual conversation was Brinkley's version of a job interview. At the end of the day he said that it was going to be a busy year with presidential elections coming up and then asked me to come and work for him for $50 a week, which he would pay out of his own pocket. There was only one answer: yes.

So there I was, playing hooky from my new job and sitting on the couch of my genuine idol. It didn't take me long to realize that David was untouchable. Everyone was afraid of him, figuratively tiptoeing around him, careful not to say the wrong thing in his presence. While his office door was always open, no one ever thought to walk in unless invited. He rarely came out of his office . . . rarely spoke to any of the staffers . . . and most, if not all, were afraid to even go near his office. Seemingly the only people he liked and respected were Wallace Westfeldt, the executive producer of the show, the hard-charging and chain-smoking Christie Basham, and the stern-minded and brilliant president of NBC News, Dick Wald. That was about it. So imagine my surprise when after grilling me about my background and talking a little politics, he said the words that changed my life, again: "I'll work it out with those people down there [in local news], and why don't you come work for me, then, as a researcher or whatever." The whatever turned into a close, personal working and social relationship that shaped my career. An extraordinary period of my life when I was lucky enough to sit inside the cockpit of news, watching world events unfold in front of me. If Doc Farber shaped my academic career, then David Brinkley was the finishing school, as I learned journalism and writing and news observation and reporting under the master. So just a few weeks after leaving South Dakota behind, I was working part-time for an influential senator and future presidential candidate and the most famous name in television. And I was attending a school at the highest level of university studies.

At the end of that momentous day I ran down the stairs to the phone booth next to the entrance and called my stepfather, Al, who was a Brinkley fanatic, and told him, "You cannot believe what has just happened to me." Then I called Linda in Denver and Dr. Farber. Afterward I went out and got drunk. Life was looking good.

It didn't take more than a few hours for me to change my title from "gofer" to "David Brinkley's assistant." A title that opened a lot of doors in Washington, D.C., social circles and especially in restaurants I had no business sitting in. But a lot was going on I could help with: with student riots in Paris, London, and Rome, Vietnam raging, and the Kent State University massacre in May 1970, where four students were shot dead by the Ohio National Guard, my youth became my passport to the inner sanctum of the NBC newsroom. I was Brinkley's link to young people, what they were thinking, how they were feeling. As I was a recent student, he thought I had my finger on the pulse of youth mostly because of my encyclopedic knowledge of the music scene. This fifty-one-year-old icon kind of channeled his new life as a divorced, successful, handsome man through this skinny kid from South Dakota. We started going out for dinner at night at the hip, "younger," restaurants . . . and he scored us tickets to the Rolling Stones concert at RFK Stadium, where Stevie Wonder and the Jackson Five were the opening acts.

In spite of our age difference—I was twenty-two—we gradually became close enough for him to ask me to set him up on a date. "It's not like I can walk into a bar and pick up someone," he said. I duly obliged. David's hobby was working with wood. He was about as close as you could come to a master carpenter. I was living communal style in a big house, and one of the residents was a beautiful young woman who was a gardener by trade. I thought they'd make a good couple. She was young. So, there we were; David and his new date and I with Linda (who was now living in Washington and beginning her teaching career) found ourselves in a swanky Georgetown restaurant. Halfway through the evening he leaned over to me and whispered, "I told you I wanted to get laid, not jailed."

David was what you would call then a classic Southern gentleman. Still, he liked to experiment. One night I went over to his house and he pulled out this beautiful wooden box and said, "Ever tried this stuff?" It was marijuana. For the purpose of selling this book, I suppose I could say he was a genuine pothead. He was not. It was a passing thing with him, but I still laugh that he rolled his joints with a large cigar-making machine. Those were big joints.

While he was arguably the most famous journalist in America, he wasn't into the celebrity angle or the power trip. Although, when maxiskirts arrived on the scene as a replacement for miniskirts, I remember him saying, with typical laconic understatement, "I wonder how I could end this trend."

He never, ever watched himself on television. Ever. I asked him why and he said, "If you watch yourself on television, you tend to take out what you think is the worst of you and leave in what you think is the best, when, in fact, what you think is the worst may be your best. So if you watch, all you do is become a poor imitation of your own version of yourself." Being famous, he got heads to turn wherever we went. I once asked him if that bothered him. "Not really," he said. "It might bother me if they stopped looking, though."

But I couldn't stop looking or learning. The office I showed up to every morning was filled with a broadcasting hall of fame. At the end of this one big hallway was Brinkley's office. Next to his was that of John Chancellor, who later succeeded David and Chet as the anchor of the *NBC Nightly News*. Then . . . all the iconic network correspondents of the day: Ron Nessen (who later became Gerald Ford's press secretary), Robert Goralski (the Pentagon correspondent), Cassie Macken (Congress and politics), Irving R. Levine (economics), Richard Valeriani (State Department), Jack Perkins (the lighter side), and the list went on. They were a great group, and they all took me under their watch . . . mostly, I agree now, because David liked me and what choice did they have? Right? I remember one of the first days I arrived; Chancellor ("call me Jack") said they were all going to lunch, I should have some coffee ready when they got back. At noon, off they went. At 1:15, I had fresh coffee perked and ready to go. At 2:00, they weren't back, so I made a fresh batch. At 2:30? Nobody. Finally, around 3:00, they all came back from their two-martini lunch and went to work on the show that aired at 5:30.

Brinkley never left his office, so that gave us work time and personal time and, for me, learning time. I marveled at the way David would write with the ability to communicate with everybody, well educated or not. He never used big words. Every sentence was incisive, but powerful, such as using the word *murder* instead of *assassination*. Often, he would hand in a script to Wallace Westfeldt and Wally would say, "Do you really want to say that?" David would reply, "I wrote it, didn't I?" David loved Wallace because Wallace got it. And Wallace became another mentor of mine, which was huge. In time, he hired me as a full-time production assistant at $15,000 a year—a handsome sum in those days, I thought.

One of this entry-level job's descriptions was, in fact, one of the most crucial elements of the broadcast: when to sign off. Seems trivial, but I was handed a stopwatch and the job to tell Westfeldt how much time was left to fill at the end. It was called pad . . . so if there was a thirty-to-forty-second shortage of news, I would tell the producers that we needed another story.

So in September of 1970, the David Brinkley Bridge in West Virginia collapsed. The bridge had been named after David because, during an election campaign, he had recorded the rickety sound made by the wooden bridge's slats, embarrassing the state authorities about their failure to maintain the bridge. Perfect Brinkley story. Well, when the bridge eventually collapsed, it became his favorite story, and he decided to end the broadcast with a play-by-play of his bridge going down. He spent most of the afternoon sitting, alone, at his typewriter and tapping away at a commentary on how his namesake in West Virginia had gone down. He couldn't wait to deliver it. At the end of that show, Westfeldt turned to me and screamed above the chaos, "Pat, how much pad?" I said, "About two minutes and thirty seconds." So we filled that amount of time, and then it was David's turn to deliver this jewel. He began, "The David Brinkley Bridge collapsed today—" And then suddenly an advertisement for kitchen soap came up and the show was over. I looked up and David was still talking . . . to nobody but the crew. The show was long over. There was panic. People started screaming at me: "You stupid fucking asshole!" "Jesus Christ, Pat, you just fucked David Brinkley." "Somebody go talk to him, now!" Fear took over the room like a bad cologne. Finally, and calmly, David poked his head into the control room and said to me, "Come see me in my office."

I walked in and he was holding a cigarette between his teeth, something he did when he was angry. He spoke: "What happened?" I panicked and said, "David, it was only a couple of seconds." And that's when I learned about keeping time in television. A few moments of silence went by (seemed like an hour), and David looked at me and said, "Buster, let me tell you about a 'couple of seconds.' If you're fucking some chickie, it's not very long. But if you have a pin stuck up your ass, it's an eternity." Lesson learned.

Washington was the hub of power and the magnet for the disaffection with the Vietnam War. The war enabled me to make one of my first significant contributions to the show. One of my jobs was to go to the film room and check on what was coming into the station. Remember, it was before the days of tape and live feeds from the field. The film was physically carried from the action to the studio and then viewed on a monitor, a cumbersome process. In April 1971 I was looking at the monitor and saw a handsome fellow in his military uniform throwing his medals and ribbons over a fence in front of the US Capitol. The military man was clearly expressing his opposition to the war. His name was John Kerry. On that day, after he threw his military decorations over the fence, he told an audience of Vietnam Veterans Against the War and other antiwar protesters, "I'm not doing this for any violent reasons, but for peace and justice, and to try and make this country wake up once and for all."

I raced from the basement viewing room to tell Brinkley of this powerful and mesmerizing sight. He walked downstairs with me and reran the film. "Let's talk to Wallace," he said, before talking to the executive producer about getting the young former navy officer on the show. That was how John Kerry, later senator, presidential nominee, and secretary of state, first appeared on the *Nightly News*. He was given four minutes—a lifetime in television—to state his views, which he did eloquently. Certainly he had had practice. Earlier that week he had spoken for nearly two hours to a Senate Foreign Relations Committee hearing chaired by Senator William Fulbright. He became the acceptable public face to opposition to the war, appearing on the *Dick Cavett Show,* writing for influential newspapers, and speaking at numerous rallies. These days when I occasionally see him on Nantucket Island, where we both have homes, I like to remind him that I gave him his first big TV break, which launched his political career. He never argues that fact.

The Brinkley days were filled with great moments, each still a wonderful, almost unbelievable, memory.

Let's revisit the Democratic National Convention in Miami the summer of 1972. That was the summer that both Democrats and Republicans had their convention in Miami. As the main researcher—actually the only one (now they have like 350)—I moved to Miami for the entire summer. A great moment during the Democratic convention occurred during NBC's one-hour updates live during the day. Usually on these, John Chancellor was the main anchor and David was brought in for his perspective. One day we were all sitting around our working suite at the famed Fontainebleau Hotel on the then-called Miami Strip, and there was the usual hustle and bustle. David was in his adjoining room reading the newspaper. Chancellor had not arrived yet, and the show was to begin in about two hours. Another hour went by, no John. Producers were beside themselves and, still afraid to confront David, asked me to go in and tell Brinkley that he might have to do the show solo. I did, and David, cigarette between his teeth, said, "No, Jack will be here." Another hour. No Jack. Another hour, no Jack, and so now it became apparent that Brinkley would be soloing. A search party went looking for Jack, but no results. Finally the producers were throwing scripts at me and telling me to take them in to David. David threw them back. "Jack will be here." Finally . . . fifteen minutes to air, as everybody around us was in full broadcast panic, David and I made our way downstairs to the set. In the elevator . . . he said, "Okay, Buster, tell me what's going on here." I was prepared, and for about five minutes I told him about the California challenge, Jesse Jackson's role, the Stop McGovern campaign, what was going on in Ohio, and any other detail I could recall. No script, and when the light came on, David ad-libbed what was the greatest political analysis I had ever heard. So great that *Time* repeated it mostly word for word, as political gospel. I'm thinking to myself, *This guy is Elvis Presley, the Beatles.* The show ended and David and I went to lunch with Jay Rockefeller in the hotel. Well into the lunch, Brinkley turned to me and finally said, "Where the fuck is Chancellor?" We never got the answer to that story. He showed up the next day, a little sheepish, but, nevertheless, ready to go back to work.

Also in Miami, Dick Wald, then president of NBC News, held a party in his hotel suite. For some reason everybody was asked to take off his or her shoes upon entering. During the party, David and I got bored and silly and picked out a pair of shoes and threw them several stories down into the pool. As the party ended, Wald, then the most powerful person at NBC News, was asking around, "Has anybody seen my shoes?" I didn't tell him until about twenty-five years later.

Then there was the time David was hosting the 1973 Nixon inauguration, and when it was over, he and I jumped into a limo to take us back to the studio so he and Chancellor could host the inaugural parade from there. About forty-five minutes into the drive, David noticed that we had left the city. Turned out, the driver got lost and we were way, way out in the middle of Virginia. We never made the parade and it wasn't a pleasant car ride. Jack did that one alone.

So many great experiences, such as talking to Henry Kissinger as he was negotiating to end the Vietnam War. One time, we were at a social dinner at David's house and Dr. Kissinger was there, along with the legendary Katharine Graham, the publisher of *The Washington Post*. David and Kissinger and I were sitting in big leather chairs in David's living room, and the two of them were discussing the plan for peace. I was overserved and was leaning back on my chair. Suddenly, the chair won that contest and I fell flat on my back right in the middle of one of David's sentences. He never stopped talking and nobody said anything. Last year I ran into Dr. Kissinger at Patroon restaurant in New York, and he remembered those days and summed them up with a simple "David was a great man."

As the Nixon administration renewed its hold on the reins of power, I pondered my own future. "It's time to stop drinking the heady wine," Tom Brokaw told me, implying that I had to be my own man. After three incredible years with David and the rest of the team, I knew Tom was right. At the end of the election season Chancellor echoed those sentiments: "You have to get out from under mine and David's wings. You have to learn the business from the bottom up. And never forget to read the sports pages; that's where a lot of stuff is happening."

My relationship with David had changed anyway. He remarried in 1972, to Susan Adolph, who earned the inevitable nickname Hitler. Naturally he wanted to spend time with his new bride rather than propping up some Georgetown bar with me.

He asked me what I wanted to do. I was anxious to stay behind the camera as a field producer. So he called up Dick Wald, then head of NBC News, and told him that I needed a job. I met with Dick and he picked up a phone and, suddenly, I found myself heading to Chicago to work as a summer-relief local-news writer for WMAQ Channel 5. My life was changing in other ways, too. Linda had moved to Washington and was teaching locally. We were living in separate apartments but seeing each other most days. I said to her, "I guess we should get married." I didn't even buy her an engagement ring, and our wedding on July 7, 1973, at St. Therese Church, known locally as Little Flower, in Sioux Falls was a modest family affair. Before the wedding Father (now Monsignor) James Michael Doyle, who officiated, helped me through the relevant classes so that I could convert to Catholicism. Inevitably my father was not present. He was now in a nursing home in Marshalltown, Iowa. So instead of a honeymoon we drove over and visited him. It had been a while since I'd seen him, and to my shock he was about a foot shorter and weighed about a hundred pounds. It was the last time I saw Joe O'Brien.

Sadly, my stepfather, Al, was missing, too. He'd died the previous year, and on the day he died I remember sitting in a bar in Georgetown overcome with a powerful need to call my mother. They say that when you die, you pass through the people you love. I called my mother and she told me what I had sensed, that Al had just died. I flew back to Sioux Falls and gave the undertaker one of Doc Farber's sports jackets to dress Al in.

As he lay in his coffin, I put a dollar in his jacket pocket. It was a reminder of the time when I was at school and needed a dollar.

Al, who never had ten cents to rub together, gave me that dollar without question. I never forgot his generosity of spirit. Or him, mourning him harder than I did my own father, who died several years later. Al's gesture, that generosity of spirit, was priceless.

Once we returned to Washington, I left my bride behind—she still had a teaching contract to honor—and I drove to Chicago alone in my new red Triumph sports car, which I had bought thanks to the outlandish expenses I'd claimed during the various political conventions in Miami.

Even though I was newly married, I was traveling alone, which was, I discovered, the way I liked it. Without any clear sense of direction, somewhere along the way I took a wrong turn and ended up in Kansas City. An inauspicious beginning to my journey along the yellow brick road of broadcasting. And for many nights moving forward, I always thought of my mentor and quietly said to myself, "Good night, David." And thank you.

5

This Must Be My Lucky Day

I was on my own in Chicago in 1973, without the comforting career blanket that was David Brinkley. In my mind, I had gone from the top of the totem pole at NBC to the bottom. In reality, I was here to learn the business, to learn how to write and edit and report on the local level with the high hope that this would continue the journalism foundation to build my career.

Working with David gave me incredible access to how the "big guys'" did it—"swimming," as Tom Brokaw described it, "in the heady wine of NBC." This was not a demotion but, in many ways, a graduate school in the business.

I quickly learned that in Chicago there were three mafias: the Mayor Daley mafia, the actual Mafia, and the WLS radio mafia.

WLS was a fifty-thousand-watt radio station that I listened to as a kid in South Dakota because the signal was so strong. It employed the legendary disc jockey Dick Biondi, whose voice and selection of songs would turn any wide-eyed kid into a radio freak with dreams of "being there." I was one of those kids and I actually got to be there, as the DJs of WLS, the mighty 89, of the mid-1970s adopted me as their pet TV guy. J. J. Jeffery, the morning guy, who had a laugh that could never be matched. Bob Sirott, the midday guy, who became one of my best friends and had the ability, I thought, to do anything . . . and he did. And to round out our crowd, the "night guy," John Records Landecker.

The three of us, with our wives and girlfriends, would gather every Friday night and rotate from one apartment to another and drink and smoke pot until the sun came up. I still remember driving home as the sun rose over the glorious city of Chicago and going to bed, counting the days until the next Friday. I don't think I have laughed as hard as we did since. In his bestseller, *Records Truly Is My Middle Name,* John referred to our group as a "click." He left out a lot of details, probably because he's a grown-up now, but those were the days when we all never, ever wanted to grow up. I'll always love and cherish those guys for inviting me into their world . . . and making me feel at home and almost making me die laughing.

Ironically, just when I left Washington, D.C., the biggest story of the century was breaking: Watergate. So right away, I was jealous that I was not part of the Brinkley crowd who were covering that one top to bottom. Instead, I was writing local news about city politics, fires, and weather. That's what kept Chicago news in business: city politics, fires, and weather. I wrote about so many fires that year my Valentine's card read, "My heart is on fire for you. Arson is suspected."

Make no mistake, this was a big-city operation, WMAQ Channel 5, operating out of a huge newsroom on the nineteenth floor of the historic Merchandise Mart, a 4-million-square-foot monument to consumerism in downtown Chicago. I did meet some early resistance as a "Brinkley Boy" from some of the old-timers there, who snickered behind my back (some of them are still there working in local news . . . the others are dead), but eventually I proved my worth, and the temporary summer contract led to a full-time job as one of the four newswriters for the Chicago legend himself, Floyd Kalber.

Just as the city's mayor, Richard J. Daley, was the big boss man in city and national politics, Kalber ruled high atop Chicago television. His nightly broadcasts would earn a 50 share of the audience, unheard of then and an acid dream in the world we live in now. The suits back east had their eyes on him to maybe even replace Chet

Huntley someday, until they started to look at the numbers: simply put, if Kalber left Chicago, the third-largest market in the country, there would go WMAQ. They weren't going to allow that to happen. As a result, Kalber's status went into another atmosphere, earning him the nickname the Tuna, after the late Chicago Mafia boss Tony Accardo, aka the Big Tuna. Just as Accardo ruthlessly ruled the Mob, the Tuna's word on the nineteenth floor of the Mart was law. With his chiseled somatotype isotope look, deep voice, and penetrating gaze, Kalber was the ultimate old-school anchorman—aloof, powerful, and untouchable.

When he walked into the newsroom, never too early, never too late, there was always a hush. He would go straight to his office and start to read the copy we had written for him that night. All-business, a man of few words—and friends—he would think nothing of slashing to pieces some script you had spent all day working on. Everything had to be perfect or it would come flying back into your face, page by page. That was about the size of it, though, after three years of working with the demanding and intimidating Mr. Brinkley, I found Floyd Kalber a relative pussycat, though a pussycat with claws. While I got to know him well enough to hang out in his office, business was still business, and many a time he would march out of his office and throw that night's script on our desks and say, "That's not news." Sometimes this would happen when the "news" was supposed to be on television in about ten minutes, so I did learn a great deal about working on a deadline.

The great thing about my experience at Channel 5 in Chicago was that I was working in the last great newsroom in America. I was part of the last days of, as Floyd would say, "real news." And like in the days of Damon Runyon, a few of the old-school, old-salt guys were still around. Guys who smoked all day while gathering the news and then, after work, went to the local tavern and smoked and drank and talked about the news. It never seemed to end. So I tagged along and gladly dove into the news scene that was Chicago. That newsroom would have made a great reality show . . . from the desk to the reporters to the writers to the camera and sound people. There was the overblown, self-serving Dick Kay, who had changed his last name from Snodgrass, who covered politics and spent every waking minute trying to get into the anchor chair. When he did, on rare, awful occasions, he would yell out, "I'm anchoring tonight." I can't remember him ever breaking a story, but he was amusing. There was Russ Ewing, whose talent seemed to be that escaped prisoners and other criminals would famously "turn themselves in to" Russ instead of the authorities. Russ was African-American and never let us forget that he was in touch with "his community." There was the insufferable Rich Samuels, who saw himself as the first investigative reporter. People like this gave me the confidence to say, "Jesus, it doesn't take much to be a star in this business."

There was the other anchor, Jim Ruddle, who was able to memorize an entire script and never use the teleprompter. A couple of clowns came and went in a hurry, such as Ron Hunter, who famously dodged a murder charge after his wife was found dead in his bed, shot by his gun. He was knowledgeable on only one topic: Ron Hunter. And then there was Len O'Connor.

Len O'Connor was the consummate newsman. Like David Brinkley, he started his career at a newspaper . . . went to radio . . . and graduated to television. Unlike Kalber, he was not your normal-looking television stereotype. He was portly, had gray hair, and talked in a high-pitched, almost whiny voice that somehow gathered tremendous authority over his long career. I loved Len O'Connor. His office was in the back, near Floyd's, and he, too, rarely stopped to talk to people. But one day I simply walked into his office and introduced myself, and he told me to sit down. "Kid," he said in that voice, "I think you've got something. I've been watching you and you just might have it." From that day on, Len became one of my biggest supporters as I was navigating the politics and backstabbing of the newsroom. And when he started doing commentaries with his signature sign-off, "And I am Len O'Connor," he put Chicago politicians on notice that somebody was watching them closely. Everything he said mattered. Like all of us, he eventually got fed up with taking instructions from people we didn't respect and left WMAQ in a storm. He was the last of a breed. I was sad when he passed at the age of seventy-nine.

Meantime, back in the newsroom, things were changing.

Kalber's view was to give the viewers only the "meat and potatoes" of news, and it worked for so many years, but changing social mores took care of that. In 1975 the station introduced what was known as a "happy talk" format, in which the anchors would not only deliver the news, but then go unscripted and talk about it. It was a relaxing approach to being hammered every night with politics, fires, and bad weather. Enter: Jane Pauley.

Jane was a local anchorwoman in Indianapolis who got the attention of the Chicago news bosses. The late Ed Planer, then news director, went to visit Jane and offered her a job on the spot. According to Ed, Jane said, "How much would this pay?" Ed replied, "Probably around fifty." Jane: "Gee, can you live on fifty dollars a week in Chicago?"

In fact Jane got to live on $50,000 a year in her first big job, and she was immediately placed right next to the Tuna. Not only didn't it work, but Jane was on a faster track than anybody expected. After just a few months, she was hosting the *Today* show from New York and became one of this country's most beloved news anchors. Jane was and is one of the smartest and nicest people to ever have picked up a script, and I will always love her personality, style, and outlook on life. There weren't many like Pauley. There was simply nothing plain about this Jane.

While the arrangement with Kalber didn't work out in Chicago, it worked out for me. The days of the single local anchor where the news was delivered as if by God were numbered. The culture was changing dramatically as the viewing public searched for personality along with information. That shift brought the industry right to my doorstep.

Meantime in the production world, I was on the move again. I was promoted from the ten o'clock newswriting assignment to produce the afternoon news. Raw news gathering got me excited, and here we were—without computers or the Internet or Google—using the old wire services and the city news service and actual telephones to gather the day's events. I was consumed by the work and was a good producer. Watching the great Wallace Westfeldt of the *NBC Nightly News* all those years taught me a few things. As I said earlier, Chicago was consumed with city politics, fires, and weather. During one balmy week in the early spring of 1974, Chicago was hit with a huge snowstorm. Normally Chicago shrugs off snowfalls. Not this time—because of the added drama of a city workers' strike, there were no snowplows to clear the roads and sidewalks. As the city lay under a thick blanket of snow, I got a call from a citizen in the suburb of Berwyn, Illinois, which had somehow mysteriously already been plowed. As producer, I also made assignments, and I searched the newsroom for a reporter to get out there and get me this story. Nobody was around. Now, let's say I wasn't your normal employee: long-haired, chain-smoking, outspoken, funny guy, first and last customer at the bar, T-shirts in the winter, jeans—you get the picture. So I handed over the show to my associate producer and said, "What the fuck, I'll go cover it." I dropped everything I was doing, put on my winter coat, grabbed a film crew, and jumped on the elevated train out to Berwyn. When we got there, miraculously, the streets had been plowed. And nobody could tell me why. Or wanted to. So I did the story as a mystery and called it "Who Plowed Berwyn?" Here I was in my first on-air job, reporting the story on my own show in the third-largest market in the country. It was a hit with the news director, Ed Planer. His first words upon viewing my first outing were "You belong on the air." I said no. But after talking it over with Linda and crunching the numbers of a $10,000 pay raise and waiting about four months to think it over,

I reluctantly cut my hair, grew a mustache for a little different look, put on a suit and tie, and accepted Planer's invitation. Within a few months I was a bona fide on-air reporter.

My first report hardly marked the auspicious beginning of a fresh, new talent. By now the TV station had a live capability—before that technological advance film was hand-delivered to the station's editing suite and then processed—and I found myself doing my first live broadcast outside a school-board meeting. My hands were shaking so badly from my nerves that my cameraman, Jim Strickland, had to shoot me in close-up. But that didn't last long. I had natural ability in front of the camera, so, from that wobbly beginning, the only way was up.

I was definitely different . . . taking from my Lutheran-church sermon I delivered as a teenager called "Dare to Be Different." I dared. And dared.

I soon became known in Chicago as "king of the live report," and I always tried to make my reporting an event within the event. At a terrible, tragic plane crash at Chicago's O'Hare Airport, it was a bright, sunny day and I was wearing a pair of round, red sunglasses to shield my eyes against the sun. The folks in the studio were screaming for me to take them off. I refused, and my cameraman, Tim Maher, agreed. I took this position: it's bright out and people wear sunglasses. I heard Tim call back to the studio from his headset, "You're wasting your time; this dude is not taking off the fucking sunglasses. You wanna go live or not?" We did.

The same position I took when it was raining . . . I made sure I was wet. Snow? I made damn sure my coat looked as if I had been out there for a while. When it was windy, I let my hair blow. When I dropped my notes during a report, I stopped and leaned over to pick them up.

I also introduced a couple things in the on-air reporting business that have never gone away. I invented the walking stand-up. While talking, I would walk from one place to another with the cameraman walking backward in front of me. It gave, I thought, the viewers a sense of being where the story was. My reporting hero Geraldo Rivera credits me with this innovation . . . but I always tried to emulate him. Geraldo had just recently become a real star in New York City for Channel 7, WABC. He had long hair, a mustache, was cocky, gung ho, made himself part of the story, and won about every award possible, including a Peabody Award for his work.

As a result, every big city had to have its Geraldo Rivera. I became Chicago's Geraldo . . . and did the best I could. I felt that I not only reported the news, I was romancing the news. I had the kind of gravitas that my colleagues hated, frankly—because I was breaking the rules with a brash style and more than a pocketful of confidence. I had the habit of showing up in everybody else's shots. For example, if Mayor Daley was leaving his building, I was usually walking beside him while the other crews and reporters begged, "O'Brien, get the fuck out of our shot!" It was my signature. I also had a breathtakingly irritating habit of walking into a story and telling everybody, "Well, you know it's a big story now, boys." My favorite was at a dinner for the visiting Egyptian president Anwar Sadat, where old man Daley introduced me to the president, who was here to introduce the King Tut exhibit. The next day at the opening of the grand exhibit, Sadat saw me and waved me over . . . and there I was, his personal guest, along with the mayor, to visit the elaborate exhibit first, while all the other stations could do was shake their heads and give me the finger. I was a born performer, but the flip side is that I was never intimidated by anybody of any fame or fortune: presidents, prime ministers, pop stars, Beatles, sports heroes. Nobody. And nothing scared me. Big fires, big crashes, gang wars, shootouts. At one hostage situation in Chicago, I stood outside with a live camera for four and a half hours while bullets were being fired all over the place between the police and the hostage takers. When Linda got home from teaching, she turned on the TV and the first thing she saw was me hunched down behind a car, reporting the story. She wondered what the hell was going on and just sat home and smiled. *That's my Pat,* she proudly thought at the time.

As a new breed of street reporter, able to inject drama and color into a story, I was a difficult commodity to pigeonhole. News executives tried to harness my abilities by forming an investigative unit to uncover off-diary stories that would win ratings in the sweeps season, those critical periods in May and November that establish a news station's commercial standing. Big ratings equal big bucks from advertisers. They hired a new producer, Paul Hogan, from PBS in Cleveland, to work with me. From the word *go* we butted heads, so much so that I tried to have him reassigned. Slowly the fences came down and we became bosom buddies. He is one of the best friends I have ever had, and when he died, in 1993 of a heart attack aged just forty-eight, I grieved him more than I did my parents. I loved him. It took me almost forty-five minutes to get through his eulogy at his funeral, which was covered—live—in Chicago.

Paul and I loved to shop together and drink together. After work, we would routinely head to the local pubs, and when we got home, we would be on the phone all night, scotches in hands, chatting away like high school kids. We were inseparable, on and off the job. When I left Chicago, Paul replaced me and was, himself, a fearless bulldog reporter and for his efforts won nine local Emmys, nine AP awards, and Reporter of the Year five times. He got me there, and now it was his turn and he deserved it.

When we worked together, we investigated gang wars, urban unrest, a neighborhood community about to be demolished for a parking lot for one of Mayor Daley's buddies, and the search for Patty Hearst, the heiress who was kidnapped by a terrorist group but then appeared to join them willingly in a bank robbery. This perfect story combined political extremism, class conflict, kidnapping, and a beautiful if elusive femme fatale. I was obsessed with her, following up every "sighting," reporting every minute lead. When she was captured, I was in Chicago, but I made sure I was one of the media pack who greeted her when she stepped out of prison in California. Years later I was on holiday at a resort in Jamaica when the elevator door opened and out walked Patty Hearst. My heart stopped. I had spent hours thinking about her, following her, pondering the motives behind her behavior. Then there she was. I stared at her frozen. I couldn't think of a word to say. So, I just stood there and finally she broke the silence: "Pat O'Brien? My God, I love your work!" Irony of ironies.

Along with Patty Hearst the other predictable ratings winner was the Chicago Mafia. I remember in 1975 when Paul and I did a weeklong series on the Mafia for sweeps. The ratings were great and we went to the Greek Islands restaurant on Halsted Street to celebrate. Halfway through the meal the manager came over and said, "Mr. O'Brien, Mr. Giancana would like to see you at his table." At first I thought this was a joke, but then I looked up and there he was. Yikes.

Now this was a big-gulp moment, as Sam Giancana was one of the most notorious Mafia bosses in the world. He had colluded with the CIA during the Kennedy administration to discuss assassinating the Cuban leader Fidel Castro. His affair with Frank Sinatra's friend Judith Campbell Exner, who was also intimate with JFK at the same time, showed how close the Mafia was to the government. He had only just returned to Chicago after surgery, but even in his weakened state he was not a man to trifle with. So I walked over and with as much bravado as I could muster said, "Good evening, Mr. Giancana, a pleasure to know you."

He ordered me a Dubonnet and ice, apologized for interrupting my dinner, looked me in the eye, and said, "I want to know what kind of man you are. I watched some of your TV programs this week. If those names had been Irish rather than Italian, would you still have done the story?'

"No, sir, I would not," I replied. He took another look at me and said, "You are an honest man. Go back to your table," and waved me away. A couple of days later, in June 1975, he was shot with a .22-caliber pistol while cooking in his basement. While theories abounded that it was rival Mafia, CIA operatives, or one of his former lovers, thirty-eight years later the killer's identity remains shrouded in mystery. In the newsroom the joke was that I had him murdered for interrupting my dinner. I'll let them believe that, but I kind of liked the guy.

My encounters with Frank Sinatra, the other familiar visitor to Chicago who was able to join the dots between the Mafia and the Kennedys, were brief, intimidating, and not especially illuminating. The classiest restaurant in town was the Pump Room at the Ambassador East Hotel. The most coveted table was Booth One, where stars such as Elizabeth Taylor, Dean Martin, Paul Newman, Judy Garland, and Frank Sinatra dined when they were in town. One evening, I took Linda along as a treat and the maître d' seated us at Booth One, all the while assuring us that Sinatra, who was in town, was not dining there that evening. This VIP treatment was one of the modest perks of being a local TV celebrity. We had no sooner ordered our meal when who walks in but Sinatra. He scowled at us, the maître d' fussed around, and to avoid a scene, we simply stood up and were seated at another table.

Not that Sinatra would have considered apologizing for interrupting our meal—he had nothing but contempt for the fourth estate. During a concert tour of Australia, for example, he described the media as "fags," "pimps," and "whores," his remarks causing a strike of Australian unions representing transport workers, waiters, and journalists. He was equally truculent with the American media. After he publicly abused the well-known syndicated columnist Marilyn Beck, I went along to the Four Seasons Hotel in Chicago where he was having dinner, in the hope of getting a reaction. As he ran to his car, I yelled, "Mr. Sinatra, can we have a comment from you?" As he got in his limousine, he spat at my cameraman. "Frank, you are a cocksucker," I shouted. So that was my meeting with the late great Mr. Sinatra.

Ironically, one of my strengths as a reporter was my fascination with the music scene, both in Chicago and beyond. I was one of the first broadcasters to bring music out of the entertainment ghetto and onto mainstream news, interviewing rock bands such as

Chicago, Earth, Wind & Fire, and the Commodores when they came to town. I put the local band Styx on the air, randomly, and a record executive heard them and the rest is history. In those days there weren't the bouncers, security guards, and other hangers-on making life difficult for fans and reporters. I remember going to see wild man Alice Cooper when his Welcome to My Nightmare tour came to town in 1975. Linda and I loved the macabre staging, which involved fake blood, guillotines, and boa constrictors. After the show we wandered over to his hotel and made our way onto his floor. As we wandered down the corridor, not a security man in sight, the man himself, drink in hand, appeared to say hello to some of his fans who were dressed as Goths and other creatures of the night. All of a sudden a lanky, drugged-out kid, kitchen knife in hand, lurched toward Cooper. I was feet away and grabbed the punk, who was clearly out of his head, and wrestled the knife from him. The incident was all over in seconds and, in the way of these things, had a dreamlike, unreal quality about it. Alice went back into his room and we decided to leave. Years later when Alice and I finally met up at a celebrity golf tournament, I sat him down for an interview and reminded him of that night. "That was you?" he said incredulously. We joke about it now, but it could have gone terribly wrong. We've been good friends ever since the tournament. He was the first big rock star I knew who stopped drinking years and years and years ago. Alice fucking Cooper not drinking? But yes, and he told me that one of the ways he did it was to take all the energy he once put into drinking and switch it to golf. He is now a scratch golfer. And when I play golf with him, I love saying, "Nice putt, Alice."

I met another hero and longtime friend in Chicago, the lead singer of the Commodores, Lionel Richie.

Linda and I had gone to a Commodores concert, and during a break, I "Pat O'Briened" my way backstage and met all the guys . . . not paying all that much attention to Lionel, who was, for all I knew, just "with the band." At any rate, somebody offered me cocaine.

While I was a heavy drinker and used alcohol to down quaaludes and all that, I had never done coke, let alone seen it. I tried a line and went back to my seat sweating with fear, wondering what was going to happen to me. It seemed to me that nothing had happened. So I tried it again. And again. And again. I discovered that the cliché about coke was true: "A line of coke made me a new man. Unfortunately, that new man wants another line of coke." Rarely a day would go by without my scoring what was now becoming my favorite drug. I was not the only one. During the seventies cocaine was the drug of choice among the upwardly mobile. It was part of the deal if you could afford it. I couldn't afford it, but somehow I managed. Lionel and I remained good friends through the years, and we tell people, "We went to college together." He's a loyal, great guy. Now, we just text back and forth like high school kids. I love the guy . . . and will always thank him for his loyalty to me.

My genuine interest in Chicago's music scene—I was out most nights at the city's blues clubs—made drinking and drugs part of my way of life. One of my hangouts was the celebrated Checkerboard Lounge on the South Side of Chicago, where on Mondays all the great blues players from Howlin' Wolf to Jimmy Smith to Buddy Guy to even the Stones would come to gig on their days off. It was called Stormy Monday and I usually took the day off to participate. The day would start at 10:00 a.m. and last into the wee hours of the morning. More often than not, I was the only white guy in the building. Indeed, my passion for music snagged me my first big showbiz interview.

One crisp November morning in 1974 I got a call from George Harrison's publicist offering me a one-on-one chat. Harrison was swinging through Chicago on what became known as his Sitar Tour, where he, Ravi Shankar, and other musicians played music infused with Eastern influences. Harrison's publicist said that George had selected me to do one of two interviews because he felt I "knew something about music."

As brash and confident as I was, the prospect of meeting George Harrison turned me to jelly. I had waited my whole life to meet these guys—when I was with the Shouters in Sioux Falls, we all drove to Minneapolis to watch the Beatles perform in a giant stadium with thousands of screaming teenagers. The chance to sit down face-to-face with a living legend—a Beatle, no less—was unthinkable until it actually happened. I mean, my life up until now was framed by the Beatles.

He wanted to do the interview on his private Learjet, so my crew and I walked across the tarmac. I told the cameraman to roll from the moment we entered the cabin. When I said, "Hello, Mr. Harrison," I swear my voice was quivering I was so nervous. He didn't seem to notice. As much as I wanted to talk to him about the music, as a newsman I needed to ask the question that everyone wanted answered: Would the Beatles, who split at the end of 1970, ever get back together? It became a national pastime—during a skit on *Saturday Night Live,* producer Lorne Michaels offered them a check for $3,000 if they would reunite for just three songs. Funny but improbable.

Of course George Harrison was sick of being asked that question and wasn't interested in answering. Before the interview started I was warned by his publicist not to start quizzing him about the Beatles. So I had to find a fresh way of asking, well, a stupid fucking question of a guy who didn't want to hear it or answer.

"I think people in this country felt a loss of identity when the Beatles broke up," I said. George stonewalled. "Why's that?" Thinking on my feet, I had to find another way of approaching the off-limits subject. "Well, my theory is that you guys arrived at a time when everybody needed something to make them happy. Our president had been killed, we were in a war everybody was trying to get out of, and, well . . . here you guys came out of nowhere!"

He responded by giving me a primer in Eastern mysticism. He told me that you can go to the Himalayas to find yourself, but if you are in a bad mood or depressed, all you are doing is taking your bad mood to the mountains. The mountains won't provide a cure. From that somewhat opaque starting point he talked a little about the

Beatles, always referring to them as *they* rather than *we,* implying that he was on the outside looking in. "Why do you say *they* and not *we*?" I asked. George just laughed. "You weren't a Beatle, were you? Oh, yeah, now I remember you!" After a chat about the new sitar sound he was exploring with the great Ravi Shankar, he began asking me what I thought of his Bangladesh Concert and we spent about forty minutes discussing George without the Beatles. The station trumpeted it as a big exclusive. Later, we caught up again in Los Angeles, and some of our interviews were run over and over again after his death. He was the first Beatle I met in person. Later on, to my supreme delight, I would meet and become friends with all of them but one.

When George died, I did his obit from in front of the famed Capitol Records building in Hollywood, the label that introduced Beatlemania to the U.S.

There was an Elvis sighting for me, albeit brief, in Chicago as well. I had made arrangements to do an interview with Elvis in one of the suburbs during his concert tour through the Midwest, and it was all set that he stop by and say hello on his way to the hotel. We set up an extravagant live shot to capture this momentous event. All of a sudden, here comes his limo, and as I was expecting it to stop and to see the King hop out . . . it sped by and all I saw was Elvis's face and his hand giving us the finger. I later got to know all his bodyguards, and they say they remember the event and tossed it away as "Elvis having fun." I did, too, and I gave him the finger back. Twice. It was cool. And they told me he loved the chutzpah.

I was a good, serious reporter in Chicago and was rewarded well. On one news Emmy night, I was up for a bunch of Emmys, and when I won my first one, I said with the air of grandiosity I was harboring, "I will thank everybody the next time I come up here to gather my next one." After two more statues, I finally said, "Thank you, and I'm going to get loaded tonight, so if anybody has a ride home for me, I'd appreciate it."

While music was my first love, politics came a close second.

Chicago was not just the home of Mayor Daley but an important battleground state for Democrats and Republicans. Big-hitting politicians were always visiting the city. On one occasion while I was covering the 1976 election campaign, I found myself sharing a bathroom with President Gerald Ford. His Secret Service, heavily armed, attempted to shoo me out, but the president waved them away. With one hand. The other was occupied.

As athletic as he was, Ford had the reputation as a klutz, especially after he was filmed stumbling while exiting the presidential jet during a visit to Austria in 1975. Chevy Chase made a career out of mocking this on *Saturday Night Live*. Ford was a reluctant candidate, and his campaign seemed to be floundering. As we used our separate stalls, the president asked how it was all going. I replied, "Mr. President, you and I might be the only people on this campaign who know exactly what we are doing right now." It got a presidential laugh.

The next day a reporter at a rival TV station snagged an interview with Ford. The pressure was on me to match their scoop. Fortunately, Ron Nessen, who had been one of the regular correspondents on *Huntley-Brinkley,* was Ford's press secretary. He took pity on me, arranging for a brief meeting in the president's hotel suite late that night so that I could legitimately say on air, "I have just left the president." The meeting was for 9:45 and was for just eight minutes. No cameras. At precisely 9:45 p.m. I was ushered into the president's suite, but there was no president. Finally a voice comes from another room: "Pat, is that you?" I replied, "Mr. President, yes, it's Pat O'Brien, Channel 5." A few seconds later he emerges with a tall tumbler of whiskey in his hand. The first thing he said was "Now you won't report that the president of the United States had himself a drink after a long day, will you?" I replied, "Of course not," and we chitchatted for a few minutes about the campaign while he sipped his whiskey. He never offered me a nightcap, but I was able to say I was alone with the president of the Free World that night. It was a big hit, and once again I had the better scoop.

While it was a thrill to meet the president, the bread and butter of my life as a city reporter was the man known as Da Mare, Hizzoner, and the Man on Five because the office of Mayor Richard Daley, Chicago's second-longest-serving mayor, was there. He is best remembered for helping to rig the 1960 presidential election, in which John F. Kennedy won a wafer-thin victory over Richard Nixon after Daley ensured the state of Illinois voted Democratic—thanks to the stuffing of ballot boxes and other chicanery. While he presided over the building of the Sears Tower and the expansion of O'Hare Airport, saving Chicago from becoming a rust-belt city, he also presided over a city machine that saw many of his associates jailed for corruption. As the last of the big-city bosses, he was loved and loathed in equal measure. He was never ignored.

For all his faults, he was open with the media, and he and I had a rambunctious relationship. He quietly admired my confidence—as well as my Irish ancestry—while publicly professing to find me a pain in the ass. One time, I dropped by his office with a ticket I had received outside City Hall and said to him, "I understand you're the guy who can fix this." He reached into his wallet and pulled out $5 and handed it to me. "You're right, Patty; now it's taken care of."

At one news conference, who couldn't forget this review of yours truly from this country's most powerful mayor ever?: "If you guys reported that Richard Daley walked on water, Pat O'Brien would say that the mayor can't swim." During one visit to City Hall I asked him, "Where did you sit on the night you stole the presidential election in 1960?" He picked up the intercom to his secretary and said, "I'll be right back." Then something magical happened. He took me to see what he called "the war room," a bare room in the Democratic Party headquarters with just two phones. One was for all the ward captains, he explained. Then I pointed to the other phone, which I think was actually red: "What's that?" "None of your goddamn business," he replied. From that moment on, no matter what people said about Hizzoner, I genuinely loved the guy. The city was thriving, the water, electricity, and roads all worked, while in winter the sidewalks were cleared. I was usually on the side of Mayor Daley for good and for bad.

If nothing else, he was good copy. It was a slow news day on December 20, 1976, so I called the mayor's office and asked if he was doing anything special. I was told that he had attended the annual Christmas breakfast for department heads, where they surprised him with round-trip tickets to Ireland for him and Mrs. Daley. At noon he was attending the dedication ceremonies for a new gymnasium on the far South Side. I thought I would swing by and take a look. At the event a youngster threw him a basketball. He caught it and looked over at me and said, "Patty, what should I do?" I replied, "Shoot it." As the camera rolled, he shot it, and it was all net. With a big smile on his face he turned to my cameraman (the only one there) and said, "This must be my lucky day."

We sent the film back to the office and headed for a noisy bar out of town to celebrate Christmas early, while first informing the news desk that we were researching a story. Then after switching off our pagers and walkie-talkies, we got down to some serious drinking. After a couple of hours of this, we headed back to the TV van to find a shitload of increasingly frantic messages all along the lines of "O'Brien, where the fuck are you?"

The news editor rapidly explained that Mayor Daley, then seventy-four, was gravely ill, possibly with a heart attack. No one knew if he was dead or alive. Apparently he was at his doctor's office at 900 North Michigan Avenue. I raced there, knowing that I'd be the one reporter who would find out what was going on.

By the time I arrived, scores of newsmen, shoppers, and onlookers were gathered outside the office of physician Dr. Thomas Coogan Jr. Rumors were swirling like snow flurries: that Daley had had a choking fit while eating with friends or that he had collapsed on the sidewalk. An ambulance was standing by outside the doctor's office, and doctors and paramedics from nearby Northwestern University had come to assist. As news spread, it seemed that the city was holding its breath in anticipation. In such a grave situation there was no room for guesswork; the report on the mayor's condition had to be totally accurate.

On this freezing-cold afternoon I went down an alley by the side of the physician's office for a smoke and to get out of the chill wind. In the alley I spotted Frank Sullivan, Daley's hard-as-nails press secretary, lying in the snow in a fetal position, crying uncontrollably. I rushed over. "Frank, what time did he die?" I was guessing. By now it was about three thirty in the afternoon. "About an hour ago," he said. So I called the office and said that I had confirmation that Mayor Daley had died. "Who is your source?" they asked. I told them about Frank Sullivan, but they weren't satisfied: "You have to get another source!" I told them I was certain Daley was dead and would stake my career on it. They agreed to run my report, figuring I couldn't be that suicidal for such a big story. As soon as I did my broadcast—beating my rivals by precious minutes—I headed back to the studio. While I walked back down Michigan Avenue through the snow, Deputy Mayor Kenneth Sain made the official announcement that Mayor Daley had died.

By now the city was at a standstill. Church bells were ringing; motorists had stopped and were asking one another what had happened. It was as if the head of state had died. After all, most kids in Chicago thought Daley's first name was Mayor. He had been there that long. Back at the office, I was told some even more depressing news—the film with the mayor shooting a basketball had been accidentally exposed and was unusable. The luckiest part of his day had been permanently erased.

The full impact of his death was brought home as I stood in line to pay my respects at the Church of the Nativity of Our Lord, which Daley had attended since childhood. I was also reporting on the number of mourners waiting to say farewell. I ended my report with this: "While there were four, maybe five thousand people here, I have to say, nobody loved a Democratic Party crowd count more than Mayor Daley. So, again, a quarter of a million people were here today to say good-bye to a great man."

Then it was my turn and I got in the long line by myself.

As I approached the open coffin, his wife, Sis, waved me through the red-rope line. "Dick loved you," she told me. "It was that Irish thing about you. He used to come home and say, 'That damn Patty O'Brien.'" I didn't know what to say, but when I got back outside in the cold and the snow, one of my tears froze on my cheek. I wanted to save it, maybe put it in a Bible till it melted. I would have put it at 1 Peter 3:14: "But even if you should suffer for righteousness' sake, you will be blessed. Have no fear of them, nor be troubled."

That chill was not just the weather—although that winter was notable for day after unrelenting day of subzero temperatures. With Mayor Daley's departure some of the fun went out of reporting the windy world of Chicago politics. I was ambitious, eager to prove myself, eager to move on—and get warm. One evening that winter as I trudged home through the snow and frost from the Belmont rail station, I made up my mind. It was time to move, my desire a mixture of ambition and my feeling, born from my insecurity, that the grass is always greener somewhere else. When I told Linda I wanted to move somewhere warm, specifically Los Angeles, she was disbelieving. We were living in a beautiful nine-room co-op, she had a great teaching job, and we had a wonderful circle of friends, so life couldn't have been better, it seemed.

Much to her dismay I called up the station manager of KNXT Channel 2 in Hollywood to see what was available. When he asked for my audition tape, I told him, with typical bravado, that I didn't have an audition tape as every story I did was good. My chutzpah got me an interview and my track record a job. Those rail tracks were beckoning once again. I was on my way one more time. That was, indeed, my lucky day.

6

Hotel California

I arrived in Hollywood in May of 1977 with a couple Emmys in my back pocket and a suitcase brimful of confidence and a point to prove to myself and my new television home and city. Because Linda stayed back in Chicago to teach, I began living the elegant Hotel California life. My first and second apartments were right on Sunset Boulevard, and there was no better way to become an instant Los Angeleno. The station had leased me a convertible Mercedes, and I had plenty of per diem money to eat and party where I wanted. On top of that, the weather was great. California dreamin' at its best.

KNXT was also on Sunset Boulevard and actually looked like a California TV station from the outside. Inside, with all the drugs and alcohol, it was definitely a 1970s California workplace.

Worth repeating again that it wasn't long before I was confronting the ghosts from my past. When I went to the personnel department, I found myself face-to-face with Phyllis Kirk, the actress who had scared me half to death in *House of Wax,* the movie I had watched as a youngster. Then married to TV producer and writer Warren Bush, she had given up acting some years before and taken a position in the CBS back office. When I told her about my first encounter with her, she was most amused.

The coincidences kept on coming. Just a few weeks into my new job I was told that a Pat O'Brien had called. When I returned the call, the voice on the other end of the phone said gruffly, 'Hi, kid, I will let you have the name in Chicago, but in this town I am the real Pat O'Brien."

The veteran actor invited me to his Hollywood Hills home, and we sat in his study—no women were allowed—smoking cigars and drinking fine cognac. He would say, "Sit right there; that's Bogie's chair," meaning Humphrey Bogart. Another chair was a favorite of John Wayne's, and after a couple of drinks O'Brien could easily be coaxed into reciting for his guests the entire Knute Rockne locker-room speech from the movie with the same name. One afternoon, we walked out and he introduced me to his neighbor: Betty White! It was my first encounter with her, but not the last, and she was always a comforting personality to interview and share a stage with for charity.

Another encounter with a hero from my youth was rather more random. I was walking to the station when Smokey Robinson, songwriter and singer, spotted me in the street outside the studio and shouted, "Hey, you're that news guy!" I was startled and replied, "I am supposed to recognize you, not the other way around." Over the years we have played a few rounds of golf together . . . and he would delight me with stories about working in the Motown song factory and writing songs for himself and the Temptations and other Motown groups. Later, when I finally met Berry Gordy, the "god" of the Motown sound, I let him confirm all of Smokey's stories. While a lot of Gordy's artists had business issues with him, Smokey remained loyal to Berry and me over the years. One night, while I was celebrating my birthday at the famed Roxy in Hollywood, Smokey spotted me and promptly sang "Happy Birthday," then followed that with a dedication, "Ooh Baby Baby." The last time I saw him, at a Paul McCartney concert, we hugged for a long time as if to say, "Well, we made it this far and we're still brothers." We both had done our share of drugs and drinking and, well, we surrendered and recovered. I always said, "You're Smokey Robinson and I am the Miracle." I love Smokey Robinson.

If marijuana and hash were the drugs of the sixties, there's no question that cocaine was the drug centerpiece of the seventies. In Los Angeles it was at every party, every office place, every nightspot, and was so available that it became a huge part of the culture. It was no different inside the newsroom of KNXT. Looking back on it, I do not know how we got the news on, but we did, and in award-winning fashion. But I'll speak for myself. The rest of my colleagues know who they are and what they did. I was doing an insane amount of coke, maybe up to $2,000 a week in today's money. And it was always followed by a healthy dose of alcohol. A typical working day would be as follows: Do some blow first thing in the morning, go out and cover the story. More blow while on the story, then around noon we would start drinking. Finish our stories and do more blow. By nine in the evening I would get home and then be back on the road again early in the morning driving to work. I never missed a day. I loved my job. And I can actually remember it.

Back then, you could go to even the most casual party and mounds of cocaine would be just sitting on the coffee tables. Many waiters at high-end restaurants were always holding, and at certain bars people would come up and say, "You've got a phone call," and take you in the back room and get you stoned. It was crazy. We all had choices and we mostly all took the wrong ones. Ironically, my interest in recreational drugs was what first put me on the media map in Los Angeles. Shortly after I arrived in the city, I covered what seemed like a routine story of police brutality. In August 1977, Sergeant Kurt Barz, a ten-year veteran from the Ramparts Division, encountered a totally naked, unarmed, but clearly hallucinating man on a street corner of Echo Park. After a brief scuffle, the man, Ronald Burkholder, was fatally shot six times by Sergeant Barz. Burkholder, a National Science Fellow and graduate of my alma mater, Johns Hopkins University, was on his knees with his hands on his head, the traditional pose for someone surrendering, when he was killed.

As part of the LAPD's defense of "justified" homicide, it emerged that Burkholder had taken PHP, a derivative of PCP or phencyclidine, commonly known as angel dust. This had transformed him from a mild-mannered Clark Kent into a raging monster, with such inhuman strength that he could not be controlled. No charges were brought against the officer, a decision that district attorneys defended on the grounds that he was "confronted by a person under the influence of a dangerous drug" and had "every right to feel that he was in imminent threat of great bodily harm or death."

I decided to investigate this claim further. The recreational drug PCP was originally created as an anesthetic for surgery in 1956, but was immediately abandoned for human use due to its strange psychedelic side effects. It was then successfully redeveloped as an animal tranquilizer but later removed from sale. The Burkholder case thrust this obscure drug into the headlines, due in most part to its reputation for causing outbursts among its users of startling violence, paranoia, and insanity. One striking description from *The New York Times* summed up the concern surrounding this drug: "PCP destroys brain tissue. It puts you either into a God syndrome or it makes you depressed and violent. It's created a situation where a young woman can kill and eat her own children."

I heard of PCP users on a violent spree being shot repeatedly and yet continuing to advance upon their victims. Police spoke of being thrown around "like rag dolls," and of needing six or more officers to physically restrain one intoxicated individual. Most notoriously, several incidents were documented in which arrestees high on PCP broke free of handcuffs by simply tearing apart the steel-link chains.

This image was popular among police officers because it provided them with a convenient excuse: when facing charges of excessive use of force, officers could claim that extreme measures were necessary to take down a given suspect. This line of argument did not wash in the civil court, or in my reports. I got the autopsy report and it showed that Ron was shot at a forty-five-degree angle, meaning only one thing: he was on his knees, probably begging for help. Gravel marks on his knees proved it. This information put the LAPD on the defensive. In 1982, after years of fighting, Ronald Burkholder's family received $425,000 in compensation. Extreme force by police officers was starting to get a bad name in Los Angeles and I was right on top of it.

During my first few months of reporting crime in Los Angeles I had been struck by the difference between the Chicago cops and the LAPD. While the Chicago cops had a reputation for corruption—as did the city—in Los Angeles the cops seemed to be out of control. Rarely a week went by when we weren't reporting a story about a cop shooting an unarmed suspect, usually black or Hispanic. The use of choke holds to restrain people, which had been abandoned in most of America because of the danger to suspects, continued in Los Angeles. I remember covering a story of a black teenager who had died after being held in a choke hold. The official cause of death was a "heart attack." Another man was accused of setting off fireworks, and the police chased this young African-American into his own house and, reportedly, administered the choke hold in his bathroom. He died. Shortly after, I had legendary police chief Daryl Gates on a live TV show, and when I asked him about it, he responded, "Well, Pat, as we all know, that young man died of a heart attack." I said, "Chief, I'd die of a heart attack, too, if the police crushed my neck onto the edge of my bathtub." Didn't go over well with Chief Gates, and from that moment on, we butted heads on almost every cop issue. And there were a lot of them.

The Burkholder case and many other examples of the LAPD's inherent racism and a willingness to shoot first and ask questions later came to a brutally violent conclusion years later in March 1991 with the beating of Rodney King, a black convicted robber and parolee, by white officers after a high-speed car chase. The beating was videotaped by a bystander and repeatedly broadcast around the world. When the officers concerned were found not guilty of assault by an all-white jury, the city erupted in an orgy of looting and killing that left fifty-three dead and thousands injured. Once again the police argued that angel dust had been a factor in their use of force.

A commission, led by attorney and later secretary of state Warren Christopher, issued a report that confirmed what many knew already. It found that a "significant number" of officers had often used excessive force, especially against members of minorities, and that these officers had rarely been disciplined; that police reports were frequently falsified to protect abusive officers; and that messages between patrol cars—many quoted in the report—documented racial animosity, contempt for official restraints, and violent attitudes among officers.

This conflagration lay in the future, but in my investigation into angel dust and the Burkholder killing I hope I gave some editorial signposts to the tensions at the time that exploded years later. My story sparked a whole series of documentaries on rival stations and networks, notably when legendary newsman Mike Wallace mounted a similar investigation into the drug for CBS's *60 Minutes*. Nothing is more satisfying for a hard-nosed newsman than seeing your rivals and colleagues follow up on your story. That, in my first year at the station, I was awarded my first local Emmy for my documentary simply confirmed to me that I had made the right decision to come to the West Coast. Just as Chicago was, Los Angeles was my kind of town.

The town was also awash in drugs, and I decided to find the source. I was inspired and intrigued after reading *Snowblind* by Robert Sabbag. His book, first published in 1976, remains one of the best accounts of drug use and drug smuggling. Think *Blow*, the Johnny Depp movie, and multiply the madness by a hundred. Sabbag's antihero was a dope dealer called Zachary Swan, whose favored smuggling routine was to use hollowed-out souvenirs imported from Colombia to transport the drug. I was eager to learn more about this illicit trade, especially how cocaine was brought to California. After tracking Sabbag down to New York—not too tricky, as he was present at a book signing for *Snowblind*—I explained that I was looking to produce a five-part TV news show on the cocaine trail. He was excited by the idea and to celebrate took me back to his hotel, where he gave me enough cocaine to make my face freeze solid. During our late-night conversation he gave me a primer on becoming a competent drug smuggler, from making the initial contact to bringing the contraband into America. He even showed me the hand signals to use on a street corner in Bogotá, Colombia, that would indicate to dealers that you were looking to score.

I convinced the station head, Van Gordon Sauter, that this series was worth pursuing and shortly afterward found myself on a commercial flight to Bogotá with my faithful crew, the late cameraman Jose Bencomo and the late soundman Dave Watts. I took them all over the world with me, and once again, this time I was the reporter, producer, and director.

We set up headquarters in the world-famous Hotel Tequendama, right in the middle of Bogotá. I had a nine-room suite on the top floor. The atmosphere in Colombia was tense because of the drug cartels, and we weren't there to help. Little did we know the wild ride that would follow. In short, I should not have survived it.

The first day, I went out to test some of the tricks handed to me by Zachary Swan. I went on a designated street corner and, using certain hand signals, was within minutes offered cocaine. It was a trial run, but it was gonna work. I wasn't mic'd up, so I told the seller to come back the next day and that I wanted a kilo of coke, an outlandish amount for a street deal. Sure enough, the next day, with hidden cameras rolling from my hotel suite, the dealer showed up and we made the deal. I told him that I would be back later to pay him, which was, of course, a lie. We had gotten great video and audio and didn't want the cocaine. I was buying cocaine on a layaway plan.

That night, thanks to Zach Swan, I was introduced to a German woman who showed us the nightlife of Bogotá. We went into a back room and smoked cocaine (research), and from that moment I was on about a three-day high. That night, we were in the hotel bar and suddenly a skinny, sweaty, nervous-looking cat showed up and started speaking rapidly in a Spanish dialect. He sat right down in our booth, and I turned to Jose and said, "What does this guy want?" Jose said, "The guy wants his money and you better come up with something, 'padre, or we're going to get killed." Meantime, the runner had brought with him a sample bag and I asked to test it. I went into the bathroom and, right out of the movie *Midnight Express,* I looked in the mirror and said, "Pat, what the fuck have you gotten yourself into?" I brazenly took the bag, put half the coke in my pocket, and filled the bag up with white soap powder. Then I stormed out of the bathroom and threw the bag in the kid's face and said, "This shit is cut with something. The deal is off!" I know what you're thinking, and, yes, I was crazy. For some reason, I scared him and he ran off to fetch another batch.

We looked at him leave, looked at each other, ordered another round of drinks, and decided it was time to get the hell out of Bogotá.

Meantime, through the drug grapevine, which I was now a centerpiece of, we found out that there was a "Get this guy" alert out on me. Jesus. So after asking around, we were told to go as fast as we could to Santa Marta, a "safe house" resort for people on the run. Just a couple weeks earlier, a reporter had been killed in that area for the same "crimes" I had been involved in. I found the very spot where this guy had been killed and did an on-camera there, one of those self-serving things we do to show we're not afraid, etc., and there was no need to get into character. I had long hair, a shirt unbuttoned to my waist, sunglasses, and enough drug-dealer gravitas to pull it off.

Meantime, in our minds, we thought everybody was after us: drug dealers, local police, government officials, and the entire drug cartel. In this environment, I thought it a good idea to get a gun. I had our driver take me to the local flea market and bought something that Davy Crockett might have used. I went back to my villa and sat on my bed, wide-awake, with the gun at my side. To comfort myself, I was doing blow and drinking scotch. All great combinations. The next morning, I called the TV station and told them we were okay and we had enough material to come home. A combination of cars, boats (up the Amazon), and planes got us up to Barranquilla on the north coast. Fearing that our tapes would be confiscated, I paid an airport worker $900 in cash to hide the tapes in the overhead storage on the plane before we boarded. Security might have changed a bit since then. Just before we were getting ready to board, we were pulled into a room, and with armed guards watching over us, we were strip-searched, fingerprinted, interviewed, strip-searched again, and finally the custom officials allowed us on board. When we got to Miami, the DEA people there were like "Where the hell have you been? We were all looking for you." Apparently word had reached them that these rogue reporters were doing insane things in Bogotá. I retired to my Miami hotel room and slept for two full days, forty-eight hours.

It was all worth it—the series got great ratings and, more than that, proved to my colleagues that I was prepared to do almost anything to get a story. Even though I was messed up all the time with drugs and drink, for some reason I was always completely lucid on air. I was still, technically, a recreational user. That would change, in time . . . but for now, I was just having a good time, I thought.

Back in Los Angeles, I pretty much had the run of the station. I got the best stories, the best crews, the best editors, and the respect of reporters all over town. Most of them didn't care much for my bravado and the "Okay, it's a big story now that I'm here" attitude, but I didn't give a fuck. It was working. Awards and Emmys were flying in. My bosses loved it. As station general manager Van Gordon Sauter once pined, "I wish I could clone Pat about twelve times." He also had the brilliant observation "If Pat's bosses don't like him, his bosses' bosses love him." So there.

KNXT had a tremendous and fascinating stable of great reporters. Most of them either were sharing an office with me or stopped by daily to see just what the hell I was doing. My office was a historic place where the likes of Jack Benny and Simon and Garfunkel once recorded. It was an old soundstage, and, boy, if those walls could talk. I could write a book about my office. Next to me was my dear friend and mentor the late, great Bill Stout. When I arrived in LA, Bill picked me up at the airport and took me to all the great Los Angeles watering holes and introduced me to all the bartenders. "This guy is gonna be good," he'd say. Bill was from the Edward R. Murrow gang that once ruled CBS and the news. I used to kid him that, sure, they were good, but, "Bill, you had one fucking story, World War Two!" Bill and I never let a day go by without sneaking out to the local pub for a few cocktails just before deadlines. We argued contantly, and when he died, I began his eulogy with "Bill, this is one argument I'm gonna win."

Behind me was Linda Douglass, who was the best-looking and the smartest person in the newsroom. She later went on to grander things, including a stint as a network correspondent and an important job in the Obama administration, and now she's the toast of Washington, D.C., and Italy, where her husband, John, serves as ambassador. I taught her well. Former *Today* show host Ann Curry was across the room, and she was as nice and smart as she looks. There were some characters, though. An African-American, little guy named Jim Gibbons, who lived in Beverly Hills and couldn't remember the last time (if ever) he was in the community. Jim had an irritating habit of speaking on the phone in fluent French. We could never figure out whom he would be talking to, but his French was perfect. He was a man in a hurry and that never, ever works in any language.

It was a curious office and because Douglass and I always got the best stories, the other reporters would always stop by to spy on us. This became so out of place that I made it a habit to punk them every chance I got. For example, around Christmastime I would sneak into Mr. Sauter's office and use his IBM Selectric typewriter for a practical joke. I would steal a corporate envelope and neatly type my name on it in that familiar executive font, then type in big letters "CHRISTMAS BONUS." Then I would stuff it with paper and put it on my desk. Before long, every reporter in the building would be complaining about never getting a bonus. I was sternly told to stop this.

Connie Chung came there for a spell to anchor, as did the great Brent Musburger, who was at CBS Sports on the weekend and doing news during the week. I was always in awe of how he could read scores and highlights and news without ever looking at a prompter and never making a mistake that we knew of. On the other hand, Jim Hill, known for his nice suits, was unable to finish one sentence without jumbling up all the words and numbers. He is still doing that at the same station. My old friend Jim Lampley stopped by, and he and I had all the obvious fun inside and outside the office. And, yes, Keith Olbermann was there long enough for everybody to hate him. No bigger jerk ever, and I don't know what ever happened to him.

There was never a shortage of stories. Big, terrible plane crashes up and down the coast, where I would find myself walking among bodies with their heads and limbs missing. Riots and demonstrations galore. Fires, fires, and more fires. Back then, even the City Council was interesting. I was consumed by local news, and the awards kept coming. So did the pay raises. One time I got such a big pay raise, the news director took me out in the newsroom and yelled out, "Okay, Pat, pick out the three people I have to fire to pay your new contract!" As the newsroom went silent, I pointed at him and said, "Well, here's one." I got two weeks without pay, but it was worth it.

In this crazy life it was pure serendipity that I ended up hanging out with the drug guru himself, Timothy Leary. I had the idea to take a look back at California in the 1960s and the much-talked-about and always poorly imitated "hippie generation." So I looked in the phone book and there he was. Timothy Leary, Beverly Hills. Leary's résumé included West Point, Harvard, the introduction of acid (when it was legal), a pioneer in group therapy, the inspiration for a couple Beatles songs ("Come Together" and "Tomorrow Never

Knows"), and the sixties philosophy to "turn on, tune in, drop out." I called him and told him who I was, and the second thing he said was "Come on over; I'd love to meet you."

Leary was a legend. First of all, he was the godfather of the hippie movement and the Walter White of the time. He was also one of the smartest, most well read, funniest people I have ever met. Ever. He had the perfect résumé for Richard Nixon to dub him the most dangerous man in America. We hit it off immediately and I would find myself at his house after work on many occasions.

One day he asked me if I'd ever tried acid. I was always a victim of that conversation that people who took acid "freaked out" and sometimes didn't come back. So, I said yes to his offer to try it. He said, "Look, if you want to write a song, write one with Lennon and McCartney. If you want to do acid, do it with Timothy Leary." So I did and I loved it. Before you run out and try it, remember that this was his acid, which had not gone through any street life and was, as we always assumed, "pure."

My first trip with Timothy ended up with him and me in my 1972 BMW with no plates flying through Los Angeles, each high on about five tabs of acid and bottles of wine between our legs. We ended up at a wrap party for a Monty Python movie, and as we walked in, Timothy said to me, "Watch this; we will be the most interesting people at the party." We were. Within a half an hour, Timothy was lying on his back swearing at everybody and I was lost in one of the upstairs rooms. When we left, a car was parked in front of mine, and Leary smashed a brick through the window and put it in neutral and it rolled down the hill. We went flying home. Later when I met up with Python member Eric Idle at a George Harrison event, I told him about that night and he responded, "That was you?"

Acid started to replace cocaine as my drug of choice. I wanted to do it more often, but Leary counseled that I wait a couple of days before starting another session—which was just as well as one time after seeing Leary I had arrived at work so stoned that the news director ordered me out of the building. Instead I used to take off a workday every week, drop a tab of acid with my friend from Channel 7, the great and talented and late Wayne Satz, and watch funny movies all day long. Even if they weren't funny, they were funny when we were watching them.

Once I was hanging out at Leary's house and a package arrived, and he said with glee, "Whoa, I think this is the new drug I've been working on." I asked what it was and he said it was a kind of love drug. "What's it called?" I asked. He said, opening the box, "I think we'll call it ecstasy." I loved Timothy and we had many, many great times together. The day after my son was born several years later, I went to an art exhibition where Yoko Ono was displaying some John Lennon art and ran into Tim. He had heard that I was now a father and came over and gave me a big, big hug. I joked, "I was counting my son's toes and fingers after all that acid we did." He replied, "You should have been counting the extra lobes on his brain." So was my friend Timothy Leary. He died a prolonged, ugly, undignified death.

The hits never stopped. In August of 1977 I was sent to Las Vegas to cover some serious flash flooding in the desert. It was basically a stakeout, since you can't schedule a flash flood. So there I was with my loyal crew sitting in a cheap restaurant outside Sin City. About the third time the waitress came over to refill our coffee, I noticed that her mascara was smudged in tears all over her face. I inquired, "What's the matter, honey?" With more melancholy than seemed necessary over the possibility of a flash flood, she said, "It says on the radio that Elvis is dead!" I raced to a pay phone (yes, late seventies—no Internet, no Google, no cell phone, etc.) and called the office and I told them that I would do this story and only me and that I was heading to the Hilton in Vegas. The Las Vegas Hilton was Elvis's residence for many years, and I figured this would be a good place to start. I was right. As I was walking in, Roy Orbison was walking out. Roy was Elvis's best friend in the music business to the tunes of "Only the Lonely" and "Hound Dog Man," the two songs he wrote for the King of Rock and Roll.

"Mr. Orbison, I have some bad news, sir," I began. "Elvis Presley is dead." He stared at me as if I were the flash flood and said, "Now, son, don't be making up stuff like that. Don't be messin' around with me!"

I finally convinced him and we did the first and probably the best post–Elvis death interview right there in the revolving doors of the Las Vegas Hilton, ending with his leaning on my shoulder and crying.

As expected, the entire country was crying. So I packed up my crew, Jose and Dave, and down to Graceland we went to cover everything Elvis. The second day there, I dropped my last tab of Leary acid and we headed to Tupelo, Mississippi, the King's birthplace. We ended up in the local hangout called Sam's Bar. I could not ignore the irony of my being stoned while covering a man who died because of his addictions to drugs. But at the moment, I had to go to the bathroom. I wandered in and went into a stall, and suddenly there was this loud commotion in the tiny room. I looked out and some guy was just beating the hell out of another man. He was pistol-whipping him with what appeared to be a .357 Magnum. At first, I thought I was, indeed, hallucinating, but found out quickly that I was, for once, at the wrong place at the wrong time. The gunman saw me and shoved me against the wall and put the barrel of the gun right into my mouth and started screaming at me. Was I gonna die in a bathroom in Tupelo, Mississippi? I let the guy scream for a while, and then, suddenly, he turned his redneck attention back to his original victim. I snuck out. It was pouring down rain, but that didn't stop me from running outside and vomiting in the parking lot. I sobered up quickly that night . . . went back in and had a hamburger at the bar and we called it a night.

As much as I was voluntarily destroying my health on this self-destructive binge, my career was going from strength to strength.

My next big series was straight out of the David Brinkley playbook. He always told me that being a journalist is about observing, not about reporting. "Sometimes there are stories right in front of you that are interesting and compelling," he once told me. This was the case with our story on male hustlers, which first aired in 1978. Our station was on Sunset Boulevard in Hollywood, and every night when I left work, I would see all these young guys strolling up and down Selma Avenue a couple of blocks from the station.

One day I pulled over and asked the guy what the deal was. He asked me if I wanted a blow job for $10. I passed, but I started talking to him about how common this was. Laughing, he told me to swing by Santa Monica Boulevard in West Hollywood, then the gay capital of Los Angeles, and take a look. Every night dozens of skinny, young kids were hanging out. Every so often one would get into a car, disappear, and return to the street a short time later. Finally I realized that they were all male prostitutes plying their trade.

The scene was straight out of John Rechy's seminal novel, *City of Night,* about a young hustler traveling around the States selling his body for money and food. When I contacted Rechy, he agreed to appear on the show, putting this street behavior in a social context. He was articulate, smart, and fearless, unafraid to speak out on the somewhat taboo subject of homosexuality in society.

At the same time my producer, Mark Litke, and I followed one street kid around for several nights. He only reluctantly gave us his name after we were with him and his hustler friends for several nights in a row. This was a piece of "news vérité," observing a street scene that many local people never gave a second thought to as they commuted home. When it was aired, the story caused quite a stir, and I was genuinely thrilled when our efforts earned a local Emmy.

For all the fluff and nonsense in the broadcast media, I realized that we could raise awareness of difficult and important issues. I was making a difference—as Dr. Farber had trained me and all the other Farber Boys to believe in.

Every story I touched now was making headlines and getting a lot of attention. But I wanted more. So, I turned to God. Doing the Brinkley theory of observing everything, as I drove around Los Angeles, I was struck just how many billboards were advertising evangelical Christian churches and ministries. The born-again movement was taking hold, the numbers swelled in 1977 by a most unlikely recruit, Larry Flynt, the owner of *Hustler* magazine and other porn operations, who announced that he had been born again after seeing a vision of God out of the window of his private jet. I spoke to my boss, Van Gordon Sauter, about this growing movement, and he was skeptical that I could convince these folks to sit down with me. I proved him wrong. Besides talking to Larry Flynt, I interviewed the tub-thumping leaders of this movement. I talked to Dr. Robert Schuller, founder of the Crystal Cathedral in Garden Grove, California, whose worldwide ministry kick-started the megachurch movement, and Jerry Falwell, the evangelical fundamentalist-Baptist poster boy who founded the Moral Majority in 1979, a movement that was pro life, family, Israel, and defense and pretty well against anything else. Then there was fundamentalist preacher Pat Robertson, founder of the Christian Broadcast Network, who opposed feminism, homosexuality, and abortion and considered Islam the work of Satan. This fascinating series described how society was changing and polarizing, the right-wing Christian conservatives and a growing liberal movement that advocated gay rights, promoted women's issues, including the right to choose an abortion, and preached peace and love rather than war and hate on the other. California, as is often the case, was at the cutting edge of the changing mores and values of American society.

My favorite moments of this investigation were my visits with Dr. Schuller. He had constructed the first "drive-in" church and built it into a monument to God and donations. His office was bigger than the Oval Office, and he had pictures of two people on the wall: Jesus Christ and Frank Sinatra. Eventually, I got around to the master himself, Billy Graham. We spent a couple hours walking and talking and in that short time got to know each other pretty well. When

I was preparing to leave, Dr. Graham put his arm around me and said, "Pat, I feel that there is something inside you that is eating away at your soul." I thought he was crazy. Me, Dr. Graham? Not me. I'm Pat O'Brien. Ha.

About this same time, a polarizing initiative was placed on the ballot, known as California Proposition 6, or, more commonly, the Briggs Initiative, as it was sponsored by conservative Orange County lawmaker John Briggs. It aimed to ban gays and lesbians and anyone who supported gay rights from working in the state's public schools or any other public-sector job. Initially it enjoyed popular support, but thanks to a coalition of liberals, gays, and conservatives, led by the redoubtable Harvey Milk, San Francisco's Mayor Moscone, and others, the public mood was beginning to alter.

When I heard of the initiative, I was incensed and begged my news director, Van Gordon Sauter, to let me take Briggs on. Forget about objectivity; this, I thought, had hidden political and human rights consequences. I knew enough European history to realize that once you put one group into a ghetto, it's not long before others are castigated as well. This issue affected everyone's basic human rights, not just the gay community's. I got deeply involved with the No On 6 campaign, interviewing the main political players, including John Briggs, a loathsome human being in my humble opinion, and Harvey Milk, the up-and-coming gay politician who organized opposition to the initiative. I went to Castro Street in San Francisco and met Harvey and marched with the gay activists. As I was screamed at for being a "nigger lover" as a seventh-grader for running around with an African-American neighbor, now I was getting "faggot lover" and all that. Still I took on Briggs and his followers, destroying the politician with my own biased coverage. This guy was not going to budge, but I pounded and pounded until the proposition was defeated. That night, I celebrated with the gay community and got congratulatory calls from prominent gays, including Harvey and people from his staff. As a result, I found myself spending time in San Francisco not just covering the No On 6 campaign but making contact with several families of the Concerned Relations group who had written to me after the born-again series. They were worried about their children, who were members of the Peoples Temple, a cult led by a well-known local figure, Jim Jones.

After the cult relocated from the Bay Area to the jungle of Jonestown, Guyana, families lobbied the authorities to visit the site, where, they believed, their children were being held against their will. While I spoke with the families, my station didn't have much interest in the story. In fact, Linda Douglass, my officemate, and I were the only ones trying to get it covered. No chance, my station said. It was seen as a San Francisco issue.

Then on November 18, 1978, came the terrible news of the murder of California's Representative Leo Ryan and journalists, and then the devastating discovery that some nine hundred cult members had committed suicide or been murdered by Jones and his intimate circle. Even though I had covered the terrible plane crash at San Diego in September that year, which left 144 people dead after a mid-air collision between a Pacific Southwest jet and a light plane, the sight of coffin after coffin arriving in San Francisco from Guyana was simply awful. As the local newspaper said, this was truly "a city in agony." The victims were innocent children or young people in search of some kind of salvation, prey to one man's warped view of existence. I covered the story and returned to Los Angeles numb and depressed. It was as if I had lost members of my own family. I was immersed in their agony and loss.

A few days later I was in the office when the assignment desk person screamed over the office loudspeaker, "Mayor Moscone and Harvey Milk have just been murdered in San Francisco. Pat O'Brien, where are you?" Well, I was already out the door and on my way to the private airport, where I rented a Learjet (on the station) for San Francisco. It emerged that the two men had been shot in cold blood by San Francisco supervisor Dan White, who harbored a political grudge against the duo and other supervisors. Dianne Feinstein, then president of the Board of Supervisors, announced their deaths to the media.

Feinstein, now California's longest-serving senator, had discovered the men's bodies after hearing gunshots. "Today San Francisco has experienced a double tragedy of immense proportions. As president of the Board of Supervisors, it is my duty to inform you that both Mayor Moscone and Supervisor Harvey Milk have been shot and killed. The suspect is Supervisor Dan White."

It was devastating news, and even journalists at the press conference were visibly shocked, some in tears. We filmed residents leaving flowers on the steps of City Hall, and that night I joined a spontaneous gathering, as thousands held a candlelit march from Castro Street, the heart of the city's gay community. There must have been fifty thousand people holding candles and marching in silence. All over the city, people were crying for their beloved mayor and Harvey Milk, who had become very beloved in certain parts of the city. The service for Mayor Moscone was held at St. Mary's Cathedral, and as his casket came out of the building, it started to rain. My cameraman, seeing the rain on the lens, said that the shot was unusable. I told him, "Yes, it is." As the camera panned from the casket to the tape, I said as commentary, "When San Francisco thought it had no more tears, it cried one more time." After that story aired, I got a call from Walter Cronkite himself, who said, "That was a hell of a piece."

It was the week after Thanksgiving, and I remember coming home so depressed and tired and emotionally drained that it was tough for me to get through the holidays. It was one of the first times I was really grateful for what I had.

The Jonestown mass suicide sparked a political and criminal investigation into numerous cults and ministries. I personally focused on a $130 million empire, the Worldwide Church of God, which was based in Pasadena. It had been founded by Herbert Armstrong, who in effect ran it jointly with his accountant, Stanley Rader. During 1979, California attorney general George Deukmejian had opened an investigation into allegations that millions of dollars a year had been stolen from the church by these church leaders, allegations that resulted in the Worldwide Church of God's being placed in court-ordered receivership for more than a year.

The two men traveled the world in a private Gulfstream jet, hired yachts, dressed in the finest suits, and generally lived the high life while their parishioners struggled with the tithes. I went after Rader big-time and it made great television. He looked like a sleazy used-car dealer and behaved like one: obnoxious, arrogant, and conceited. Under investigation by the IRS for nonpayment of taxes, he dismissed all criticism of him as the work of Satan while he drove around Beverly Hills in his Ferrari. I had many legendary interviews with Stanley Rader, going after him with facts and disgust. On a couple occasions he just took the mike off and walked away. Great television. Once I went out to the Pasadena headquarters, and while I was in there, they locked me inside! Also great television and great for my "Geraldo" profile. Then Mike Wallace from CBS's *60 Minutes* picked up the story and on prime-time TV in April 1979 skewered the smooth-tongued shyster. I was proud to have been part of that takedown. But there was some collateral damage. Stanley Rader was a ruined man, but his son was a parent of a pupil where my son eventually went to school. Rader's son told me, "Do you realize that you ruined my childhood?"

Chance encounters, luck, and serendipity are what life is about and, certainly, what great stories are about. Great stories are people stories in the end, and I loved people stories: you couldn't make them up. So it was that I found myself hanging around the courthouses in Los Angeles on my off days, hoping to see something that piqued my interest. It was kind of like ambulance chasing without the premeditation. On a hot summer day, I found myself sitting on the steps of a Los Angeles superior court and Ed Masry appeared. Ed was a familiar local defense lawyer who took on a lot of cases for little or no money. He represented the "little people" for a living. He sat down and pulled out a cigarette, and after a while I asked what he was working on. "Well, Pat," he said, then dragged on his cigarette, "right now, I'm going to go home and tell my wife that I'm done with all this." He explained that he was tired of the merry-go-round and tired of going nowhere riding it. So, he was collecting his thoughts to go home and tell his wife he was moving on. I'd seen Ed at work many times in victory and defeat, and so I weighed in on his life without invitation. I told him he couldn't quit. "What would all these people do without the Ed Masrys of the world?" I lectured. "You're a public servant, Ed, and that should count for something. I just don't see a guy with your passion giving up so easily." We then had this philosphical discussion about defense lawyers and people without voices and Ed and life and why we shouldn't be smoking and on and on. Ed thanked me and walked into the courtroom. He sort of half laughed and said, "Okay, Pat O'Brien, you've saved humanity for another day." We shook hands and off he went.

Later I learned that was the day when Ed Masry ran into a local activist named Erin Brockovich. One thing led to another, and together they launched the famous lawsuit against Pacific Gas and Electric Company for its groundwater contamination in the high desert of California. They got a $333 million settlement, and so dramatic was the case that Hollywood followed it up with the Oscar-nominated movie *Erin Brockovich*. I had forgotten about my conversation with Ed until many years later when I was covering the movie, starring Julia Roberts, on the red carpet. Julia came up to me and said, "You know, Pat, you might be the reason we are all here." Then, right behind her, Ed Masry strolled into camera view, and it all began to click. Ed told all the cameras on the red carpet about our conversation two decades earlier and that I'd talked him "into staying in the game." It was wonderful. A chance encounter, luck, and serendipity had brought us all together again. Julia won the Oscar for her role (more on her later), and Ed Masry and Erin Brockovich went on to help thousands and thousands of other victims. You could never have made this up and the lessons learned were these: to hear everybody out, listen, and maybe spend that extra moment or two with a down-and-out person.

My status in Los Angeles news circles was being elevated to heights I'd never imagined, and the one thing that kept me on top was that I could cover the dark, tragic stories with heart and soul and then turn around and cover things that made people happy. But I always connected with the dark and tragic stories. I liked stories that made people think, reflect, and digest. It was also a way at looking at myself, I know now.

Enter, again, the Beatles. I was lucky enough to be on the list to go to New York and interview John Lennon, who was making a huge comeback with his album *Double Fantasy*. John had been in seclusion as a stay-at-home dad, and now he was back to bring us great music.

Though the album had been trashed by the critics, I didn't give a damn, I was going to meet another of my four heroes. Then it happened. I was driving home in my little BMW from a bar when, on the 101 freeway, the speaker in my little beeper screamed, "Pat O'Brien, John Lennon has just been murdered; come back to the station." It was a Monday night, December 8, 1980. Trembling, I made the greatest illegal freeway U-turn in automobile history and headed back to the office. As a journalist, I was worthless. I simply couldn't function, utterly devastated by the news. That night I tried to write his obituary and ended up typing "John Lennon's Death." Then emptiness. The next morning, after I had composed myself, I wrote a very personal appreciation of the man we lost to the deranged Mark David Chapman:

"I've known John Lennon for sixteen years. I met him after school when my best friend showed me a picture of John Lennon and the Beatles and said to me, 'One day we'll look like that.' I turned to him and said, 'You've got to be crazy.' Through these years, though, I think we have all found out that there's a little bit of revolution inside all of us."

I flew to New York to cover the funeral, discovering New York City to be a giant open-air shrine to the singer who changed the world. In every bar and restaurant his music was playing. It was inescapable. The selfish part in me was that I regretted I would never meet Lennon. Later, Yoko Ono would say to me, "I bet you and John would have been great friends." We lost an outspoken genius whom we really, really could have used in the eighties, nineties, and into the twenty-first century. When I got home, I got sympathy cards from people, including my boss, Van Gordon Sauter, who simply wrote, "Pat, time will heal the pain." It never did.

Meantime back in Los Angeles, life was good. Linda and I were starting to plan a family. I was out and about and taking advantage of the Southern California lifestyle as much as I could. So, one familiar sunny Southern California afternoon, I was playing pickup basketball with the brothers down in Venice when suddenly a shout rang out. Guys were screaming and high-fiving, and when I went over to see what the deal was, they screamed, "We got Magic Johnson. We got Magic Johnson." I didn't know who Magic Johnson was, but I threw out a couple of high fives of my own. (Ironically, I would later learn from Magic that he was the first person to perform a high five on national TV.) At that very moment, my beeper went off to call the office. (It seems so funny and ancient to talk about beepers, but that's what it was: no cell phones, no computers, no Internet, etc. Somehow we got by.) I called from a pay phone and learned that Van Gordon Sauter had been promoted to president of CBS Sports in New York. So two major blasts on that sunny, sweaty day playing basketball in Venice that would soon connect.

Wanting to get into the Magic-to-LA story, I decided to go with him to his first practice at Marymount College in Los Angeles. As we pulled up, he wondered, "Why are all these people lined up around the building? I wonder who's here?" I reminded him, "You are!"

Later that season the Lakers found themselves in Game 6 of the NBA Finals against Philadelphia. That week, the mother of our sports reporter, Jim Hill, passed away, and Sauter asked, since I seemed to be a basketball fan, if I would I go to Philly to cover the story. It was supposed to be a guaranteed loss for LA because their center, Kareem Abdul-Jabbar, was staying back home because of a bad ankle. I traveled in fine form, jumping on a private plane with Capital Records chairman Joe Smith (the most famous Lakers fan this side of Jack Nicholson), legendary record mogul Richard Perry, and others. Before the game it was announced that Magic would replace Kareem at center, and I asked Magic, "You ever done this before?" He said, "Yes, in high school." Well, Earvin performed his magic that night in Philly, the Lakers won, and I returned on the team plane. The first one to greet us was Kareem himself, who said to me, "Hey, you would make a pretty good sportscaster." I laughed. Little did I know.

Soon Sauter called and wanted me to fly to New York for a meeting. When I arrived, he said, "Why don't you leave news and come and be a reporter for CBS Sports?" I told him I didn't know enough about sports to give me any credibility. He said that a reporter is a reporter and I should be able to handle anything. Then he laid out an offer that was triple my already comfortable salary. It was a turning point, I knew, but I didn't want to do it. I stood at his huge office window and looked down on the New York streets. After a long time he said, "Well, what are you thinking?" I said, "Honestly, I was wondering how people get across town in this traffic." He said, "You asshole, you should be thinking about driving on a freeway to a local news station the rest of your life."

I turned, shook his hand, and said yes.

I walked out into the streets of New York City and looked around. I was on my way again. This time, to network television.

7

You Cannot Be Serious

A few years into Conan O'Brien's late-night show, Conan and I were sitting around in his dressing room, picking on his guitars and talking about what it's like to actually be on television. "I thought it was easy," he told me. "I would watch you and Costas and Musburger, even Johnny Carson, and I'd say to myself, 'This looks so easy!' Then I realized that it looked easy because you guys made it look easy. I have to tell you, I found out quickly, it's not easy. I wanted to get under my desk and hide the first few times I did it."

Well, I thought the same thing. At least Conan was entering a world where he had some knowledge of the format, in his case comedy. I signed on to be a sportscaster, something I'd never done, never wanted to do, didn't have the skills to do, or the passion. It would be my biggest challenge so far. It was a bumpy transition from covering fires and cops and lost dogs to having a national audience expecting me to be the expert on, well, everything sports. Don't try this at home, kiddies. I immediately soaked in a new admiration for the guys who spend their weekends behind the mics. For those first few months the characteristic O'Brien brio and chutzpah were in short supply as I grappled with new names, teams, and strategies. Baseball players didn't just hit . . . football players didn't just run and tackle . . . basketball players didn't just put the ball in the basket . . . and boxers didn't just pummel. In South Dakota when I grew up, there wasn't much in the name of sports to lean back on. The only professional team I ever saw was the Harlem Globetrotters, about twice a year. Yes, there were the nearby Minnesota Twins and the Vikings, but no interest here. When you don't have a dad to move you in that direction and your only sport is tap dancing, you don't pick up a lot of heritage. But, as my dad always said, "You're an O'Brien; figure it out." So I began to do just that.

One of my early forays into this whole new world was as a commentator on a boxing match. Now, back in those days (early 1980s), we did a show called *Sports Spectacular*. As I always joked, little of it was sports and none of it was spectacular. In those days sports fans were somehow drawn to big, muscular guys racing with refrigerators on their backs, wood-chopping contests, world's-strongest-man contests, and the kinds of events you can, today, barely find on YouTube. But we did do a lot of boxing back then, and for *Sports Spectacular,* most of it was on tape delay. My bosses thought this would be perfect for me . . . sitting in a booth and calling the action, and if I made a mistake, going back and doing it again. After I told my producers that I had never even seen a boxing match, they strapped me in a booth and away I went. The fight began and I just stared at the monitor. My veteran producer, John Faratzis, yelled in my ear, "That's a right hook and he's wobbled, early." I then said, "That's a right hook, and, folks, it looks like he's wobbled early on in this game." Stop tape. "No, Pat, it's a match, not a game. Okay, take two." We continued, with mostly silence from my end. "Pat, there's a mouse under his eye." I had no idea what a mouse under the eye meant or how this could even happen to somebody. This went on for hours, and when they had finally dragged me through it, I felt as though I had just gone twelve rounds. Indeed, my ego was battered and badly bruised. This, clearly, wasn't going to work.

But Van Gordon Sauter had other ideas. Taking a page out of ABC Sports where they famously described the "thrill of victory—and the agony of defeat," Sauter decided that CBS Sports would attempt to grab on to that journalistic feel and put some depth and girth and passion behind the action. In other words, to report on the sports instead of offering just the play-by-play. I was on board with a healthy six-figure salary and apparently not going anywhere else as I learned on the job. Sauter also brought in a New York reporter who had almost the same background, the great and authentic and incredibly fun John Tesh. We were there to help define the sports and fill in the blanks. John and I hit if off immediately, but we weren't stupid. We knew we were invading a sacred fraternity of hard-core, grizzled veterans who didn't want their games to be tampered with. These were guys who had lived and breathed sports since they were kids. So their bemusement at the arrival of Tesh and me was entirely understandable. Some, such as Jimmy the Greek and Brent Musburger, accepted us with good grace; others were more hostile. Pat Summerall was thinking it over . . . Billy Packer hated us ("Don't ever tamper with the NCAA") . . . and up and down the CBS roster, the book was out on this new approach. It wasn't a comfortable place to work. Still, Tesh and I were not going anywhere, and Sauter believed that he had made the right decision to hire these two hotshot local reporters who didn't know a curveball from a knuckleball, but had a nose for a good story . . . and the Emmys to prove it. He was right.

At the time, CBS Sports had a terrific menu of sports that included the NFL, NCAA basketball, the NBA (on late-night tape delay), and a full slate of boxing. They also had all these "filler" franchises, including the Tour de France and the Iditarod Trail Sled Dog Race. To give these events some higher profile or a different look, Tesh was assigned to the Tour de France across the rolling plains and mountains and vineyards of France, and I was assigned to the Iditarod across the frozen tundra of Alaska, nearly twelve hundred miles of it. Good trade, right?

The Iditarod was billed as the "Last Great Race on Earth," and I found out quickly that it lived up to this marquee name.

So, in February of 1981, I set off for Anchorage, Alaska. The race is a grueling venture across Alaska from Anchorage to Nome. The route, through dense forest, rugged mountains, and forbidding tundra, is based on the route that miners, fur traders, and gold diggers used to get across a state short on winter transportation. When I say brutal, I am understating it. Temperatures dip well below zero and the windchill can be more than minus one hundred degrees. The race is the most popular sport in Alaska and is dedicated to the long history of mushers. Normally about fifty mushers participate and about a thousand dogs. Nobody in his right mind would try this, but there I was with my crew of grizzled cameramen, soundmen, lighting experts, producers, and production assistants. We correctly described our crew as the "hell crew." CBS Sports dedicated a lot to this event, including bush planes and pilots, helicopters, snowmobiles, and, on occasion, our own mush crew. It was quite an operation to follow the mushers from Anchorage up through Alaska, along the Bering Sea, and into Nome.

Our mission: to make a one-hour documentary on the journey. I was armed with enough winter gear to outfit an expedition to the north pole, gallons of Jack Daniel's, and bags of drugs. A man's gotta survive, right?

Well, the tone was set for this twenty-day adventure on night one. We all gathered in the bar at the Sheraton Hotel in Anchorage to have a couple cocktails and get to know each other. I noticed that the guy who was most served at the end of the bar wasn't saying much, so I asked my cameraman, Peter Henning, "Who's the drunk at the end of the bar?" Without missing a beat, Peter said, "That, my friend, is our pilot."

It was the legendary Tony Ony, perhaps Alaska's most famous bush pilot. Tony was a local dentist who flew all over Alaska offering free treatment to Eskimos in out-of-the-way areas, and he was also the pilot of choice for politicians and celebrities who wanted to hunt and fish and see Alaska close up. Tony has two stuffed grizzly bears, arms extended upward, in his living room. He killed them with one shot. He also knows where the fish are, where the wolves walk, and how to hunt and eat just about anything. He's also a great dad and husband and at age seventy looks forty. Tony was (and is) the "man" in these parts.

By now, our group had morphed into about a dozen guys who had simply stayed out too late. I suggested we go get something to eat, and Tony quickly invited us all to his house for an eleven o'clock dinner. "You think you might want to clear this with your wife?" we asked. Tony said there was no need, that Rita was used to it. So we all showed up, drunk and hungry, just before midnight without notice, and the lovely Rita fixed us a meal fit for kings: fresh salmon, salad, beef, veggies, dessert, and plenty of drink. Rita was the epitome of the Alaskan wife: a great mom, a great wife, a great cook, great sense of what she was surrounded with, and nothing—nothing—appeared to bother her.

The next day we were off and running through God's country, and I have to tell you in the simplest terms, Alaska is a big fucking state. Every mile seemed like three, and every drop in the temperature seemed as if it were always ten to twenty degrees. We went where the mushers went, so our accommodations weren't exactly what I was used to. If we were lucky enough to each have our own room, it was so small that the door hit the bed when you opened it. One shower. Little or no heat. It was brutal . . . so to pass the time, we drank and drank, and some of us snorted enough coke to get us through the fourteen-hour days, we thought, with energy. There are so many Iditarod stories, I could fill a book, but some stand out.

One time we came on a sled-dog team that had gotten tied up with a moose. If you don't know how big and powerful a moose is, think tractor with four legs and no way to turn it off. The dogs had somehow wrapped themselves around the moose's legs, and the moose was going nuts. Somebody handed me a .357 Magnum and said, "Shoot the moose while we free the dogs!" What? Now, I had never even fired a weapon, let alone shot a moose . . . and while I was organizing this thought, people were yelling, "Shoot the moose. Shoot the moose." I wasn't about to kill anything, so I held the gun above my head and fired in the air. The kick on the gun forced the handle into my cranium and down I went. The moose got scared and ran off. We were safe. I was concussed.

At the time, I had a tremendous fear of flying, so to get in Tony's single-engine Cherokee and bounce around the unstable air above the ice, I had to take Valium. One trip up toward the Bering Sea, my Valium was just setting in and suddenly Tony was poking me and screaming, "Wake up, wake up, we're gonna crash." I looked out the window and all I could see was white. We were above the Yukon River, hundreds of miles from anywhere. Oh, and the other thing I saw was all the fuel flying out of the wing. Tony informed me that if we could find a place where there was no jagged ice, we'd be okay, so we circled and found an area clear enough to land safely. We did. Tony, I learned, could land a plane just about anywhere. When the plane came to a bumpy stop, he turned the engine off, and suddenly it dawned on me that I was, indeed, in the middle of fucking nowhere. I said, "Now what?" Tony explained that he'd filed a flight plan, and if they didn't hear from us in six hours or so, they'd come look for us. (Remember again, there were no cell phones or even GPS at this time.) So I said, "Now what?"

"Well," he said as if he'd done this every day, "we have to get out of the cabin or our breath will freeze the instruments, so let's unpack." It was minus twenty-seven degrees, so we began a process I was a little unaccustomed to: we pulled out one sleeping bag, one rifle, a gallon of Jack Daniel's. Oh, and some extra ammo. I asked where my sleeping bag was and he explained that the only way we would survive would be to take our clothes off and get in one bag, and the warmth of our bodies would keep us alive. Never did that before either. As for the rifle, as soon as the sun started to go down, out came the wolves. Where they came from I had no idea, but there they were staring at us with those eyes only Stephen King could describe. It wasn't long, thank God, before another bush pilot flew over and came to our rescue, and off to our next stop we flew. Our next stop was a little seaside village called Unalakleet—where there was one hotel/café, no runway, no stores, a school for Eskimos, and about four houses. We stayed in Unalakleet for about four days during one of the fiercest storms I have ever witnessed.

One night . . . oh, about three in the morning . . . one of my crew guys came in and woke me up and said, "Hurry up, get your gear on; we have to go outside." The windchill was at least minus one hundred degrees, and our plane was blowing away and we had to go out and tie it down. When we finished, he said . . . come on, let's go for a walk. We trudged out about a hundred yards on the Bering Sea ice and he said, "Look up." And there it was, the aurora borealis, the northern lights, the most amazing and overwhelming thing I'd ever seen. We opened up a fresh bottle of Jack Daniel's and lit a joint and enjoyed the show . . . in the middle of the night in 110-below-zero weather. Life changing.

The Iditarod experience was like a religious experience, except for the guy who tried to kill me with a champagne bottle after he accused me of hitting on his wife (I didn't) and the time I flew with Tony up near the north pole so he could visit a village of kids who needed dental work. When we landed, he handed me a bottle of Jack Daniel's, and when I asked what that was for, he said, "I don't use novocaine and the screams get a little annoying."

When we got home and began editing our award-winning story, the news came quickly. President Ronald Reagan had been shot in Washington. Here I was, the hard-core newsman, writing a story about dogs, and the president of the United States had been shot. I came within two glasses of red wine of resigning and going back to news. But that, too, passed.

I did two more Iditarods, and to this day our "hell crew" stays in touch and looks back oh so fondly at the great adventures we shared.

The assignments came and went, and before long Tesh and I were ready to cover "real" sports. We were both famously assigned to be the reporters at the US Open Tennis Championships in Flushing

Meadows, Queens. This would be the big test. The Open was a mainstay at CBS Sports and one of their jewels, along with the Masters; unlike football and basketball, these were once-a-year events, and CBS put a lot of money and strength into what they called "the civil sports."

My first day, and every day, covering the Open, a limo was waiting for me outside the Loews Regency Hotel. On this day, I jumped in, and right there in front of me were the late Pat Summerall and Tony Trabert. Pat was by now a complete living legend, having played with the New York Giants and pretty much being the play-by-play voice of the NFL. He'd done everything and he'd done it well. Tony was a former US Open champion and pretty much the last sportscaster, along with Billy Packer, to hold on to the old school: love the past and hate the present and future. I slipped in the stretch limo and Pat greeted me with "Hello, kid, want a beer?" It was 10:00 a.m. I passed this time, but I quickly learned that part of the culture of covering the US Open was drinking. Back in the day Pat and Tony would have a cooler in the booth with beer and vodka and white wine and they drank pretty much all day. I did not judge and do not now. (Pat did beat me to rehab, which we'll get to later.) I'd always thought that Summerall's style of saying almost nothing during play-by-play was on purpose. Now I didn't think it was. But nobody was better, with or without a drink, to bring America the toughest tennis tournament in the world.

My job was simply to interview players going on and off the court. This wasn't done much before my arrival, but Sauter thought it was time the audience got to know the athletes in a more personal way. This assignment wasn't easy. Up till now, in every sport, the athletes were simply not used to seeing somebody before and after they played. It just wasn't done . . . so right away I was a novelty to them.

When Tesh and I arrived, we were not the most popular boys in the room. We were loud, flamboyant, partied hard, and drank harder. In the beginning, though, we were reduced to presenting an occasional feature about the ridiculous price of hamburgers at the tennis center. During our first Open, our main goal was to get through the postmatch interviews without harming our careers or the sport.

Our orders were to bring out the heart and soul of the game, how athletes and their families were feeling and behaving before, during, and after a big match. Way too much of sports coverage, be it basketball, football, or baseball, was reduced to bald statistics. Even though Sauter, Tesh, and I were inexperienced, the breaking of the sports broadcasting mold came at exactly the right moment in the history of sports. The union of sport, celebrity, and branding took the reporting in a foreign direction. We were poised to expose the good and the bad of the modern-day athlete. We were taking ABC Sports' "up close and personal" approach and running with it. Not for the first time, I found myself at the right place at the right time.

Overseeing the daily broadcast was our abrasive executive producer, the late, great Frank Chirkinian, christened the Ayatollah for his take-no-prisoners approach. Known as the "father of televised golf"—and tennis—he was, as his nickname suggests, a tough boss. Whatever he was thinking he said out loud. It was Frank's world, and to him Tesh and I were greenhorn visitors. If we made a mistake, he would simply say, "Listen, you cocksucker, if you ever do that again, I'll cut your balls off." As much as he tried to hide it, he recognized that sport needed a fresher look, which Tesh and I were prepared to offer. Again as luck would have it, we were parachuted into the game when two gladiators, the shy but magnificent Swede Bjorn Borg and the brash, outspoken American loudmouth John McEnroe, were at the peak of their epic skills. One hated talking; the other hated the media. My job was to try to get them to answer a couple of questions.

When they met at the US Open in the 1981 Final, there was a bit of a rain delay, so I found myself standing in the tunnel with both of them. Neither one knew who the hell I was or why I was there. McEnroe was unapproachable and pacing back and forth and at one point said to me, "If you think I'm going to talk to you, you're fucking crazy." Borg meanwhile was leaning against the wall, adjusting his racket strings with his fingers. On a whim, I asked him if I could check his heartbeat. It was forty-five. In a few minutes, he would be playing in a grand-slam final. Forty-five.

My test, though, was always to try to interview McEnroe. In the early days, it was impossible, but as time went by, John learned about the media, that we weren't all his enemies. He would become the greatest analyst . . . not just in tennis . . . ever. Over the years, John and I would become friends, and in 2011, when I was covering the US Open, he said to me on live television about those days, "Yeah, Pat, I was just toughening you up for the rest of your career." We worked together again at the 2012 Summer Olympics in London, and as we were veteran colleagues by then, it made for good television. I told him then and I still believe that whenever John is covering tennis, I learn something new.

I think one of the seminal moments in John's relationship with the public came after we convinced him, in the late eighties, to sit down and do an in-depth interview to explain himself to the American public. Up until then, people knew him and loved/hated him for his outrageous outbursts and his "You cannot be serious" episode with a chair umpire. The first time he went on one of these displays at Wimbledon, he got a call from his new sponsor, Nike, from Phil Knight himself, the founder and president, who said, "You know that screaming you did today? Do it again tomorrow." It was good for business and they both knew it. People forget now that tennis had some really, really bad boys in those days. McEnroe was the bad-boy team captain . . . but don't forget Jimmy Connors, who was actually meaner than John, and the ever-so-entertaining Ilie Nastase, I guess the original bad boy. Connors would never figure it out and, after he retired after a brilliant career, remained bitter about the sport. Nastase became an ambassador to the game itself. And then there was my dear friend Vitas Gerulaitis. If McEnroe was the bad boy, Vitas was the playboy. Nobody was more flamboyant than Vitas on and off the court. A ladies' man and a man's man, he was arguably the nicest athlete I ever knew. After his playing career ended, and after I was eventually named the host for the US Open, Vitas became my broadcast partner. Prior to our working relationship, Vitas and I had a fairly active party relationship. We were regulars at the famed and dangerous Studio 54, where, when we went in (especially him), everything was available to us. Everything. And he and I would go to fights in Vegas now and then . . . him wearing a white fur in eighty-degree weather.

Vitas, it's well-known, had a lot of demons, and about the time I really started to get to know him he had settled in and confronted all of them. One night we were having a quiet dinner in Manhattan, and he was so happy and so proud of himself. He said, "Now that all that shit is over, I'll probably get hit by a truck." The next week, he was dead. He was staying at a friend's house and went to the guest room to watch TV and eat a sandwich. In the most bizarre set of circumstances, he fell asleep from carbon monoxide and died right there. That day, Linda and I had gone to an event for President Clinton in Los Angeles, and I had been out of touch for several hours. (Again, no cell phones, Twitter, Internet, etc.) I got home and poured myself a glass of wine and switched on the television. On CNN, they were showing shots of Vitas and me in the stands at the US Open, laughing and carrying on. I couldn't figure out the context. I looked up, and Linda was standing in my office doorway and said, "I'm so sorry, Pat." Vitas was dead. I couldn't believe it.

I still can't. So much life. Too much life.

I also was gifted to have been around the great Arthur Ashe for a time. While McEnroe was the bad guy, and Vitas the party guy, Arthur was the good guy, the thinker. I always admired the way Arthur carried himself, and he was the first athlete whom I spent time with discussing Africa and the Middle East and world events. His enthusiasm in getting the game into African-American communities and putting rackets in the hands of the less fortunate, black or white, was so inviting that you couldn't help but feel "small" around him in your personal accomplishments. If you've never read his book *Days of Grace,* pick it up and learn what it's like to be a real man, a real father, and a real participant in the world. When we lost Arthur, we lost not only a tennis champion, but a champion of rights and humanity.

In the eighties, tennis started to change. No longer was it necessary to have a serve-and-volley game, as long as you had a 125 mph serve. The big servers and the baseline boys arrived at the US Open, including a young, unknown Czech by the name of Ivan Lendl. All of a sudden he arrived at the semifinals, and so, naturally (albeit late), we wanted all we could get of him. I was getting ready to interview him live, and I decided to ask him how to pronounce his name: "Is it Eye-van or Uh-van or EE-van?" He replied, "It doesn't matter." I said, "Well, is it Eye-van?" He said yes. We go on the air and I said, "Well, I'm standing here with Eye-van Lendl—" and he interrupts abruptly, "My name is Ivan!" So began my long-lasting war with foreign names. I would later learn that whatever the player's name was, the way I pronounced it the first time would be his or her name. Period. Which I learned from Musburger . . . "the big left-hander." "The big fella."

Well, in reality, Brent was the big fella. I knew him from our days together at KNXT in Los Angeles, but to work with him as a sportscaster was, for me, like going to graduate school. Nobody was better in handling the rigors of the sports studio; nobody was better at selling a game, delivering a story, and talking to the fans. The greatest. Brent would tell me that when he made a mistake, he would just keep talking until the viewer thought he/she had made the mistake. It was brilliant. I stole that one, too, from him.

After some success at the US Open, the big door was opened for me: *The NFL Today.*

The NFL Today wasn't broken and clearly didn't need to be fixed . . . but Ted Shaker had bought into Sauter's vision to add a little more texture to our sports by way of "sports journalism." I was put on the show as an addition to Brent, Phyllis George, Irv Cross, and the irrepressible Jimmy "the Greek" Snyder. It was an honor. Later, I would become one of the hosts, but for now I was just thrilled to be part of television history. Brent was Brent. Phyllis was one of the first women to be assigned a studio job. Irv Cross was sort of an after-thought. When you look back at that show, it was the first show to shoot a big wink out there to the gamblers. Brent would sneak in the lines on the games in some casual way, and the Greek would just out and out talk about gambling, which at that time was a television no-no.

The first time I met Jimmy, he said to me, "I've heard about you, kid. I'm told you're a hustler, so I'm gonna make odds that I'm gonna like you." He did, for a while, and we'll get to the drama later . . . but for the time being it was quite the learning curve to see how the big boys (and girl) did it. The Greek did little or no preparation before going on the air. His info came from friends and other hustlers he met on planes, at the track, and in bars. One time we were discuss-ing the San Francisco 49ers on the air and he said to Brent, "Yeah, I really like that kid, uh, that guy, uh, that kid . . . you know," and Brent would jump in, "You mean Joe Montana?" "Yeah, that's the kid." It was hilarious . . . but that was Jimmy the Greek. When he snuck the odds in, the executives cringed along with the NFL, which tried to pretend at that time that people didn't gamble on football. It was pure hypocrisy, but done with a wink and a smile, and America loved it. Brent would say something like "Well, Greek, let's say the 49ers win by six," and so on. That was the cue for Jimmy to give his assessment. I remember going to the track once with Jimmy at Bel-mont. He would walk to the window with a thick roll of $100 bills, like a roll of paper napkins, and drop $10,000 on a horse. Invariably the horse won. I asked him once how he knew the horse would win. He winked and said, "I talk to the horses."

8

Float Like a Butterfly

I was moving and I was moving fast. The idea of sports journalism was catching on at CBS Sports and I was in the middle of it. At the same time, I was called back to KNXT in the early and mideighties to anchor the news, so I was doing double duty. It wouldn't take long for my nickname to become Double Duty after the legendary Negro-league player Double Duty Radcliffe, who caught one game and then pitched the next in a Negro World Series doubleheader in 1932. Damon Runyon gave him that name and I wore it as an honor. But with the honor came lots of travel and a lot more national exposure.

Many times people and stories came right to my front door. In Los Angeles, right when I started at CBS Sports, a serious financial scandal surrounded the Santa Monica Track Club in Santa Monica, California. Ali had loaned his name and his Muhammad Ali Sports Club to the outfit, and with that they began spending money like Floyd Mayweather Jr. The cast of characters was long, from Don King down. The group was paying fighters many times what they were worth, and the money flowed so quickly, Ali finally looked at the books and pulled his name. He turned it into an old-time Ali rant, as in "The FBI is after me; the CIA is after me." He was in, in name only, but oh, what a name for the headline writers. Now the great one had to come forward and speak about it, even though it appeared he wasn't directly involved. There were two stipulations:

he wanted to do the interview with me, and he wanted to do it on live television. This was big. Here I was, just on the national stage, and I had to pick on the most famous and beloved athlete in the world. I was no stranger to Ali. He and I had met through our friend Jesse Jackson in Chicago in the 1970s, and from the beginning we got along famously. Ego meets ego. But now, some of the luster had been removed from his image, and so we were about to clash. I simply could not let our friendship get in the way of asking him tough questions about what had gone on behind the scenes at the track club, where the money was going, and what did he know and when did he know it.

I was nervous. About five minutes to airtime—with the New York producers nervously screaming in my ear, "Where is he? Where is he?"—in walked the great champion. When he saw me, he winked but didn't say a word. Instead he sat down next to me and clicked his long fingers together right next to my ear. Twice. I said, "Hey, champ, what's that about?" He said, "Can you do that? Click your fingers together and make that little noise?" We were thirty seconds to air and I tried it, but because I was so tense and nervous, my hands were sweaty and I could not make that sound. "You're nervous," he said, smiling. "Your fingers are wet and you think you're going to pick on Muhammad Ali on live television?" In my earpiece they shouted, "Ten seconds, Pat. Nine, eight . . ." Ali clicked his fingers again. I was getting annoyed. Finally we were on and I asked all the right questions, he gave all the right answers, and that was that. Afterward, he gave me a big hug and explained that that snapping thing was an old trick of his to see who was nervous around him. And off he went into the night.

In December of 1981, Ali was trying another comeback, and this time it was against a fellow Olympic boxer, from Jamaica, the hard-hitting Trevor Berbick. I was sent down to Nassau in the Bahamas to interview my friend and to cover the fight. The day of the fight, I walked up the beach to Ali's villa and knocked on the door. It opened and there he was. He was happy to see me and invited me in for some cereal. I didn't want to overstay my welcome, so I said I'd see him at the fight. "No," he said, "you stay here." Then, for an amazing three full hours, I watched him go through all his little magic tricks—the kind you learn when you're ten years old—but something about that day was both sad and happy. Clearly, he was nervous. Clearly, he needed somebody to talk to. Clearly, I was at the right place at the right time. We went for a long walk on the beach and the fight never came up. He wanted this fight and, in his mind, needed to win this fight, but I could see the Ali bravado was falling short of the mark he always hit so well. After about four hours of this—he showed me his new trick, levitation—I went back to my hotel and he went for a nap.

Later that night about an hour before the fight, I wanted to go to his locker room and say hello. A mob of reporters were standing there, including the little legend of print, Dick Young himself. Dick, who hammered away at the New York *Daily News,* was one of those ink-stained veterans and was, to say the least, polarizing. When he died, *The New York Times* described him this way: "With all the subtlety of a knee in the groin, Dick Young made people gasp. . . . He could be vicious, ignorant, trivial and callous, but for many years he was the epitome of the brash, unyielding yet sentimental Damon Runyon sportswriter."

So there I was, the new kid on the national block, standing there with all these journeymen who had been covering Ali his entire career, and we were all knocking on the same door. Ali's longtime friend and photographer, Howard Bingham, opened the door and pointed at me: "Pat, you can come in." All hell broke loose. Dick Young began screaming, "You motherfucking, cocksucking asshole, get the fuck out of here," or something close to that, and then someone, maybe him, picked up a chair and threw it at the door. It was crazy. I closed the door, walked over to Ali, and said, "Got any more magic tricks tonight?" He laughed and said no. Then, I put my fingers together and made that little noise in his ear. He looked at me with those steely eyes and said, "You got me, I'm nervous."

He had every right to be on this night. He took a hell of a beating for ten rounds in what proved to be his last fight. Those events, however, sealed our friendship for years, and he was always there for me and I was always there for him. After he was diagnosed with Parkinson's disease we became even closer, as my mother, Vera, contracted and died from that very same illness. Ali and I would meet up at many charity and fund-raising events. One that I will always remember was at Hickory Hill, the estate of the late Bobby Kennedy, where Ali and I found ourselves sitting on a couch in what was once Bobby's library/den. I sat down and said, "Well, champ, after all these years, we still look good." He said, "What do you mean *we*?" We had a good laugh, and somebody caught that moment in a photo that remains one of my favorites. From that moment on, every time we saw each other, we repeated that exchange. "We look good, right?" "What do you mean *we*?" I absolutely love Muhammad Ali.

Oh, one more magic-trick story. We were in a mall somewhere, and as it usually happened, Ali was surrounded by a mob of young people. He decided to show off his new card trick. He pulled out a deck of cards and had a ten-year-old girl pull one out and put it back in the deck. Then, he dramatically threw all the cards in the air and they landed all over the place. He walked over and picked up the queen of hearts. "Is this your card, young lady?" Silence from the crowd, then she nervously said, "No." Silence again. Then the great Muhammad Ali replied, "Young lady, then you don't know card tricks."

Boxing, at the time, was the Saturday-afternoon jewel at CBS, known as the Tiffany Network because in 1950 the first color TV transmission ever originated in the Tiffany building on Park Avenue. I was paired up with producer David Michaels (Al Michaels's little brother), and our mission was to produce big, expensive stories outside of the live events. We were a perfect match in that we loved to travel, loved the texture of our subjects, and loved and respected each other. And we both loved a good steak house. We traveled all over the world together and during many twenty-hour days

together never had a fight or a disagreement that affected our relationship. We became best friends.

I say all this because it's important for a producer and a reporter
to actually agree more than they disagree. In television, decisions are
made by committee, so there we were going from London to Paris
to Moscow and beyond deciding and thinking about what millions
of Americans should also be thinking about.

About this time in boxing there was the never-ending search
for the next Great White Hope. Jerry Quarry had failed that test
and others bounced in and out of the ring before a young Italian-
American named Ray "Boom Boom" Mancini made it his turn. A
good-looking, tough kid from Youngstown, Ohio, Ray was a television dream. He had the kind of story we all loved; his father, Lenny,
was a contender for a world title, but those dreams were crushed by a
World War II injury. So Ray took his wild fighting style into the
ring and was doing it "for Dad." Suddenly, he would get his shot at
the WBC lightweight title against the champion, Alexis Argüello,
another handsome stud from Nicaragua. It was to be our perfect
next big story, so Michaels and I got on the Boom Boom train. We
watched all his fights and did all the research and were in Atlantic
City to watch what would become the fight of the decade. The fight
lived up to the incredible hype, and Mancini looked sharp and very
much a champion in the early rounds. The crowd was clearly on his
side. We had our story. Then in the fourteenth round, Alexis lived up
to his nickname, the Explosive Thin Man, and unloaded a lethal
punching combination that literally knocked Mancini's head right
off the television screen. The fight was stopped . . . and with Mancini's father looking on in his wheelchair, the two warriors met in the
ring for the postmatch interview with Tim Ryan. While Mancini—
still the attraction, even in the loss—was talking, Argüello interrupted
him, and instead of the usual chest-thumping we hear from punks
today, the world champion said, "You are a great man and your father
was a great man." He went on to say how he felt for Mancini's family,

and then afterward in the pressroom he embraced Boom Boom and said, "It was the best fight so far this year, my friend. I think my heart is special. But his heart is bigger than I have."

Michaels and I looked at each other and at the same time said, "We're covering the wrong boxer." The next day, we booked tickets for our journey to Managua, Nicaragua.

First stop was Phoenix, where Alexis was already training for his next bout. He was on a journey to become the first boxing champ to win world titles in four different weight classes.

Not only was Alexis Argüello a fierce and wicked boxer; he had the whole package: charisma, rugged Clark Gable looks, an insane physique, and a smile with enough wattage to light up Times Square in the middle of the night. He was also not only street-smart but book-smart and had the kind of style and defiant grandiosity that men would pay money for. But we learned quickly not to be deceived by the handsomely wrapped package. His manager, the legendary Eddie Futch, told me that Argüello's appearance beguiled many of his opponents: "Guys get into the ring with him and he doesn't look that big, right? Follow me, son? Then they take that first punch and they say to themselves, 'What the hell am I in here with?'"

Arizona was going through one of those, well, Arizona hot spells, about 110 degrees, and while Alexis worked tirelessly in the even hotter gym, I went outside to lie under a tree for some shade and quickly fell asleep. All of a sudden, I felt this aura of somebody standing over me and staring. It was Eddie Futch, who asked, "What's the matter, boy?" I told him that we'd been from New York to California twice, then back to New York and then Phoenix. As I squinted in the sun, I explained to Eddie that the road was getting to me. Futch thought about it for a second, then said, "That's no road, son. Going from New York to Detroit and back and forth from Manila and then Africa to train champions, now that's a road, son!" I was learning what the hell I am in here with.

Outside the ring Alexis was a gentleman; inside the ring he was an animal, his fitness and endurance legendary. When I joined him at his Miami training camp, he would encourage me to punch his stomach as hard as I could. My fist came off worse—it was like hitting a concrete wall.

His training and focus in those days were insane. I once went down to Miami, where Alexis had a nice yacht, and we decided to go for a run. As we began, he began breathing in hard, then starting from his neck began flexing his entire body down to his toes. Try it. I asked him what this was about and he explained that in a fight your body is usually always flexed, so he runs "flexed." He ran like that for two hours. I did not. All was going well for Argüello except for one major thing: he couldn't go home. He had a deadly fear of the revolutionary Sandinista government. In one interview with me, he put his fingers to his temple and said, "Boom," to indicate his fate if he went back. So David and I went for him.

As a guide we were fortunate to hook up with an amazing man by the name of Sucre Frech. Sucre was the Brent Musburger—the Howard Cosell—of Nicaragua. Sucre was a broadcasting legend. There wasn't a major fight in decades that he didn't call in Nicaragua. He had read the book and seen the movie. He loved Alexis and confirmed why the great Gentleman Fighter couldn't return home. Sucre pointed us in the right directions, and David and I visited Alexis's old neighborhoods and family and friends and saw poverty we didn't think existed. Some of the homes had cardboard floors . . . but they all had a television or a radio, and the people followed their countryman with a passion. We went to his old gyms and to the outdoor rings where he honed his skills. They were usually just put up the night of the fight in some vacant lot, and after they built it, the people came. Sucre, however, lived in supreme luxury in a mansion complex that was heavily guarded by guys with machine guns. One night, in his palatial home on the outskirts of the capital, he graciously hosted a cocktail party for his American visitors. On silver trays, he served this delicious fried meat, and after I had about six of them, I asked what it was. "In your country, Patricio, I believe you call it Spam." Spam! Spam, as I knew well, was chopped pork-shoulder meat and ham and more salt than a city uses to clear streets. I was familiar with it because back when I worked in the meatpacking company, I was on the Spam line. Irony kicks in when you least expect it.

I drank and drugged my way through the Managua trip, but we came back with a terrific story. Our special report on Alexis Argüello was called the best sports journalism story of the year by *Sports Illustrated*. Howard Cosell said it was the best example of a profile he'd ever seen. When it aired on CBS, Brent, not a big favorite of profiles (he was a game man), praised Michaels and me.

But the best thing that came out of this adventure was a long friendship with Argüello. But his flaws were starting to surface. He started drinking too much. He was using cocaine too much. His family life fell apart. Then he was just destroyed by Aaron Pryor in Miami, a fight billed as the Battle of the Champions.

Argüello finally retired and went back to his homeland and became mayor of Managua in 2008. A year later he was dead. The reports were that he committed suicide. I still don't believe that. He was too vain and too proud. I still keep in touch with his son, Alexis Argüello Jr., and I keep telling him that his father was, indeed, a great, great man. I loved Alexis and I miss him. He handed me a journey that made me a better man and made me realize that hard work, works . . . but that hard play has its inevitable consequences.

I was getting comfortable with this sports job, and just as Van Gordon Sauter and John Chancellor before him had predicted, sports was news and news was sports. The line was getting erased. Nowhere was that more evident than when Tesh and I were sent to cover the Pan American Games in Caracas, Venezuela. This was some fucking trip, which made the Iditarod adventures look like a Gymboree class.

These games were notorious for the number of athletes who pulled out of the tournament, citing a variety of injuries. However, the real reason was that the authorities had, for the first time, introduced comprehensive drug testing. There was no hiding place.

The developments cast a shadow on all of track and field, confirming the long-standing rumors of widespread drug use in the sport, which had never been widely reported by the media—sports or news. Suddenly sounding distressingly plausible was the statement made by world-record-holding hurdler Edwin Moses that 50 percent or more of America's world-class track-and-field athletes were using drugs to try to improve their performances. "I didn't want to believe that," said US hurdler James King. "After this, I have to."

Effectively it was the biggest drug bust in the history of international amateur sports—and I was part of the TV team that exposed the scandal. I remember going to the airport to try to interview these athletes as they headed home, citing dubious business meetings. I ask you, who has a business meeting just before representing their country? On the tarmac at the airport I remember the American pole-vaulter trying to take me out with his pole when I asked why he was leaving. He missed my head by about a foot, but his actions allowed me not to miss the story. At that moment I realized that the wild rumors had to be true.

The story was rank hypocrisy on our part. If there was drug testing for broadcasters, the games would never have been aired. I was doing prodigious amounts of cocaine. Nor was I the only one. As soon as we landed in Caracas, half the staff went looking for drugs, knowing that they were much cheaper in Venezuela than the States. I bought about a kilo of coke from a dealer named Raoul, took it back to my room, and poured it into the top dresser drawer. Anyone who came into my room would grab a handful. The scene was right out of *Scarface*. Somehow, I never missed a day of work or an assignment.

One night Tesh and I were sitting in my room, drinking the minibar dry and doing lines, when all of a sudden we got into a violent argument. At first he refused to leave, but eventually, both of us out of our minds, he went back to his room and I crashed. Just as I was drifting into a drug-and-drink-addled sleep, Tesh knocked on my door. "Pat, I want to apologize," he begged. Foolishly I opened the door. He was standing there in gym shorts with a TV camera on his shoulder, which he used to simultaneously film and hit me. He started to beat the shit out of me. Blinded by the camera light, I beat a hasty retreat to the bathroom, taking a couple of nasty falls. The fracas reached the bathtub, and as I grabbed on to the shower curtain for support, the entire curtain and rod came crashing down on my head and I fell backward into the marble tub. Eventually Tesh left. The next day I wandered down to the pool, covered in bruises. Tesh was lying there, recuperating from the night before. He looked at me through his sunglasses and said, "What the hell happened to you?" He couldn't for the life of him remember what had happened.

From that moment on, I decided to stop doing cocaine, going completely cold turkey. I gave away or threw away massive amounts of the stuff. Surprisingly, it never bothered me to stop, and I didn't do another line of cocaine for twenty years. Then it changed my life completely—but we will come to that. In spite of all the booze—we all drank the local Polar beer—and drugs, we never let our extracurricular activities get in the way of our professional careers. I don't know how we did it, but we did. As I say, my powers of recovery must be in the genes—on my father's side. When we all signed off at the end of the final broadcast, we were live in the studio. Everyone was thanking his team, and so on live television I said, "I would like to thank my junior high Spanish teacher, Mr. Gonzalez, and the makers of Polar beer," shocking Brent, sitting next to me. That kind of irreverent banter is commonplace these days, but in the early-1980s sports commentary, it was, to say the least, unconventional. We got out of Caracas alive and without incident, but having had no honest sleep and not being in any physical or emotional shape to do anything. All I wanted to do was lie down and close my bloodshot eyes, but when I arrived home Linda had organized a welcome-home pool party at our home with all my friends. My sweet, adorable wife woke me up halfway through the party and sent me to bed, where I slept soundly for a day.

Looking back on those games, I lived two or three lives. During my off-hours, I did the corporate thing, having long dinners with former treasury secretary William Simon, who kind of took me under his wing down there. By day, he and I would sit by the pool and discuss economics and coin collecting. One day, we went to a coin store and he was delighted to buy all these mint dollars with his name on them. It was surreal.

One night, the entire CBS crew was invited to some heiress's home for what amounted to a state dinner. The home, rather, mansion, was as big a residence as I had ever seen with what must have been $50 million worth of artwork on the walls. Each room was devoted to a different country, and it was like a museum that nobody ever got to visit. A couple of red flags, though. There was only one bathroom, and so many of us were using cocaine, the lines were long and irritating. I was somehow seated at dinner next to our hostess. During dinner, she confided that she knew the legendary Evita and that they were dear friends. I said, "Are you telling me that Evita has slept here in your house?" She replied, "Oh, honey, this isn't our house; this is just where we entertain. Our house is up the hill." The house looked like a castle that had been built during the Magna Carta years. Behind it was a replica of Dodger Stadium. It was a kind of reckless display of wealth I had never seen, nor have I ever seen again.

The other highlight was meeting a young man named Michael Jordan. Michael had just made a name for himself by hitting the final shot to give his North Carolina Tar Heels the 1982 national collegiate basketball championship. I was doing a live report on the atmosphere around the athletes' village when all of a sudden I saw him walking toward me. I said, "Mike, come on over here." He strolled over and we had this wonderful, smart conversation. I remember after I threw it back to Brent he said, "If that young man can play basketball anywhere close to the way he conducts himself in an interview, he's going to be a big star in the NBA." Little did we know. And little did I know that the NBA and Mike Jordan, along with a couple guys named Larry and Magic, were about to define my career and frame it for the rest of my life.

Those tracks were taking me to another big stop.

9

Be Like Mike

The great German philosopher Arthur Schopenhauer noted, "Talent hits a target no one else can hit. Genius hits a target no one else can see." That brings us to Mike Jordan. That's what we called him back then, and he, too, was on a sports journey we didn't know existed. At one time, not many people paid attention to Mike; he was a reasonably unknown college basketball player at North Carolina as the 1980s rang in. It all came together at the Superdome in New Orleans at the 1982 Final Four. It was a big gamble for CBS, which owned the rights to the games . . . and for the NCAA, which had never before held a Final Four in a big, domed stadium. But there they all were—a standing, sold-out crowd of fifty thousand, unheard of for a college basketball game. The clock showed sixteen seconds left in the game with North Carolina, Mike Jordan down by 1, and Carolina with the ball. The legendary Dean Smith coaching the North Carolina squad and the legendary John Thompson guiding Georgetown. Coach Smith was well-known for his emphasis on the team and not the player. That's why Carolina's jerseys only had numbers on them. Mike's was number 23. A year earlier, when Jordan arrived at North Carolina, he sat in the back of the locker room as Dean Smith addressed his new team. "I know most of you are McDonald's All Americans, and all of you were stars in high school, but here at Carolina, it's about the team." Then Smith repeated the age-old cliché: "There is no I in team." Jordan raised his hand. "Coach, there is an I in win."

So now we're back to sixteen seconds on the clock and now we're inside the North Carolina huddle. They were all waiting for what kind of play Smith would lay out for his team, which included the nineteen-year-old freshman Jordan and junior James Worthy. On the other side of the floor was another nineteen-year-old freshman, Patrick Ewing. All three future Hall of Famers. Jordan, Smith, and Worthy all told me the same story: They got into the huddle and there's silence from the coach as the crowd is on its feet going wild. Silence in the huddle. Also, it was well-known that Dean Smith never favored a freshman to take the final shot. That was a rule they all lived by in Dean's world. As the time-out ended, still nothing from Dean. As they broke for the last sixteen seconds, Coach Smith said to his team, "We'll let our freshman take the shot." As they walked back out on the court, Coach Smith walked up to Mike Jordan and said, "Son, you'll be wide-open." He was. Number 23 hit a jumper to put Carolina up by 1, and then as Georgetown was taking the ball down the court, their guard Fred Brown inexplicably threw the ball to North Carolina's James Worthy, who held on to it as the clock ran out. We never called Jordan anything but Michael after that. He was on his way to superstardom almost unmatched in the world of sports.

Hard to believe that only three years earlier the NCAA championship game that featured Indiana State's Larry Bird against Michigan State's Earvin "Magic" Johnson garnered only fifteen thousand fans at the University of Utah's Huntsman Center. And hard for some to believe that it was not Michael Jordan who made the NBA, it was Larry and Magic.

As noted earlier, at the time CBS was putting the NBA Finals on a taped delay at 11:30 p.m. Now, with Larry and Magic on board and with the high-flying Julius Erving doing his own magic in Philadelphia, it was time for CBS to take advantage of the franchise it owned. I remember the day when CBS executive producer Ted Shaker grabbed me in the hallway and said, "We're going to assign you to the NBA half-time report." I had no idea what he was talking about. First of all, there was no such thing as halftime as we know it today. Back then, the report was all done at the same place the game was played, with people such as Brent or Gary Bender repeating recent history by reading stats from the first half. CBS decided that it was time to jump the shark.

We all met with then NBA commissioner Larry O'Brien to talk to him about what we had in mind: putting a face on a sport that needed an identity and an audience. O'Brien seemed confused. We explained that with Dr. J already in place and with the Larry-and-Magic and the Celtics-Lakers rivalry, it was time that America heard from the players. We sat there and actually asked the NBA's permission to interview its players, go to their homes, and "humanize" the game. Larry liked it, and right there and then "At the Half" was born. We then introduced the American sports fan to a new dimension in covering the games: that the players were as interesting as the game itself, and that with any luck Larry and Magic would take the Lakers-Celtics rivalry to new levels. We were right.

Fortunately for us, Magic Johnson turned out to be the greatest personality ever in sports and he was happy to oblige us at every turn. As luck would also have it, Larry Bird was the complete opposite: he hated the media, hated publicity, and rarely spoke in public. It was perfect. Meantime, Dr. J was willing to do what we wanted, too . . . having spent most of his basketball life with nobody knowing what he thought about the game, what he did after and before the games— his likes, dislikes, passions, family, and all that. We were there to introduce America to all of this. We took the ABC Olympics "up and close and personal" format to another level and, this time, a new sport. The NBA on CBS was about to become a household phrase and, to everybody's surprise, so was "At the Half."

The early 1980s were halcyon days for sports fans. Golden years when, it seemed, every sport was overflowing with tension, sensation, heartbreak, and triumph. Sure, we had Magic and Larry and Dr. J, but we also had Scott Hamilton winning the gold in the World

Figure Skating Championships; the Walrus, Craig Stadler, wobbling his way to a Masters championship; Jimmy Connors grunting his way through Wimbledon; Martina and Chrissie trading tennis titles; and Joe Montana showing us his MVP credentials in Super Bowl XVI after Diana Ross sang the national anthem.

But for the time being, we had an NBA to navigate and market. It soon became apparent to television viewers and to the athletes that "At the Half" was the place to be. Not necessarily because we were so great at presenting it, but because we were the only ones presenting it. Now, with cable and DirecTV and all the regional channels and sports networks, viewers have their choice of games and announcers. Back then, they had one choice: us. And we didn't disappoint.

Under Ted Shaker's leadership, we had a pretty free hand to experiment and deliver what we wanted. We drove to practices with Magic Johnson, we shot around with Larry Bird, we took a tour of Dr. J's Philadelphia mansion, we hung out with Charles Barkley, we walked through a forest with Dennis Rodman, we played tricks on players on airplanes, and on and on. Players began to realize that "At the Half" was a place where they could create their own personalities, heal all wounds if necessary, and just have fun.

When Michael Jordan was drafted by the Chicago Bulls, I immediately set up an interview with him, and off to Chicago I went. We decided to meet in a Chicago park. I got there early, and about an hour later up pulled a shiny new Corvette Stingray and out came Jordan. No press people, no posse, no handlers, no bodyguards; just Michael. As we strolled through the park that day to talk about his hopes and dreams in the NBA, not one person approached him. On this day it was just Michael and I going for an afternoon stroll and unknowing kids and adults pretty much ignoring us. That would soon change, dramatically. One night after a home game, Michael and I went to dinner, joined by no fewer than six bodyguards and crowd handlers. I used to kid him that he had more protection than the president of the United States! We'll get to Jordanmania later . . .

but it was amazing to see and watch him go from obscurity to a global phenomenon. I have never, ever seen other celebrity of that magnitude.

When we first started "At the Half," the print media reaction was a combination of fear, stupidity, jealousy, and unmitigated disregard for the fans' right to get to know their players and their game. I was blasted as a joke and a buffoon, and the entire idea was wildly reviewed as a waste of airtime. Many complained that this was sports and "What is this guy doing laughing and hanging out with players? What? They are having fun at halftime? How dare they! It's about the game, not about a halftime show." It was that sentiment over and over and over. The sports TV critics were beside themselves. Nobody in the media thought it was groundbreaking or even a service to television viewers. Nobody, anyway, except the television viewers themselves.

It soon became clear to the network executives and the people who slaved over ratings and trends that sports fans were not using halftime anymore to go get another six-pack or run errands. They were watching! And to put an exclamation point on our decision, for the first time the halftime show was getting sponsored. One of our first sponsors was Prudential, and I knew it was working when a busload of kids pulled up next to my car in California one day and in unison screamed, "Prudential 'At the Half.'" Now, that's marketing. There were also some less subtle changes in my life. I used to walk into arenas with play-by-play man Dick Stockton or Brent and people would yell out, "Hey, Dick!" or "Brent Musburger!" I was the "third guy." But one day we walked into the Seattle Kingdome for a game and some people started yelling, "Pat O'Brien! 'At the Half'!" I still remember the look on Stockton's face.

Being the grandiose guy that I was to begin with, I relished all this and rolled with it big-time. Before long players were coming up to say hi to me and search me out after the game for drinks or dinner. For the players, this new approach to covering sports was a bonus. What was once a league perceived as a bunch of guys in shorts doing cocaine and playing basketball was now becoming a league of human beings with real lives, real problems, moms and dads and opinions and fears and joys. We made it all happen. When the NBA eventually went to another network, NBC, I got a letter from the father of Detroit's bad boy, Bill Laimbeer, which said, "I don't think the players will ever realize how much you did for them, financially, professionally and socially."

When all this began to happen, Lakers coach Pat Riley told the *LA Times,* "Pat has a very open personality. He's loose on and off the air. He doesn't take himself too seriously." No shit. With my signature mustache and long hair that didn't appear coated with paint or hairspray, I had a distinct look, too. As Los Angeles radio personality Jim Healy always described me, "You know, that sportscaster who looks like a porn star."

During the early eighties, when Kurt Rambis came on the scene with the Lakers, they gave him the label the Clark Kent of Basketball, for his big, thick glasses he wore on and off the court. He had come from playing in Greece, and I was finishing up a story on him at the end of one of the halftimes that ended with his saying, "I could never figure out what they were writing about me because it was all Greek to me." Funny, yes . . . but just as the halftime was ending, a guy walked past me wearing big, thick black glasses. I said, "Quick, hand me those." Surprised, he handed them over, and when I came back on camera, I had the Rambis look. I didn't have to refer to the joke. With the big glasses on I simply said, "That's 'At the Half' for today, enjoy the second half, as the NBA rolls on right here on CBS." Somewhere in the corporate offices of CBS's headquarters located in a black skyscraper known as Black Rock in New York, Howard Stringer, then president of the network, was at that moment walking by a TV set and said to somebody, "Who's that?" The person explained and Stringer said, "I think we found a new personality." A week later out of nowhere, they tore up my contract and gave me a new one. It was working.

But what made "At the Half" was certainly not me, but the people

I was introducing to the American sports fan. And nobody helped the NBA grow and flourish more than Earvin "Magic" Johnson. I think the first thing I ever said to him was "I hope you can live up to that nickname!" As we all know now, he did and more . . . but in the beginning, he was arguably the most refreshing new athlete to ever hit the scene. Magic had that "it" factor that was irresistible. The basketball audience couldn't get enough of him, and he embraced his role as the face of the NBA with grace and humor and humility. I don't think I ever did a bad interview with him, and I must have interviewed him over a hundred times. America got very used to Magic's playing basketball on Sunday, and that before and after the game he would be standing with me, win or lose. I was his television caddie. I was there for him and he was there for me.

In Magic's rookie season, he led his Lakers to the championship. But the very next year, the Lakers lost to the Houston Rockets in the play-offs. The next year, head coach Paul Westhead was fired early in the season and replaced by Pat Riley. It was widely known that Magic was publicly and privately behind the firing. So amid all these happy, smiling interviews, his public stock dropped, and when I asked if he wanted to sit down with me on TV and talk about it, he did not hesitate. In today's world, no athlete would do that. But there was such an uproar that Magic felt he had to face it and he did. I didn't hesitate to ask the tough questions of my friend, and he didn't hesitate to answer them. That sit-down chat on a national game on a Sunday afternoon made Magic a bigger man and gave me a lot of credibility.

For the most part, I became the "Lakers" guy and one of the first sportscasters in history to actually own up that I was also a fan. It was never a secret. Even though I made every attempt to be neutral on the air, one time while giving the score when the Lakers were down at halftime, I said "we" instead of "the Lakers." But even though everybody knew I was that guy, it was cool with all the players and coaches. They trusted me.

It was no secret that I was close to the organization. When the late Dr. Jerry Buss bought the Lakers and the Forum, he and I sat in the empty arena and he told me and a national audience how when he finally closed the deal, he ordered the Forum emptied and one spotlight to shine on the middle of the court. "I just sat there with a bottle of Jack Daniel's and got plastered and couldn't believe my good fortune," he said. In fact, it was the fans' good fortune. Dr. Buss (he had a PhD in chemistry) changed the way sports franchises operated. He adjusted the ticket prices, using simple supply and demand. The rich people and the celebrities wanted to be close to the action, either on the floor or in the first few rows. He made that happen and they paid for it. In return, he spent the money building championship teams and began by signing Magic to, basically, a lifetime contract. At the time his salary made outrageous headlines. It was $1 million a year. A few years later, Michael Jordan signed for $30 million a year.

My relationship with the Lakers and my being in Los Angeles paid off big-time for CBS, since every weekend we featured the Lakers and whatever team they were playing. Pat Riley had developed and orchestrated "Showtime," and we were right there to give it a platform. Showtime was a stark contrast to the Lakers' historical rival, the Boston Celtics. There literally was not enough airtime to tell this story. It was Magic vs. Bird. The inevitable Hollywood celebrities vs. the regular working people in Boston. Stretch limos vs. public transportation. Champagne vs. beer. Those historic weekends produced goose bumps and thrills and books and documentaries and eventually a Broadway play. The NBA couldn't have been luckier to have all these things fall into place . . . and my being in the middle of it was ridiculously great.

But let's not forget what led up to the Magic-Bird era. In basketball, plenty of legends helped set the stage and shaped the sport. I was fortunate to get to know some of these guys as well.

The first time I met Bill Russell, it did not go well. My relationship with perhaps the greatest big man in NBA history was, at best, strained. Bill was not exactly a social animal around us and had little or no sense of humor or perspective on what he meant to sports fans. When he first started working as an analyst at CBS Sports, I was nothing more than a blip on the screen, but in my mind, I felt that Bill needed my counsel. Right? After a game one night I pulled him aside and said, "You know, if you could ever let the audience know how great some of these players are and admit that there was an ounce of envy, you might connect better with the audience." He just stared at me. Nothing. I continued, "You know, when you're watching Kareem, let the audience know how difficult the sky hook is even for a guy like you." Nothing. My thinking was that even the greatest players ever have to marvel at somebody, right? Not in Bill's mind. Later, a group of us were at an upscale Chinese restaurant in Beverly Hills for dinner. Things were going great and Bill was in a better mood, but then it happened: my biggest pet peeve in sports and a learning lesson for me, as well. A little kid gingerly walked up to our table and stood there waiting for Bill to finish a sentence; then he asked for an autograph. Bill stared at this kid, who was about ten, and said, "Did your dad send you over?" "No," the young boy responded, now probably sorry he'd garnered the nerve to approach the table. Russell looked at him and said, "I don't sign autographs, but thanks for asking." I told Bill I thought it was rude to turn down a little kid, and again Russell just stared at me. I don't think we ever had another conversation longer than hello and good-bye.

The whole autograph scene has always been puzzling to me. I have a pretty sweet collection of autographs of some of the greats, and my theory was always "five seconds of my embarrassment in exchange for a lifetime of memories." But I do have a considerable number of autograph stories through the years. In May of 1981, Cleveland Indians pitcher Len Barker pitched only the tenth perfect game ever, so as part of our "sports journalism" efforts, CBS sent me to Cleveland to interview him. While we were there, I decided to do a piece on all the famous pitchers who had thrown from that mound from Cy Young to Satchel Paige to Bob Feller and now Len Barker. After I interviewed him, I asked him to sign a ball for me, which he did. The next day, I interviewed the great Bob Feller and asked him if he would sign the same ball. He did, but not before he said, "Why would you hand me a ball with Len Barker's name on it? What did he ever do?" Feller was a prick. I had heard stories of his literally pushing away little kids who wanted autographs, and he was infamous for being a not-so-in-the-closet racist. In fact, when I was doing my report, I was standing on the mound and said, "A lot of the greats have pitched from right here . . . ," and when I said, "Satchel Paige," Feller interrupted, "You're mentioning him before me?" Bob was a bitter young man and equally bitter old man.

One time I got a call at home from former Dodger manager Tommy Lasorda, who began the conversation with "When the fuck did you become a Hall of Famer? Are you a fucking manager?" I was perplexed. He then explained that he was signing balls at a stadium and some kid handed one that had my signature on the between-the-seams spot reserved only for Hall of Famers and major league managers. I never did it again. Some players didn't sign a whole lot of autographs but didn't go for the Bill Russell "don't come near me" approach. Two of those were Ted Williams and Joe DiMaggio. Now, here were two guys a lot of people just didn't approach for whatever reason and I knew that. I was in Boston one time and walked by a room and noticed the door was open. As I passed by, I saw Ted Williams himself sitting alone on a chair in the room. I knocked and said, "Hello, Mr. Williams, I'm Pat O'Brien." He was polite, so I took a chance. I pulled out a ball and said, "Gosh, my son is a big fan of yours and I want to start a collection for him of all the legends." It worked. He signed. One slight detail: I didn't have a son at the time. The same story worked with Joe DiMaggio later when I did have a son.

Reggie Jackson loved to sign balls. But I learned a lesson from him, too. One time we were leaving a stadium and people were mobbing Reggie for autographs, and only because I was nearby did a few ask for mine as well. I was signing as fast as I could and as many as I could. It was crazy. Finally Reggie grabbed one of my autographs and said, "What the hell is this, Pat?" I looked at the paper and it looked like one of those unreadable doctors' signatures on prescription notes. Reggie said, "That's your father's name; respect it." From then on, I learned to sign a "Pat O'Brien" that Joe O'Brien would have been proud of.

Eventually, money and demand changed the autograph scene. I once met up with Michael Jordan in Phoenix for dinner and golf, and when we landed in his private jet, he and Charles Barkley and I were whisked away to Michael's hotel suite. Inside, some hundred balls and jerseys and posters were waiting for his signature, either to be sold or given to charity or from his sponsors and so on. The soon-to-be-Michael-Jordan-signed memorabilia was neatly stacked against the wall in the suite's dining room He looked at it and said, "Let's go to dinner; I'll do this later." He explained that somebody would arrange for all this merchandise to be at his next stop. But for all his insane celebrity and the public demand, I never saw him turn down a kid who wanted him to scribble something.

That night at dinner, we were sitting around drinking and laughing, and a little kid approached Barkley. He said, "My dad and I came all the way from Brazil to watch you play. Can I have your autograph?" Barkley looked at him and, as only he could, said, "Not now, kid, can't you see I'm with my friends trying to relax?" The young man was devastated and looked about to cry. Jordan and I looked at Charles and said collectively, "What the fuck is wrong with you, boy?" Jordan said, "That's rude." Jordan got up and grabbed the kid, brought him back, made Charles sign . . . then MJ signed and we all signed and took pictures. It turned out to be a cool moment for all of us. Afterward, Barkley said, "I hate that when I'm eating!" So Michael said to him, "Here's what I do sometimes. They usually come over and say, 'I hate to do this, but . . . ,' and then before they can say anything else, I say, 'If you hate to do this, why do you do it?'"

Michael once told me that nearly 90 percent of the "Michael Jordan" autographs are fake. So he designed a way to self-authenticate them, by subtly working the number 23 into the *M*. Go check your Michael Jordan autograph right now! We'll get to Michael in depth in the next chapter, but I honestly felt sorry for him for all the demands the public put on him. He didn't like it, but he accepted it as part of the territory. And by the way, half of everything Barkley says is with a wink and a smile. He's a cool guy and deservedly now the face of the NBA—from a chair on TNT.

And then there was one of the great pioneers in the modern NBA, Julius Erving, who was also centered enough to know that the fans were the people who were supporting his elegant lifestyle, and he couldn't spend enough time with them. One night after a play-off game that went late, Julius and I were leaving the Spectrum in Philadelphia, and a gaggle of kids were waiting for the great Dr. J. He stopped and said, "Why aren't you kids at home, don't you have school tomorrow?" Then as he signed each scrap of paper, he mingled and chatted and every now and then would ask a simple math or geography question, and if the kid got it, Dr. J would sign. If the kid didn't, Dr. J would answer the question and then sign. Yes, Dr. J was a class act from top to bottom. Like a lot of the players, he welcomed me into his life, one time opening up his Philadelphia mansion for our cameras and a private tour not unlike Jackie Kennedy's famous tour of the White House. During that tour he showed us a Ming Dynasty vase that he'd bought in China and was so afraid it would break or get lost, he carried it between his legs the entire trip. Dr. J was the first player to transcend sports with his high-flying style on the court and his grace and personality off the court. When the Doctor made a house call, every arena was full. His hands measured fourteen inches from the tip of his middle finger to the wrist, and his dunks . . . nearly every one of them . . . were legendary. He became my first close friend in the NBA, and I was honored to know his beautiful wife, Turquoise, and their kids.

CBS did a lot of Philadelphia games in the early eighties, and I got to know the team well, a unique group of guys that included Mo Cheeks, Bobby Jones, Moses Malone, and Charles Barkley. They all welcomed me into their inner circle. When they swept the Lakers in the 1983 NBA Finals, I was invited to their victory dinner in Los

Angeles and got so drunk, I ended up spending the night in jail. Apparently, a policeman had been trying to get me to pull over for about a mile, and I was so wasted, I didn't hear the siren or see the lights. I was handed a DUI, but it never made the newspapers or the gossip columns, and this is the first I've ever mentioned it. When I went through many more problems later in life with my drinking, everything made the news . . . but this time, nothing. I was nearly three times over the legal limit, and I thank God every day that I didn't kill somebody that night. From that awful night, believe it or not, I never again drove after I had been drinking. I was fortunate to have a driver most of my career, which was lucky for everybody who was on the road. And for me.

The next year, the 76ers lost in the first round to the New Jersey Nets. It was a shocker. Nobody could believe it. After the final game, I walked into the 76ers' locker room and most of the players were drinking; some of them were throwing garbage cans around and kicking things. I asked Mo Cheeks where Julius was and he silently pointed to the bathroom. I walked in and there was Dr. J, just finishing tying his tie. I said, "You okay?" And he said, "You got to put this in perspective. I look at this as a blessing; I get to spend more time with my family." I'll never forget that. Subsequently, we traveled thousands of miles together and used to joke that we should write a book called *Last Gate on the Left,* as it seemed our plane was always the farthest one down. Dr. J's journey had its bumps and bruises and tragedies. When his son Cory suffered a drug-related death in 2000, I dropped to my knees and prayed and cried for my friend. Julius navigated through that tragedy with supreme grace, putting an exclamation point on how he once summed up his career: "Respect is a lot more important, and a lot greater, than popularity."

I truly wish I had listened more carefully.

10

Larry and Magic and the Mick

Being a sports fan in the 1980s was like being a seven-year-old on Halloween night, a ten-year-old on Christmas morning, and a teenager the night of the prom. It seemed everywhere you turned, there was athletic magnificence. But when the last book is finally written on this era, the Magic Johnson vs. Larry Bird story will overshadow it all. Even though Magic was the guard and Larry was the forward and they never matched up against each other, we all felt as if every game between the Lakers and the Celtics was simply Magic vs. Bird. That's the way we promoted it, that's the way we covered it, and that's the way it was, except in the minds of two important people in this drama: Magic and Larry. Not until it was all over, after they went their separate ways, did they finally admit that, yes, it was special. Until that happened, all they cared about was helping their teams win. They left all the drama and talk up to us, and we didn't disappoint. In the hundreds of interviews and conversations I had with the two of them separately, not once did they bring up the other guy. To them there really was no I in team. They didn't talk much at all during the games, and from what I saw, they never walked out together or chatted after the games. They were literally in two different worlds.

After a Lakers/Celtics game, Magic would return to a locker room full of teammates and coaches and media and celebrities, who were allowed to come in and mingle. Over in the Celtics locker room,

Larry would retreat to the massage table in the training room and pour over stats from the game. Magic would walk into the Southern California night surrounded by adoring fans and celebs and his own people, such as the ever-present Lon Rosen (his longtime faithful manager and troubleshooter and all-around good guy) and maybe Arsenio Hall and that crowd. Larry walked into an empty parking lot outside the old Boston Garden and all by himself got into his car or truck and went who knows where. If there was any dirt or gossip about the two that I thought was worth sharing, I would . . . but there isn't. Okay, we do know that Magic loved the ladies maybe too much, but the only thing you probably didn't know about Larry is that he liked champagne and an occasional cigarette. One time out of nowhere, after a game when everybody else was gone, he came up to me and borrowed two cigarettes.

When CBS lost the NBA to NBC, Larry gave me a home-jersey number 33 and signed, "To Pat, thanks for the memories." Magic signed a number 32 jersey with the name Irish on it and wrote, "To Pat, thanks for all the good times in the 80's." But my favorite memory is the picture of Magic and Larry with me in the middle at an All-Star Game. They were shaking hands across my body and smiling at each other. It was one of those looks that I'm sure McCartney and Lennon had one day when they knew they had something going on that was pretty special. It also reminded me of a conversation I had with Bob Woodward of the famed Woodward and Bernstein duo that brought down the Nixon administration. I asked Bob just when they knew they had the story of the century, and he said, "One day after we linked some White House names to the Watergate break-in, we just looked at each other. We didn't say anything." Larry and Magic never had to say anything because they did it the old-school way, with their actions on the court.

From a reporter's standpoint, though, they both got what my role was as well. It got to the point where after a game Magic would find me while I was looking for him . . . and when I needed Larry, he was always, albeit reluctantly, willing to talk. They both knew that

I was their pathway to the fans. It was never about "We need to talk to Pat O'Brien" . . . it was about "I want the fans to hear what I have to say about this game." I did have their trust, but that's the way it used to work. Not anymore. Now the players only talk to TV reporters after the game because they are mandated by the NBA to do so.

To both of them it was all about the game, but there was one major difference. Magic adored and relished the public spotlight; he always knew when the light was on and loved the glow. Larry ran the other way. Still, they both played up the Showtime Lakers vs. the Working-Class Celtics. It worked. Every now and then the two cultures would clash. In 1985 during the Finals, Larry had an ordinary night in Boston; ordinary for him, anyway. So now the Celtics came to the Forum in LA for the next game, and early before the game Larry was out on the court shooting around. A group of African-American Lakers fans on one end were heckling him: "Where you been, Larry?" Bird walked over to them and asked that they come on the court. Sheepishly, they all walked out to the top of the key, and Larry said to them, "Where have I been? With your mamas." That, to me, was funny brilliant. But Larry could be scary brilliant on the court, as every fan of the NBA knows. In 1987 in Game 7 of the Eastern Conference finals against Boston, it appeared that with five seconds left, the Detroit Pistons were going to win. With the Pistons already celebrating and inbounding the ball, Larry came out of nowhere for the famous "Larry steals the ball" highlight. He brilliantly tossed it to DJ and game over. After the game I said to Larry, "I'm gonna tell my son someday that I knew the greatest player who ever lived." He responded, "Well, at least the luckiest." On the other side, when the Lakers forced a Game 7 against the Pistons in the Finals, I grabbed Magic about thirty seconds after the game, and on live TV he was screaming, "I'd like to thank CBS and Pat O'Brien and everybody for letting us play a Game Seven!" He picked me up off the ground and hugged me and then ran into the locker room.

They could both be quite contemplative, though. I once asked

Bird what made him think he was better than everybody else on the court, and his brilliant answer was "I know the difference between 2.8 seconds and 3.0 seconds." Brilliant. But then on another occasion when he was double-teamed at the end of a game in the Eastern Conference finals and uncharacteristically froze, the team lumbered back to Boston for a long practice at the Celtics' facility. After the practice, Red Auerbach himself walked in and kicked everybody out. He screamed, "Clear the gym!" When I walked past him, he said, "Pat, you can stay if you want." Then Red called Larry out on the court and started to draw an imaginary play on Larry's chest, telling him, "Son, when you are double-teamed, you have to pass the ball to an open man." Red's explaining one of the fundamentals of the game to one of the game's all-time greatest, and Larry just stood there and listened. I snapped a picture right at that moment, and it might be my favorite image from that era. When it came to the game, no matter how inane the point, Larry always wanted to listen. But the two of them had more confidence than a Kennedy on election night. One time at the All-Star Game in Houston, the score was tied and Magic had the ball. As time wound down, he threw up a prayer from about forty-eight feet away. The ball hit the rim and bounced off and the game went to overtime. Magic screamed and got on his knees and started pounding the hardwood. Afterward (Magic led the West to victory) I asked him about that shot: "You didn't really expect that to go in, did you?" His reply was classic: "Irish, I expect them all to go in."

Of all the characters I got to know during those years, one of the oddest was a young kid named Dennis Rodman. He was the sixth man at the time on the Detroit Pistons and had a complicated life, to say the least. Before arriving in Detroit, he was at a small college, Southeastern Oklahoma State, and was living with a "surrogate family." I liked his story and so I arranged an interview. The Pistons said he wanted to do it in a nearby forest. In Detroit? So anyway, we arrived there and we sat down under a big tree. My first question was simple: "So, how did you get into basketball?" All of a sudden he stretched out his arm and started crying hysterically. We ended up conducting a great interview, and I never did ask him what was wrong that day . . . but his journey had been rough. No father, raised by another family, uncomfortable in his own skin and about everything else. In this introduction of Rodman to America, he was kind of "normal," with no tattoos or piercings; all that would come later in what turned out to be a very public, complicated life . . . filled with addiction, including tabloid marriages and just plain circus chaos 24-7. I always loved Dennis, but he is one complicated motherfucker. One time backstage at a Stone Temple Pilots concert, Rodman came running up to me out of nowhere with a chair over his head. He wasn't kidding. As he was about to hit me, somebody in the band stopped him just before the chair landed on my head. Dennis had found out that his former wife Carmen Electra and I had just had lunch at the Ivy in West Hollywood, and apparently this didn't sit well with him. Like everything else in his life, this drama passed as well. He'll go down in history as one of the game's greatest rebounders, the guy who got Michael Jordan the ball, and as far as I know, but in this day and age we can't be sure, Dennis is the only member of the Basketball Hall of Fame to appear in public in a dress and later become a favorite son in North Korea.

Through those late 1980s and early 1990s, the Detroit Pistons became a great team to watch bounce other teams around, and some of the most personable men in the NBA—Bill Laimbeer, Rick Mahorn, Isiah Thomas, and company—were, to say the least, a rough group on the court. They had never heard of finesse basketball, didn't play it, didn't want it, and proved it every single game as they knocked people up and down and around the court. So because it was true and because it had terrific alliteration, I started calling them the Bad Boys of Basketball. I'd like to say I came up with it . . . but I do know that I was the only one saying it on television. While at their Palace of Auburn Hills, I once opened a play-off game with "And tonight, live from Auburn Hills, another episode of the Bad Boys versus the Celtics." After the game, the late, great Chuck Daly approached me and said, "Hey, can you leave that 'bad boy' stuff alone? It's really not a great image and I don't want that to get into the refs' heads." Now, Chuck was one of my best friends in the coaching fraternity, but I had an audience to please and so I kept pushing the name. Finally, the league itself asked me to stop it because they were cautious about giving the league, growing in popularity, a bad name. So, I stopped. But then, marketing took over and somebody started printing Bad Boy T-shirts and hats, and soon there were league-approved "Bad Boys of Basketball" highlight reels and they became famous, forever I suppose, with the moniker. They also won a lot of games.

Coach Daly was cut in the same stylish mode as Pat Riley of the Lakers. Daly enjoyed good suits. He enjoyed the tailored look. He thought about such things as "If I wear a double-breasted suit, Pat, do you think I should have it unbuttoned when I'm sitting down?" One of the great stories is, during a Game 6 in the Eastern Conference finals in Detroit against the hated Celtics, the Pistons were behind and Daly was standing up, coat buttoned, waving his team back down on defense. He was out of his mind and coaching the hell out of the game. During one of these moments as he was waving them down, arms flung all over the place, he spotted me right behind him. While he still yelled at Isiah to get the transition going, he turned around and said to me, "Hey, Pat, did you know that there's a cream now that makes you tan? I tried it and it's great." And then he went back to "Let's fucking go, guys; we got this." Legendary story that we laughed about until his death. Chuck Daley was another one-of-a-kind from that era. He gave me a line I'll use forever. When he left Detroit to coach for Orlando, I called him a couple weeks in to see how it was going. "New job, same fucking problems." Thanks, Chuck.

Of course, Pat Riley was the perfect look for Los Angeles. Movie-star looks and body, a killer swag, great smile, Zen quotes, pop-culture sensibilities, and a terrific coach. We hung out socially a lot, and I was with a group at a black-tie event once where Riley and all of us greased back our hair for that, well, "black-tie greased-back-hair look." All of us looked like fools except Riley, who decided that was the look and kept it. Soon half a dozen coaches were trying it, and I went into a story meeting to pitch a story about all these coaches who were copying Pat Riley's style. My bosses reminded me that I was doing the same thing and said, in what soon became a CBS mantra, "Stop with the Laker loving." Okay. How'd that work out for everybody? Safe to say, the Lakers were on every single Sunday no matter what. Americans wanted Showtime.

Getting along with coaches is never easy, but I made them all part of the story, helped build their characters in the eyes of America because they were all great characters, not just a bunch of guys who never smiled on the sidelines. I nurtured them to be "cast members" of our coverage. Nobody covered ejected players and coaches the way we did. I followed them and stalked them in the hallways to bring their immediate thoughts to American fans. During the pivotal fifth game of the 1985 championship series between Los Angeles and Boston, for example, I followed Celtics coach K. C. Jones to the room for exiled coaches after he was tossed. He locked himself in. I grabbed a live camera and told the truck to come to me immediately. Here was my report: "The door says VISITORS. It should say NO VISITORS. K.C.'s locked us out." I knocked. "I know you're in there, Coach, so if you are watching, and I know you are, come out here and talk to me." He came out. It was great television. Vintage "At the Half."

There were also some vintage fuckups. Back then there wasn't YouTube or the Internet, so a lot of them are best forgotten. Live television is live television, and only those who have ever done it at this level will understand the kind of pressure there is to be perfect mostly all of the time. Our executive producer, Ted Shaker, was strict on perfection and took most mistakes personally. I love Ted, but under his leadership, people were always walking on eggshells. And as the popularity of his announcers grew, it seemed Ted became more critical. I admit that I was getting a big head, but I was paid to have a big head: that's what on-air people do. There's not a human being alive who doesn't believe his own clippings. Not one. We could go four hours live and Ted would usually bring up the mistakes . . . even if there was one or two. It made us better, but it was management by fear, and he didn't make any friends there.

I made a lot of mistakes. I was a master at covering them up, but I had my share of them.

Our standard opening was "This is the NBA on CBS" . . . and one time in Milwaukee, I yelled out in excitement, "This is the NBS on CBA." "Pat, call the truck." Ted: "Don't ever do that again; pay attention." Shaker had the inability to roll with the punches, even though they never hit him.

He was also beginning to dislike my friendships with all the players and the coaches. I never understood this. Last year on my radio show, Dick Stockton was talking NBA hoops and said, "I will say this about Pat O'Brien. He got to know the players and they got to know him. Before the games, he would be out there while they were stretching, talking to them, laughing with them, and he became very connected. He was always ready. Now, our sideline people hide in the tunnel memorizing what they are going to say." High praise. John Salley, one of the Bad Boys, echoed that: "Pat was like one of the guys, you know? He used to interview me all the time and the other guys would say, 'What's he like, man?' I'd tell them that Pat knew the language. A cool guy. One of us. He was a smooth brother, Pat was. In fact, Pat could get into some of the black clubs we couldn't. He'd just walk past the ropes and we were right behind him. No questions."

Shaker didn't see it this way. He thought for a "journalist" I was getting too close to the players. Before games, players such as Kevin McHale and Larry Bird and Bill Walton and Isiah Thomas and Magic and Jordan and Kareem and Worthy and on and on would stop by my set to say hi and chat a few minutes before air. This drove Ted crazy. I was getting, in his mind, too popular. He started to tell my producers to make me "settle down" and to "reel him in." I always wondered, For what? Being popular? Getting the stories? Reel me where from where?

So there I was, Mr. Big Shot, at Game 2 of the Eastern Conference finals in the legendary Boston Garden. Michael Jordan, who had missed three-quarters of the season with a broken ankle, was back in the NBA play-offs and we couldn't have been more thrilled. We decided to open up the game with Jordan and me. Unheard of now to get a star like that to go live before a play-off game, but there we were. So I began with the dramatic words "Michael Jordan, welcome to the NBA play-offs." So far so good. So now, I wanted to be that neutral guy and so I said, "But I have to ask you, can one man beat the Lakers?" Then, like a bad dream, I heard these words from Jordan's mouth: "Well, Pat, we're playing the Boston Celtics today." I didn't flinch . . . we finished the interview . . . and at the end I said, "Well, you don't have to remind me you're playing the Celtics and in their way are Michael Jordan and the Bulls. This is the NBA on CBS." Jordan put his arm around me on national TV, and as I walked off the court, my producer, Bob Mansbach, was shaking his head: "Call the truck." It was Ted Shaker. "You make one more mistake like that and you're fired." Fired? Fortunately for me, there was not much to-do about it in the media because, thankfully, Jordan scored 63 points in that game and that was the story. Afterward, I went back to my hotel and began to drink and worry. Ted Shaker wanted to fire me. I was devastated. I got on the plane, and when I got home, I had a call from Michael. He wanted to see if I was okay. We laughed about it and that was it. It lives on, on YouTube, and is played every year on the anniversary of that game. I didn't get fired. Eventually, Ted did.

Looking back on all this seems like a dream now. As much fun as we were having and as cool as I thought I might have been . . . I don't think I ever realized just how big a deal it was to have this kind of access to the superstars of sports. That kind of access is unheard of today. But remember, back then, there was no ESPN, no

Internet, no blogs, no YouTube, and so on. When people come up to me and say, "We miss you on the NBA," I say, "You don't miss me; you miss the era and the players and the simplicity of owning the coverage." It wasn't me; it was the fraternity atmosphere that was the NBA in the 1980s. All of us who were part of that just look at each other and say, "Now, those were the days, man."

They sure were, and I'm grateful every day to have been part of it. I hold to the Dr. Seuss theory "Don't cry because it's over, smile because it happened." But I wasn't done because, by now, I was completely embedded in the fabric of CBS Sports. CBS Sports had, at great long-term expense, the finest franchises in America, and I was in the middle of them all. Most of my energies were devoted to the NBA, but now the network was putting me anywhere it could. I was now officially a big-time sportscaster, which was about as far away from my original life goals as possible. Obviously, Musburger was, as we called him, the Big Dog at CBS, but I was the puppy. I was hosting the NBA . . . doing sidelines on our college football packages . . . and was one of the hosts of the famed *NFL Today*. All this included the NBA All-Star Games, college football championships, the NCAA Final Four, the US Open Tennis Championships, and CBS Sports Saturday and Sunday. Along the way I hosted the Super Bowl and eventually Major League Baseball and a couple of Olympics. Glory days.

The final sentence in the great Scorsese movie about the Band called *The Last Waltz* was this from Robbie Robertson: "The road is one goddamned impossible place." It was. I was traveling about three hundred thousand miles a year . . . from one hotel to another . . . one limo to the next . . . and two bars to the next two. It was a fun but hard-driving life. I found out that you can do two things on the road: work and drink. And that's what we did. It was men being men, and what men did then was drink—a lot. Mine was not out of control yet, we'll get to that, and I never missed a day of work or an event, nor did I ever show up drunk or drink on the air—but we did put our bodies to the test at the finest bars and restaurants in the country. It was fun, and there was another bonus: I was making a lot of money. So things were, by the looks of it, good. But, as always, there were things missing. For starters, once again, a dad. All the guys I worked with on the air would routinely call their dads after the game and hash it over, play by play. Sometimes their dads would show up and I could see them beaming with pride. There were dads everywhere. Even though players always say "Hi, Mom" on TV, I got to know a lot of their dads along the way. During interviews, the players would always share a story or two about how they wanted to make their fathers proud. One of my favorites was James Jordan, Michael's father. James was not much of a public kinda guy, but he was always there, and he and I would stand in the tunnels before games and laugh and talk about life and, of course, about his famous son. James Jordan was a cool guy and his real passion was baseball. I am confident that Michael went into baseball to fulfill perhaps a promise, but certainly a wish, directly connected to his dad. Sadly, he never got to see his famous son give it a Jordan try in the big leagues.

As for my father, he, too, was full of life with lots of dreams for himself and for his family. One by one, he poured them into a bottle and drank them. One by one and two by two and, as the years droned by, three by three. I remember the time he was full of life, with money in his pocket and a job worth telling the fellas about. But it wasn't enough. He had wives who loved him and they were never enough. He had kids, including a son who wanted what my father could never give: a father to share life with. As a boy, visiting him in Knoxville, Iowa, where he lived with his fifth wife, I do remember a sports moment. He was in his big chair in the living room, and on the RCA television set was a basketball game featuring Bill Russell against Wilt Chamberlain. My dad loved basketball, and on this day in the sixties, we had our first and last conversation about sports. He never took me to a game, never suggested I play a game, and, outside of the nearby Knoxville Raceway, which he loved, never showed much of an interest in sports of any kind. So, neither did I. That's how it worked. So anyway, he's telling me about these two giant guys who play against each other all the time. During the sixties, Wilt and Russell met 142 times, more than 14 times a year in the regular season and the play-offs. I remember him saying to me that afternoon, "Now, here's a game you should like, Pat. These guys are so big and so goddamned good at what they do. Jesus!" And that was my only sports conversation with Joe O'Brien. So how much irony are we looking at here? My dad never saw me succeed beyond being a good tap dancer. I can only hope that it would have been my father's dream to watch his son land right in the middle of the sports world and, yes, eventually be good friends with Wilt and work with Russell. I could have introduced him to all the players of his era: I'd spent a lot of time with Havlicek and Cousy and Baylor, bringing their stories to my halftime show about the genesis of the NBA. I can see Joe now at the end of a bar somewhere saying, "Hey, that's my boy up there!" It makes me so sad that that never happened.

Linda and I were on vacation in Mexico when I got the call that Joe had had his last drink. He was living at a Veterans Administration–supported nursing home, and despite being down to about eighty-five pounds and his body's falling apart, molecule by molecule, he still couldn't stop drinking. I had received a call a couple weeks earlier from a military doctor saying they were going to kick him out (again) because he was smuggling whiskey inside a cane he had hollowed out. But the day they called me to say it was, indeed, the last call, I was in Mexico watching Marquette win the NCAA National Championship in basketball. The coach was Al McGuire, and as everybody around him celebrated, Al just sat on the bench and cried. So I'm on the phone hearing that Joe had died and I'm watching McGuire cry. Fast-forward to the late eighties when Al joined the CBS broadcast team and one night we went out to Elio's on the Upper East Side in New York for dinner and drinks. So I finally told him the story and that every time I see him I am taken back to the day my dad died. He had an Al response: "Oh, fuck, that's awful. I'm really sorry, man. Fuck!" Al was a character and was becoming quite a media star by that time. After surveying my work, he pulled me over during one of the CBS basketball seminars and said these haunting words: "You know, Pat, you are really, really good. Way ahead of everybody. But, let me tell you, son. There's something about being too far ahead. Be careful."

My dad had died on April Fools' Day, a confluence of events I attempted to use as an opening joke in my eulogy. Nobody laughed. Joe would have laughed. He left no money, no property, no cars, no assets, no journals to read—nothing. He had given me his only two material possessions: a gold Bulova watch with a stretch band and a gold ring with the Irish crest on it. But no memories to speak of. A couple gems here and there, maybe just enough to hold on to, but probably not. At any rate, just like that, he was gone.

Obviously, fatherhood was always important to me . . . but Linda and I didn't initially have a passion to start a family. The same argument: we were busy. She was building her teaching credentials and I was running around the world building my career. Finally when we were both thirty-five, we said, "Let's do it." So we tried and tried and tried—and no baby. We went to Ireland for a serendipitous try. Nothing. Finally after about four years of this, we consulted a fertility doctor, who told us we were both fine, it was just a matter of "timing." After a bunch of "timing" routines, he settled on an exact date and hour for us to try to conceive. The exact time was between 10:00 p.m. and 4:00 a.m. on the night of September 27, 1986. Calendar check: the prime-time Miami-Oklahoma game at the Orange Bowl in Miami. Prime-time CBS game featuring the Jimmy Johnson–led Miami Hurricanes and the Barry Switzer–led Oklahoma Sooners. To say there was a future Pro Bowl, Hall of Fame group on that one field on that one night is an understatement. There was Brian Bosworth (who only had 22 tackles that night) . . . Vinnie Testaverde, the Miami quarterback, who sealed his Heisman Trophy that very night . . . Bennie Blades, Keith Jackson, Michael Irvin, and more. In the booth, Brent Musburger and Notre Dame legend Ara Parseghian.

On the sidelines: me. Linda giddily flew down with me to Miami for our baby-making duties and went to the game, which turned out to be a classic. Arguably one of the greatest college football games ever played. Oklahoma fell apart late in the game and Miami went on to win 28–16. The stadium was bedlam.

After the game, Linda and I went to the Miami party with Jimmy Johnson and his team and had a glorious celebratory night. Afterward, as CBS staffers and the Miami team cheered us on . . . we left for the hotel. And that was the night Sean Patrick O'Brien was conceived. That game is still played over and over on ESPN Classic and was featured in the famous ESPN documentary *The U* . . . with a young, long-haired, confident-looking me on the sidelines—not realizing that I was about to conceive our first and only child. It's a good little treasure to have in the Internet cloud to celebrate that night. I am sure, though, that Jimmy Johnson and Vinnie Testaverde and Michael Irvin and the Boz watch it for radically different reasons.

Lots of college football games have been notable and historic, I guess, but none more so than a Division III contest between Baldwin-Wallace and Wittenberg on October 3, 1982. Your calendar will show you that October 3 that year was a Sunday, an NFL Sunday. Your Google search will tell you that 1982 was the year of the NFL strike, and with no NFL games to televise, CBS went with a college football game it was supposed to air anyway as stipulated in its massive NCAA contract. It was brilliant. To make it even more so, CBS opened the game with *The NFL Today* and shipped Pat Summerall, John Madden, and me to Springfield, Ohio, to cover the game. So there we were: the two big guns of CBS and me to treat this little "nothing" game as if it were the Giants and the Cowboys. We obliged. We rolled into Springfield and everywhere we went, people came out to see Pat and John, perhaps the biggest celebrities to ever grace the town. We ate at their restaurant chains, toured the campus, and did the game from a stadium roughly twenty-five times smaller than the average NFL stadium. We had a great time. Both Pat and John love to tell the story . . . and have told it often . . . that during the game, some kid scored and they went down to me with the kid's dad for an interview. About a minute later, another kid scored on an interception, and I grabbed that kid's dad. Only thing, it was the same dad. Pat and John got about twenty years out of that story. Baldwin-Wallace won the game on a fourth-quarter field goal, 16–14. I interviewed the dad of the kid who kicked the field goal, too. I think.

In the late fall of 1986, I was doing a Michigan football game in Ann Arbor when my trusted driver and assistant, Chris, grabbed me and said I had an important call in the CBS truck. It was Linda: "Honey, you're going to be a father, I'm pregnant!" The Miami night had been a success. I was going to be a dad! I walked outside and ordered Chris to go find some champagne, and the two of us celebrated. He had found some of those little airplane-size champagne bottles, and we sat in my hotel room and toasted the big moment. Not exactly the perfect celebration for such a life-changing moment, but I didn't care. My head was swirling and my heart was pounding. I couldn't wait to get home.

Sean was born right in the middle of the NBA Finals on June 9, 1987. We had gone through all name possibilities, boy and girl. We didn't know which it would be. We kind of settled on Daniel Patrick O'Brien if it was a boy, but the night before he was born, I had a dream that John Lennon approached me and said, "If it's a boy, you have to name him Sean, which is Gaelic for John." That was it! We welcomed Sean Patrick O'Brien into the world about two o'clock that morning. Our pediatrician, Peter Waldstein, was there, but he was in a hurry. Peter was not only the best pediatrician in Beverly Hills, whose clientele included the Hollywood A-list and several athletes, but he was also the biggest Lakers fan in LA. He had a private jet waiting to take him and some buddies to Game 4 of the NBA Finals between the Lakers and the Celtics in Boston. Sean was born, Peter snapped a Polaroid, and then like a modern-day Paul Revere he carried the news to the CBS truck outside the Boston Garden. As we watched the game from our Cedars-Sinai room, all of a sudden the broadcast came out of a commercial and showed

Larry and Magic standing in the middle of the court side by side. The game had stopped. All of a sudden Dick Stockton said, "You probably noticed that James Brown is here tonight filling in for Pat O'Brien. That's because Pat and Linda last night welcomed in Sean Patrick O'Brien. Everybody is healthy, and congratulations to Pat." Up came the first baby picture of Sean with the subtitle "Sean O'Brien: future sportscaster." Then they faded back to the game and Larry and Magic were still standing there. I always told Sean that his birth announcement held up two of the greatest athletes in the world on their biggest stage.

The next night, I went to that Yoko Ono art showing in Beverly Hills, and that's where I ran into Timothy Leary, who famously said, "You should have been counting the extra lobes on his brain, not his toes and fingers," alluding to all the acid we had done in the seventies.

Linda and I brought Sean home the next day. He had all his fingers and toes. On the way home, I had a cassette of "When You Wish upon a Star" . . . determined that this would be the first song he ever heard. As we walked into an empty house with our new baby, we looked at each other and said, "So, what do we do now?" Parenthood had begun. Fatherhood had begun. Sean Patrick O'Brien had been handed over to who I hoped would be the best dad ever. I was about to step into the greatest journey of my life.

I had been studying hard, though. During Linda's pregnancy, on many of my interminable plane flights, I'd discussed fatherhood with everybody I sat next to. On one flight, that person was Bill Cosby, who had for some reason always taken a proprietorial interest in my career. He told me the number one thing to remember as a dad is to hug your kid every day. I started doing just that on June 9, 1987, and now, every time I see him, I still do it, and the best part is, he hugs me back.

As we approached 1988, I was at home as usual playing with Sean and contemplating the forthcoming TV sports season: postseason football, a slate of NBA games, and the NBA All-Star Game. Then the phone rang.

It was my boss, Ted Shaker. "Did you hear about the Greek?" Isolated as we were back then without the Internet and Twitter to keep us informed minute by minute, I said, "No, now what?" Ted quickly told me that Jimmy the Greek had been in a bar in Washington, D.C., talking to a reporter, and that during what was reported as a drunken conversation, Jimmy rolled into a racist rant about African-Americans and how their slave ancestry made them better athletes. He said, "The black is a better athlete to begin with because he's been bred to be that way, because of his high thighs and big thighs that goes up into his back, and they can jump higher and run faster because of their bigger thighs, and he's bred to be the better athlete because this goes back all the way to the Civil War when during the slave trade'n the big . . . the owner . . . the slave owner would, would, would, would breed his big black to his big woman so that he could have, ah, ah, big, ah, big, a big black kid, see . . ."

Yup. That's what he said to WRC-TV reporter Ed Hotaling. I was mortified. My mouth dropped in shock almost at the same time as my instinct for self-preservation kicked in. My second thought was *How the hell am I going to deal with this? All I do is interview African-American athletes!* Already, I was getting calls from a couple NBA guys and several NFL players. They were wondering what we were going to do about this. Fortunately, it was not my problem. It was Shaker's.

Even without today's twenty-four-hour news cycle, the news spread relatively quickly, and there was nothing positive about it for anybody. Finally, a couple weeks later, on Sunday, January 16, it happened. I was in Denver hosting an NBA halftime show. Just before the show, my producer said, "They've just fired the Greek and you have to announce it. Do it right off the bat." Thirty seconds to air I told the booth, "There's no fucking way I'm going to ad-lib this thing. I want something written and approved by top management, and I will then read it word for word on the air." They agreed.

By the first commercial I was handed a card that did, indeed, announce that Jimmy was no longer with CBS, with as little explanation as possible. At the end I read, "'In no way did Mr. Snyder's remarks reflect the views of CBS Sports, and the relationship has ended.'"

Then, not on script, I looked into the camera with one of those "What the fuck was this cat thinking?" looks. That look ended up as part of his nearly $100 million lawsuit against CBS, which he lost. The Greek went into seclusion in Vegas, if seclusion was possible for Jimmy, and died right there in the gambling capital of the world. He probably meant well, and if he did, those were the worst "I meant well" remarks in the history of misguided comments. He had a good run, but nobody, no matter how much bigger he or she is than the room, goes undefeated.

Yes, in the world I have worked in, I've seen a lot of talent, but every now and then there are those people who are so out front, they are lonely. Howard Cosell was that man. Howard was arrogant, pompous, obnoxious, vain, cruel, verbose, and a show-off. Those are his own words describing his personality and his broadcast style. With his catchphrase, "just telling it like it is," he changed the world of sports broadcasting. He had enough talent to figure out that a new, young fighter named Cassius Clay had enough of his own talent to go one-on-one with Cosell before and after fights. Their interviews were legendary, and looking back on it, it's hard to figure out who made whom. They were the perfect couple. When Howard eventually took over ABC's *Monday Night Football*, it became the number one show of the week, with fans tuning in as much to hear what he had to say as to watch the game. He was, indeed, rude and obnoxious and was loved and loathed in equal measure. His special talent, to me, was that he somehow pulled this off with perfection. To me, Cosell was a god.

So one night I'm having dinner with some friends at McMillan's on the Upper East Side in Manhattan, and right in the middle of the restaurant, there he was, holding court with about ten people. I had never met him and I couldn't take my eyes off him: one of those guys who just always seemed unapproachable. Finally, our eyes met, and from fifty feet away I said, "Hello, Mr. Cosell." He was drunk. He then stood up at his table and yelled across the restaurant, "Don't you patronize me, young man!" in his legendary, clipped style. I cringed. The restaurant stopped. He wasn't done: "Pat O'Brien, stand up and show yourself." I was now scared, but also kind of honored that he even knew who I was. Right there, though, it was just Howard and me. The old and the young. He looked around for his next line and spotted a priest sitting in his cloth at a nearby table. Cosell screamed out, "Padre. Padre! Do you hear me? Say a prayer for this young man who is trying to take over my business. Say a prayer that he comes over to my network, a real network, and gets a real job." Everybody laughed. Then he winked at me, raised his glass in a mock toast, and went back to entertaining his table. The next time I saw him, he was coming out of the press box at Dodger Stadium and breezed by me as if I were a panhandler. Eventually he was let go by ABC, proving that even legends wear out their welcome in the fickle business of television. There are no untouchables, and once again, nobody goes undefeated.

I used to hang out in a bar called Ferrier on Sixty-Fourth Street between Park and Madison. It was one of those places where people knew your name, and I drank enough there that they knew my name, height, weight, birthday, Social Security number, and how many glasses of red wine I could consume in one night. Well, one night, about midnight, I decided it was my last call, and I set out to walk back to the Four Seasons, a few blocks away on Fifty-Seventh Street. When I got outside, it was pouring down rain. I mean, one of those New York monsoons that not even an umbrella helps. So, I'm jaywalking at a rapid pace and traffic was at a standstill. As I was crossing the street, a window on a Volvo station wagon rolled down and the guy inside yelled out, "Pat, Pat, come on, quick, I'll give you a lift." I welcomed the invite, and when I shut the door, I looked over and the man behind the wheel was Joe DiMaggio. He was alone. I had never met Joe and was in awe. I said, "Oh, hi, Mr. DiMaggio, thank you so much." I told him where I was going and he put the car into gear and off we went. Not another word was said. First of all, what do you say to Joe DiMaggio at midnight in the rain? "Hey, do you think anybody will ever get a hit in fifty-six consecutive games?" No, I didn't say anything. Neither did he. I remember stopping at a light for what seemed like forever with just Joe and me and the windshield wipers going back and forth, back and forth, back and forth. We pulled up to the Four Seasons and I got out. I said, "Thank you, Mr. DiMaggio!" He said nothing and drove away.

The thing about being on television is that, well, everybody has got one. Including the late John Gotti. Back when Mr. Gotti was head of the Gambino crime family in New York City, I was having a quiet dinner on the East Side with former coach and current broadcaster Bill Raftery. All of a sudden, there he was, the head of the Mob in New York, leaving the restaurant and heading for the door. The entire restaurant stopped. As he walked by my table, he stopped and pointed a well-manicured finger at me and said, "Pat O'Brien! I love your work!" I was at a loss for words, so I stood up and said, "John Gotti! I love your work." With that, he walked out the door, and to this day I'm trying to figure out which part of his "work" I actually liked, but it was worth the story. A couple years later, the Dapper Don died in a Missouri prison

To me, the head of the baseball family was and always will be Tommy Lasorda. The former Dodger skipper and I met in the early eighties and developed a close friendship. I don't think I ever saw him in a bad mood, and we never, ever had a conversation that didn't include two things: how great baseball is and how great Dodger baseball is. When Tommy was the Dodgers' manager, it was routine to hang out in his office before and after the game. Frank Sinatra, Tommy's longtime friend, and every other big name would visit to pay homage to Lasorda. There was always Italian food and wine and as many Tommy stories as he had time for. I once asked him how many stories he had tucked away, and he said, "If we got into a car and drove from New York to Los Angeles, I could go the whole trip without stopping, and then we'd have to get on a boat to Hawaii so I could finish." That's a lot of stories. Of course, everybody has his or her own Tommy stories. My favorite is the time I brought my son, Sean, down to the clubhouse. Sean was about six years old and Tommy asked him if played baseball and Sean said no. So, Tommy took a glove from one of his players and handed it to Mitch Webster, gave Sean a ball, and said, "Let's go." So we went out to the field and Tommy told Sean to throw the ball. Sean had never thrown a baseball, so his form was a little short of Lasorda's scale. Tommy was gentle. He said, "No, son, bring the ball back to your ear and follow through." Sean tried it again, still not to Tommy's liking. About the third try Tommy got frustrated and screamed, "Goddamn it, son, throw the fucking ball!" I said, "Tommy, he's six!"

Actually, Sean had quite the sports heritage growing up. He learned to throw from Tommy Lasorda, learned to hit from Mickey Mantle, got his first tennis lesson from Rod Laver, his first basketball lesson from Michael Jordan ("Sean, nobody plays defense. When you get the ball, shoot it! If you don't have the ball, steal it from one of your players and then shoot it!"), played catch with onetime neighbor Keyshawn Johnson, and hung out in some of the great locker rooms of the eighties and nineties. We never told him this was unusual. One day, he came home from school and said, "Is Michael Jordan famous?" Apparently he had told some classmates that he met Michael and they didn't believe him. I told Jordan this story and Michael called Sean and invited him to the premiere of *Space Jam*. Jordan insisted Sean bring a friend to walk the red carpet with him. Nobody questioned Sean again about all this.

Sean's baseball lesson from Mickey Mantle was quick and simple. The Mick told him, "If you don't see the ball hit the bat, the ball will never hit the bat." Simple, but effective.

I first met Mantle in the mideighties when my CBS team and I traveled down to Dallas for an "at home with Mantle" feature. As I was walking up to his doorstep, I was saying to myself, "I'm going to knock on this door and on the other side is fucking Mickey Mantle." I knocked and I was right. He said, "Come on in, Pat; can I get you a beer?" It was 10:00 a.m. And that began a long friendship with one of the greatest Yankees ever. We hit it off pretty well right away: talked on the phone a lot, played golf, drank in New York bars, dined in fine restaurants, and did a lot of laughing. During our first, of many, interviews, I asked him what he thought about when he was driving around alone and the song—his favorite—"It Was a Very Good Year" came on the radio. He paused and then his eyes started to swell up with tears. The Mick was racing through memories of years of self-destruction right before my eyes. He once famously said, "If I knew I was going to live this long, I would have taken better care of myself." It was no secret that Mantle had a drinking problem that was getting worse. He beat me to rehab, so he was a hell of a lot smarter than this self-destructive drinker. Nevertheless, after that interview ran, I ran into Yankee fan extraordinaire Billy Crystal, who shouted at me, "You made Mickey Mantle cry!" I could never figure out if Crystal was amazed or angry. Mick and I played in a golf tournament together once with Hank Aaron, and when Mick approached the first hole, he got into a stance that was low enough that he could use his baseball swing off the tee. It worked. He hit the golf ball a million miles.

Mickey went through his health and alcohol problems very publicly; not his choice, but that's the way it was. About four days after he was released from an emergency visit to a hospital for recurring liver problems, I was in the bar at the Regency on Park Avenue in New York, and Mickey and Billy Martin were at the end of the bar slamming drinks down as if there were no tomorrow. Mick spotted me and said, "Come on, Pat; join us." I enabled.

One time, my best childhood friend, Greg Blomberg, had made his first trip to New York and we were sitting at the Regency bar when Greg excitedly said, "Hey, I think that's Mickey Mantle over there and he's waving at us." Sure enough, Mickey was sitting alone and trying to get our attention. As we sat down, he leaned over and said, "Pat, I don't know where I am. I've been on a four-day bender." Selfishly, and wanting my friend Greg to have the story, I said, "Mick, let's get a round." So we all sat there and drank and Greg and I ended up carrying Mickey Mantle to his apartment in the hotel. It was sad: two lifelong Mantle fans trying to navigate their idol to bed.

As the years went by, a Mantle renaissance swept the country and his many fans, who had detached themselves from him, were now coming back for more curtain calls from number 7. He loved it. He began to understand how much he meant to people. I give pretty much all the credit on this one to Bob Costas, who was closer to Mantle than anybody else and, perfectly so, delivered his eulogy.

When Mantle graduated from rehab successfully (I never thought he would last, but he did), he called me and wondered if I would come down and play golf in Dallas. On the first hole, he placed his ball on the tee and just stood there and stared at it for several seconds. I said, "What's up?" He said, "That is the first time I have ever put a golf ball on a tee and it stayed on the first try." He had gone through life with such bad shakes from the booze that this one little chore was simply impossible. That was also the day when he pulled me aside and said, "Pat, do you play anything else? Because you really fuckin' suck at this!" He was right again.

I will say this: he stayed sober, even after the death of his son. That's an accomplishment. And he died sober.

I think the way I'll always remember him is the time I took him to dinner at a crowded Four Seasons restaurant in Beverly Hills, and when he walked in, the room stopped; everybody just stood up and started applauding. A look of sheer joy came over his face, and maybe some regret. He died knowing that people really, really loved him for better and for worse.

But the athlete who we all thought was going to die young was, ironically, Magic Johnson.

In mid-October 1991, Earvin missed a couple of games and nobody thought much of it. But when he missed the third game for what they were officially calling "the flu," I said to Linda, "This is a

guy who never misses games. Something here has got to be wrong."
There was. On October 25 he underwent a routine life-insurance
physical and the doctors checked everything. When the results
came back, he was told that he had contracted the human immuno-
deficiency virus, HIV. Magic was so disbelieving that he ordered
two more tests; both of them came back positive for HIV.

Hard to believe now, but even in 1991 AIDS was considered strictly
the "homosexual" disease or the "drug addict disease" or something
that was only in Africa or Haiti. That was basically the narrow definition of AIDS.

I got a call from a close confidant of Earvin's, who began, "Magic
wanted me to call you." Then he said, "Are you sitting down?" Within
seventy-two hours, so many rumors were floating around that Earvin
was forced to hold a news conference on November 7. The morning
of the news conference, Dan Rather called me from New York and
said, "You're the only person around here who is close to Magic.
Why don't you cover this for the *CBS Evening News*."

The news conference was held inside the Forum Club, the restaurant and bar where so many celebrations had been held after so
many great Lakers victories. I had met Magic there for drinks after
games. But now, hundreds of reporters were crowded into a tense
room. The hidden thought on everybody's mind was that Magic
Johnson was going to die. Period.

It was not your normal gathering of news and sports people. There
was no laughing, no comparing notes, and barely any conversation.
When Earvin came into the room, the noise of the cameras' clicking
was deafening. He walked in with a purpose, and when he walked
by me, he stopped and I hugged him and gave him a kiss. (This had
been our normal greeting.) He put his arm around me and said,
"Tell your boy I'm going to be all right."

We later learned that Magic hadn't known the difference between
being HIV-positive and having AIDS. He was told there was a difference fifteen minutes before the press conference. He told his team
in the locker room and they all broke down. Then he came before

the hard-nosed press and we all broke down. But Magic sternly said, "I will battle this deadly disease," and promised to become a national spokesman. At that moment, AIDS had a face. And the message had been sent that AIDS could be transmitted through heterosexual sex. The news conference was delivered live to the country, and afterward Dan Rather and I had a conversation on the air about it. I was back in my news mode, and when I was finished I went for a walk to the end of the Forum parking lot and broke down and cried.

I thought of the John Lennon verse "Life is what happens to you while you're busy making other plans."

The hug and the kiss with Earvin were caught on CNN and other networks and ran for days. I got mail: "You kissed a Nigger with AIDS" and "You're going to die, too, nigger lover," and the usual sad, ignorant crap that comes from morons. I poured myself a drink and burned the letters one by one.

11

The Best Seat in the House

As the last decade of the twentieth century rolled around, I was blessed with an insane amount of work. Not only was I embedded in the NBA and college basketball and football; I was also still hosting the US Open Tennis Championships and working on the sidelines for NFL games. Then on the night of April 1, 1990, my life changed again. Brent Musburger was fired from CBS. Brent was the face of CBS Sports and in command over every sport we covered. No problem. In my mind nobody was better, and to this day he is still at the top of his broadcasting game. But Ted Shaker and some other executives had different ideas. In truth Shaker thought that Brent was wielding too much power at CBS and, of all things, was too popular. Ted liked to keep his talent close, and Brent wasn't close. He was getting away—or, in their minds, he was running away—with too much power over the network. Yet the ones saying all this were the very executives who were handing Brent all the assignments. He was also in the middle of a contract negotiation, and with the purchase of Major League Baseball rights and two Olympics, Brent was, rightly, asking for more money. The CBS solution was to cut off his head, which they did on April Fools' Day. As the rumor spread, we all thought it was, indeed, an April Fool's joke.

About midnight, my phone rang at home and it was Brent. "What do you think, kid?" I told him I felt bad about all this, and then he said, "This is the best thing that ever happened to you." I was pretty happy with what I had, but Brent was basically telling me I was his heir apparent. This had never crossed my mind. The next night, Brent did the play-by-play of the 1990 NCAA men's basketball championship game between Duke and UNLV, before a curious audience: even without Twitter and Facebook, this story was everywhere. At the end of the broadcast, he stood next to his partner, Billy Packer, and for the first time acknowledged that he was gone. As he said good-bye, all he said was "I had the best seat in the house, folks. See you down the road." And that was the end of the Musburger era. Boom. Suddenly everything changed. Jim Nantz replaced Brent as play-by-play announcer on hoops. Greg Gumbel replaced Brent as the host of *The NFL Today,* and I was named host of pretty much everything else. It was frightening. I felt that I had skills, but not at the Musburger level.

I hardly had time to ponder the seismic shift inside CBS and the sports world when I was called in to replace Brent as host of the last of the CBS Sports NBA Finals, between the Detroit Pistons and the Portland Trail Blazers. I immediately suggested that we hire Bill Walton to sit next to me. Trouble was, we couldn't find Bill. After a couple of calls, I found out he was in Las Vegas. Bill was not a gambler and not a big drinker, so I wondered what the hell he'd be doing there. I did know he was on crutches, nursing his nearly career-long foot injury. I also knew that Timothy Leary was in Vegas, and I knew that Tim and Bill were good friends. So I started calling hotels. On the third one, I asked for Dr. Timothy Leary, and they said, "Hold on please." I was in. I later learned from Bill that the legendary writer Ken Kesey answered the phone. Ken was a Merry Prankster, one of the riders on the famous bus described by Thomas Wolfe in *The Electric Kool-Aid Acid Test,* and the author of the classic novel *One Flew over the Cuckoo's Nest.* I said, "Is Bill there?" I heard Kesey muffle the phone and yell, "Bill, it's Pat O'Brien!" Got him. Bill said he was on crutches and couldn't get around so much, and I said, "There will be a limo waiting for you downstairs in a couple hours. You're coming to Detroit." Bang! That was the beginning of Bill Walton's television career.

Not only was this my debut fill-in for Brent; it was also the national debut of the Palace of Auburn Hills, a jewel of a new arena. While we were waiting for Bill to arrive in Detroit, we found out about a problem with the singer to perform the national anthem. My friend Bobby Colomby, drummer and leader of Blood, Sweat & Tears, was sitting with me and said, "I've got a kid you might use." I said they were desperate, but not that desperate as to bring out an unknown singer. Bobby said, "She's probably one of the best singers I've ever heard." Enough for us, and suddenly Mariah Carey had her first big national job. I was on a roll. After she finished the anthem, which she nailed, I said on live TV, "The Palace now has its queen." That quote went all over the world, and eventually so did Mariah. She and I still laugh about how it all came together that night.

That series was won by Detroit in only five games, a terrible ending to such a great run for the NBA on CBS. When the series ended so abruptly that night in Portland, I had to race to the locker room to interview the players and coaches. I knew from experience that this was always the part of the job where you get soaked with champagne. As I was running to the locker room, I passed Jim Gray and said to him, "Quick, Jimmy, I don't have a coat, loan me yours." I put his on, went in and did all the interviews, got soaked with champagne head to toe, and, when I was done, returned Gray's cheap-champagne-soaked coat to him. Finally at the end of the broadcast, we gave a farewell address to the NBA and thanked them for the memories and played the Band's "The Last Waltz" and then the historic Marvin Gaye version of "The Star-Spangled Banner." It was the end of a beautiful and meaningful era for us.

Meantime, CBS executives had some shoes to fill. Jim Nantz was promptly placed as the play-by-play voice of the NCAA Tournament and the Final Four. I was made the host. A new *NFL Today* was formed with Greg Gumbel replacing Brent, and Terry Bradshaw,

Lesley Visser, and me filling out that set. I suddenly was the host of CBS's college football studio.

Now, being a sports studio host requires its own skill set. It is miles from sideline reporting, and it's on the other side of the world from play-by-play, which I do not have a talent for and never will. The sports studio made household names out of Musburger, Bryant Gumbel, Bob Costas, and Jim Lampley. The best. Hard to top because nothing in your life prepares you for the sort of rhythm it requires.

This is a snapshot of why the job does your head in: First of all, there is no script. You go on and say, "Hi, everybody, welcome, and let's get you caught up on today's scoreboard." In college football, that scoreboard could be thirty-five scores. You would be handed a card with the two teams, the score, and a sheet telling you, say, who made the big play. The knack is to keep it moving, interesting, and not to get behind.

The entire time you were talking to the audience, your producer would also be speaking in your earpiece. When people ask me what that was like, I say, "Okay, say your name and your age and your home address and what your favorite color is while I talk into your ear." So they begin. As soon as they start with "Hi, everybody, I'm Jim Smith," I say, "Okay, Jim, switch to score three now and we're not going to do highlights. Then do scores three to nine and then move to a live interview." They all stop. Panic.

That is precisely what happened to me the first time I tried to host a show, the first time I tried to emulate what Brent Musburger did so effortlessly. My producer, David Winner, could see the panic in my eyes and screamed, "Go to commercial, go to commercial." So I limped my way to a commercial break. "And we'll be back right after this." David brought me off the set into a private part of the studio and said, "Okay, you are not going to ever do this by thinking about all the things you have to do. You cannot think the big picture here. Take it one thing at a time. One score at a time. One highlight at a time. One interview at a time." It was the best advice I ever got, and eventually I became one of those guys on the elite list.

In time, guests who sat to my right thought I was some kind of magician, juggling the instructions from the control booth while keeping the show on the road. For example, the first time legendary coach George Raveling (Iowa, USC) sat next to me in a college basketball tournament studio, this is what he heard in our ears: "Okay, Pat, we're gonna say hello, then set up the day, then scores one to five with highlights on number three. On camera and talk to George. Then scores nine, eleven, sixteen, twenty-three, thirty-two with highlights. We haven't finished yet so we'll tell you. Then go to the screen and there will be a coach to interview, but we're not sure which one yet. Okay, in ten, nine, eight, seven . . ." After listening to this almost indecipherable cross talk George had the look of somebody with a loaded gun in his face. Later, he laughed about it and would always say he could never figure out how we did it.

Everyone else felt the same way. Pat Haden, former USC great and onetime quarterback of the Rams, once said to me, "I would rather have the front four of the biggest Viking team chasing me down than do that." Coach Dean Smith of North Carolina was intrigued to know how I kept talking without stuttering.

I realized that the technique was never to study the teams too deeply, as there was enough to do just keeping up with the scores. Instead I used my analysts to fill in the details. So they had to be ready. Once I was flying from Los Angeles to New York to host the weekend college basketball. Coach Raveling was the analyst, and as I enjoyed a couple of glasses of red wine George was wading through a pile of newspaper clippings, poring over all these basketball stats, personalities, and histories. I said to him, "Coach, do you know why you are reading all that?" He replied, "No, honestly, I don't." I said, "You're reading that because I'm not."

As the 1980s came to an end, CBS went on a shopping spree. First, the network purchased the rights to broadcast Major League Baseball for a ridiculous price (at the time) of a billion dollars . . . another billion bought us two Winter Olympics in 1992 and 1994, bringing the total investment in these sports to over $3 billion. The executives and us were calling it the Dream Season. The accountants and the critics were calling it the Nightmare Season. The hottest sport in the country, with Michael Jordan and the return of Magic Johnson, had found a new bankroll at NBC, so CBS was, as we say, under the gun to pay for all this stuff. As for baseball, Brent was replaced by the great Jack Buck, and that left hosting Major League Baseball to me. Not only was my plate full; so was my kitchen. I thought to myself at the time, *Are these fuckers crazy?* Making me the host of the All-Star Game, the postseason, and the World Series was like having Garry Trudeau paint the next Picasso. (And, yes, I know, he doesn't do the drawing, but that makes this better.) So, let's say it together: Pat O'Brien was now in charge of the National Pastime.

I think that by this time in my life I had been to a total of half a dozen baseball games, maybe . . . and watched perhaps two. My most prominent baseball credential was that I pretended I was Mickey Mantle when I was a kid and then, later in life, got drunk with him several times. Then I played golf with him when he got out of rehab. So there I was about to host the MLB All-Star Game at Wrigley Field, one of the glorious shrines of baseball.

This was CBS's first big jewel in baseball, and the network went all out for its baseball look and feel. The late Jack Buck was certainly a grand start, as he was one of the jewels of the announcers' booth. A legend in St. Louis, he was in many ways the Mayor Daley of baseball announcers. There hadn't been many like him. To analyze the game, CBS brought in Tim McCarver, a former catcher and at the moment the best analyst, kind of the John Madden of baseball. Then for this inaugural event, they brought in a lot of other legends, such as Ernie Harwell, who had been calling the game for thirty years in Detroit. Harwell, Buck, and Vin Scully were the current living legends calling America's Pastime. And me. So you might imagine how (for me) meek I was as I walked out onto the field for the first time the day before the game as the All-Stars were gathering. As I walked over by first base, a gaggle of reporters with their notebooks were listening to every word by somebody crushed in the middle of the fifty or so baseball writers. It was Ernie Harwell, holding court. Suddenly, right then and there, my image changed. As I approached, Ernie, whom I had never met, caught sight of me and pointed me out to all the writers, who by their very trade hated broadcasters with a passion and especially the image I presented: grandiose, entitled, long hair and a mustache and Armani suits. Not many could relate to any of that except entitlement. Certainly not the wardrobe.

So, Ernie pointed and said in his deep, beautiful voice, "See that young man over there? You're gonna like him. He's gonna bring some fun back to this game. I show you Pat O'Brien." I felt as if I were coming up to bat without any clothes on and then handed an Armani suit, then hit for the cycle. The writers glared at me. This off-the-cuff comment by one of the greatest baseball announcers ever had thrown them. How could Ernie fucking Harwell like Pat O'Brien? It was great. Five seconds of minor embarrassment for a lifetime of a memory. Later in the season, I strolled into the New York Yankees locker room, and there in front of his locker was the Yankee captain, Don Mattingly, known always as Donnie Baseball for the way he played and represented the game. He, too, was surrounded by these wretched ink-stained boys of the press. He was leaning back on his chair talking, and all the beat writers were transcribing every word. I'd never met Don, but he got out of his chair, stood up right in the middle of a sentence, and said, "Gotta go, boys; the King is here!" These were the New York writers, who tend to be a little more cosmopolitan, and I think they got the irony. But let's get this straight right here. Back in those days, by definition any network that owned baseball or basketball or football was like a monarch. It was, literally, exclusive coverage. Today there is no singular voice of any sport—that's just the way it is. Every network has dozens of faces and voices, and ESPN has thousands. So we were always thought of as the elite, by everybody else's definition. Little did they know, must of us were scared to death. As for this generational feud with writers, I once asked Norman Chad, who wrote a syndicated media column, a gambling column, and later became a broadcaster, why writers hated broadcasters so much. He didn't miss a beat: "You make more money, you drive better cars, and your wives and girlfriends are better looking." As they all do, Chad finally gave up his writing and became a television guy. As a television broadcaster, he was worse than his writing. And he was really a bad writer.

The first season of CBS baseball was a disaster. Fun, but a disaster. In the World Series we ended up with two teams nobody cared much for: the Cincinnati Reds and the Oakland Athletics. Both teams had some personalities and some superstars, but television needs either big markets or seven World Series games to make money. We had two small markets and the Reds swept the A's in four. A billion dollars didn't buy what it used to. But I used the hosting position to not only set up the games as best I could but also bring forward some stories that had long been ignored in baseball. For example, we did a long-overlooked story on the Negro leagues and where some of those pioneers were today. We tracked down such guys as Double Duty Radcliffe and Buck O'Neil. O'Neil invited me into his home and the first thing he said was "I'll tell you one thing: our pussy was better than today's." We didn't air that, but we got a tremendous selection of stories of what it was like to be, arguably, the best players ever and not be in the big leagues. The train rides, the humiliation of not being able to eat where they wanted, the near-poverty pay level, and so on . . . but what came across is how they built the game and how nobody cared. That story, which ran in one of our pregame shows, sparked a new interest in the Negro leagues, and eventually the players were allowed in the Hall of Fame and, equally cool, their old logos and gear sold off the shelves for MLB. However, in doing the story, I was struck again at the overt racism this country had thrown at these spectacular artists who laid the foundation of the game. One of those founders, "Cool Papa" Bell, said he was so fast he could turn the light switch off and be in bed before the light went off. And he said it with style.

CBS's years being the caretaker of baseball had a lot of memorable moments. For me, they revolved around the Minnesota Twins. When I was growing up in South Dakota, the nearest baseball team was Minnesota, and even though I had little interest in the game, I did retain some of the names from my childhood, specifically Jim Kaat and Harmon Killebrew. Perhaps my favorite sports picture growing up was an action shot of Kaat throwing the ball. CBS hired Jim to be part of our team. So suddenly I found myself hanging out with the guy who was on the picture that was in my drawer. As for Killebrew, it would have been tough to grow up in South Dakota and not know about Harmon. The power hitter, All-Star, and Hall of Famer was the Mickey Mantle of the Midwest. In the late eighties, I was at a celebrity golf tournament with Mantle, and this guy behind me said, "Mr. O'Brien? Mr. O'Brien?" I turned around and, boom, it's Harmon Killebrew. I said, "I don't think you should be calling me 'mister.'" He laughed and asked if I would take a picture with his granddaughter. Everybody has a television, and, more important, most sports legends tend to be sports fans . . . but it always humbled me when these things happened.

The first time I met Reggie Jackson, he was playing in Oakland on a team that was managed by Billy Martin. The years had not been kind to Billy and Reggie's friendship, so CBS sent me to Oakland to see how this deal was going. The media-savvy Reggie knew exactly why I had shown up, and when I introduced myself, he said, "I know who Pat O'Brien is and I know you are new to the game, and don't think you're going to make a name for yourself off of my name." Always the smart-ass, I retorted, "If I wanted to make a name for myself, I'd be interviewing Dave Winfield." How do you think that went?

But, through the years, Reggie and I became great friends, and he gave me the nickname the Chairman because, he said, every time he turned on a sporting event, I was sitting in "the chair." Made sense to me. For a while, it was Reggie Jackson himself sitting right next to me. One time, while we were doing an Oakland game in the

1992 season, somebody threw a baseball at us while we were doing the pregame and it hit me squarely in the head. I didn't even flinch, made no mention of it, and kept on talking. Afterward, Reggie was marveling that I had the resolve to just keep on talking with the fans throwing stuff at me. I said to him, "In what fantasy world do you think that ball was for me?"

Reggie and I had long talks about our dads. His dad was nurturing and attentive . . . in fact, he saw most of Reggie's home runs in person. I, of course, didn't have many dad stories. I think that's why Reggie told me to always honor my father when signing an autograph. I do.

I was certainly thrown in at the deep end. Within days of introducing the new queen of pop, I had graduated to a president and a prime minister, in April 1990 interviewing George Bush Sr. and Canadian prime minister Brian Mulroney after they had thrown the first ceremonial pitches at the home season-opener inside Toronto's new SkyDome. The two world leaders were ushered into my booth, both clearly enjoying themselves and the occasion. I had them seated on a ledge overlooking the stadium, but just before we went to air I was told that they had to be moved to face another camera. With only a few seconds before we went live, I said, "Hey, guys, we've got to get up and turn around quickly; let's go." The White House protocol people and certainly the White House press corps were disgusted that I had addressed the president of the United States as one of the "guys," but I apologized immediately afterward for being so abrupt. "Don't worry about it," George Bush told me, then graciously invited me to join him in his booth to watch the game.

As I was hosting the game rather than doing the play-by-play, I had some extra time. When I was ushered into the president's booth, he was sitting with several baseball greats, including my former driver Joe DiMaggio and Ted Williams. If that weren't enough of a thrill, the president then offered me a hot dog. I tried to be polite and decline, but he insisted and made me one. A White House aide brought in a dozen baseballs for the president, the prime minister, and the baseball legends to sign. As I left to continue broadcasting, the president offered me a ball as a souvenir. I did something stupid: I declined. It was an attempt at being polite, but I went against my own theory of "five seconds of embarrassment for a lifetime of memories." That ball had the signatures of a president, a prime minister, DiMaggio, and Williams. Good ball. But the experience of that evening will last a lifetime. I had come a long way from my days back in South Dakota when I worked at KSOO radio as the late-night DJ.

I returned to the broadcast right after the replay of the day's Twins game . . . but in my rush and excitement to get on, I fast-forwarded the game and shortened it. So Ray Scott and Halsey Hall would say, "And so we have two innings in the books here at the Met." And the next thing listeners would hear was "Top of the sixth, now . . ." At the time, I didn't know the difference.

When I hosted my first World Series, in the first billion-dollar baseball contract for CBS Sports, everybody was skeptical. As I said earlier, the jewels of any sport are the All-Star Games, the play-offs, and the Finals or, in this case, the World Series. Our first one was a sweep of Oakland by the Reds. As I said at the time, it was Marge Madness, after the irrepressible Marge Schott. One time I was waiting for the VIP elevator to take me up to the booth and Marge was standing there. She was frustrated that the ride wasn't there, so she took it out on me by kicking me in the ass. That's the first owner who ever or has ever physically attacked me.

No charges were pressed. She was quite the character.

Perhaps the highlight of my baseball experiences involved the broadcasters I worked with: McCarver, Jack Buck, Tommy Lasorda, and Jim Kaat. Lasorda and I had known each other for years and we always cherished our dinners. One night we were going to Bamonte's in Brooklyn, an old Italian spot that Tommy loved. We were driving through a rather uncertain neighborhood, and suddenly we were stopped by the police. A cop arrived at the driver's side and said, "Mr. Lasorda and Mr. O'Brien, what the hell you doing in this neighborhood?" We were lost. The officers escorted us to Bamonte's and we had a fine genuine Italian meal. Once in Minneapolis, I took Tommy to an Italian restaurant that didn't have soup. He was screaming, "What kind of a fucking Italian restaurant doesn't have soup?" We had to leave.

Minneapolis was always a special place for me to host play-off games and the World Series, and my favorite was that Game 6 inside the loud Metrodome in the 1991 World Series. This Series goes down in history for the basic statistics: three of the games went to extra innings. The home team won every game. The outcomes of five games were decided by 1 run on the final play. Game 6 was Puckett's night beginning to end: including a highlight catch, a triple, a single, and a sac fly. So Lasorda and I are sitting in our perch watching this unfold, and suddenly here comes Charlie Leibrandt, the left-hander for the Braves. Kirby at bat. Tommy pokes me and says, "Put your coat on; the game is over." A few seconds later, Puckett hits a convincing home run into the delirious hometown crowd. As the ball was still in the air, Jack Buck made his legendary call: "We'll see ya tomorrow night." The next morning, I called Kirby at home and asked if I could come over. He said yes, and I arrived early for a breakfast of cereal and milk. Then we walked down his long driveway to see all the flowers and cards at the bottom. The great Peter King of *Sports Illustrated* said this was what he always remembered me for: getting the big interviews when it counted. Again, it was a time when we owned the Series and nobody else was aggressively covering it . . . but my relationship with Kirby was what got that one. Kirby's life didn't go so well after that and resulted in blindness and then a stroke. He died with his family and teammates from that team surrounding him. The good often die young.

The baseball experience pretty much rounded out my sports résumé. I had all the sports covered. All except one big one. And that, too, was about to become another stop on the tracks.

Just after the 1991 World Series, Ted Shaker and I were sitting at the back corner table at Perry's on Union Street in San Francisco. We always enjoyed being together socially, and we still do. However, as the executive producer of CBS Sports, Ted had been my best friend and my worst enemy, depending on his mood. Although responsible for my meteoric rise at CBS, he also threatened to fire me more than once. He had told producers to "reel me in" and had, indeed, reeled Brent in by leading the parade to fire him at CBS. On this night, Ted was my best friend as we sipped California red wine in this legendary sports bar. Not our first time. Usually after a 49ers game, the crew would end up here for late-night burgers and drinks. Perry's was always a good time and another of the million reasons to love the Bay Area. Still is.

Ted and I were congratulating ourselves on what we believed to be our success in hosting Major League Baseball and debating what the future looked like without the NBA on CBS. The loss of the NBA demanded more than a couple glasses of wine. But we were rolling, especially heading into 1992. It was to be our Dream Season: the Major League Baseball All-Star Game, MLB play-offs, the World Series, March Madness, the Final Four, college football, the Super Bowl—and now CBS had added the jewel of jewels: the Winter Olympics. In a financially controversial move, CBS picked up Albertville, Lillehammer, and Nagano.

Ted leaned over to me and with authority said, "I'm thinking you will also host the Olympics for us." Well, it made sense, since I was hosting everything else—for good or for bad—at CBS, but then they didn't let Shaker anywhere near the Olympics games. Those duties were handed to two veterans: Mike Pearl and Rick Gentile. Ted had been publicly "reeled in." And that was the beginning of the end of the Ted Shaker era.

In his absence, CBS stunned everybody by going way out of the box and naming Tim McCarver and Paula Zahn to host the 1992 Albertville games. Every moment of the games would be tape-delayed except for the *Late Night* show, which, thankfully, was handed to me. I was thrilled. I'll get to that in a moment . . . but first . . .

Paula Zahn. By her own description, totally unequipped to host a sporting event, let alone the premier sporting event on the planet. Paula was a tremendous newswoman and anchorwoman, and I coanchored with her locally in Los Angeles for a while. We had a problem, though, as we could not get through any sentence without laughing. I'm serious. We were great friends, and somehow every time we started to deliver the news one of us would break into laughter, then both of us would, and then they said, "There goes the O'Brien-Zahn era." It was quick. I respected her then as I do now, but she had no business hosting the Olympics.

Tim McCarver. By his own description, totally unequipped to host a sporting event, let alone the premier sporting event on the planet. McCarver, to this day, in my mind, was the greatest baseball analyst ever, but hosting is a different gig, and he found out quickly. It's one thing to be bad at something, but to know that you are bad at it while doing it is the worst feeling ever. I've been there. Tim has one of the most wonderful personalities in broadcasting, but as a prime-time host even he will tell you he struck out looking. He was thrown to the wolves. The two of them were handcuffed to the teleprompter, and CBS left them no room to escape. Their taping sessions were legendary, with take after take after take, and on one night Tim was under such public and professional scrutiny, he fainted right on the set. It was ugly.

But while it was going on, Tim was a man about it. Every day we would meet around noon and have these long, wonderful wine-soaked lunches on the deck of our hotel with the Alps looming over us. We laughed, worked on our tans, got loaded, then went for our naps before we forged through the snow in the middle of the night to do the shows.

My favorite McCarver stories revolve around the years he and Jack Buck and I did Major League Baseball. Nobody better to learn from . . . to hang out with . . . McCarver is a man's man. We were doing the World Series in Toronto at the same time Tim turned fifty years old. That day, I found a place that sold (legally) expensive Cuban cigars, so I bought him six of them, put them in a nice leather case, and handed them to him in the booth before the game. A group of strangers then walked in and one of the men said, "Wow, cigars!" Tim says, "Right, I have a bunch here, help yourself," and handed out $125 (American money) cigars to these startled bystanders. I told him three days later.

In the early nineties, McCarver punked me about as great as anybody ever has. I was a guest on our friend Don Imus's radio show, and I was telling Imus that McCarver had a razor-sharp temper, and Don and I got a big kick out of it. About a week later, I was in London to interview Paul McCartney for the first of many times, which was perhaps, in my mind, the highlight at the time of my career, given my love for the Beatles. So I was on cloud nine until I checked my answering machine at home. An authoritative-sounding guy said he was representing Tim McCarver: "Buddy, you'd better surround yourself with a battery of lawyers because my client is coming at you hard. We are suing you for libel and defamation of character and we will not be stopped." Click. Don't ask me why or how, but I bit and I bit hard. I tried calling McCarver. No answer. For the entire week I was in London on one of the greatest assignments of my life, I had to live with the thought that Tim McCarver was going to ruin my career in the courts. I would lose all my money. I would lose my job. I made up so many things in my mind and I was so distracted, I could barely work. I faked my way through the McCartney interview, but that was one miserable week. Tim finally called me when I got home and was laughing so hard he could barely hold on to the phone. It's funny to me now, but wasn't then.

Safe to say, though, Tim never had a happier day than when he escaped without much injury from the Olympics.

I was so grateful to get the *Late Night* show, which was live and comfortable, mostly unscripted and fun. CBS gave me my two favorite producers, Bob Mansbach and Rob Silverstein, and it was the greatest time, as we were given massive freedom to develop, present, and deliver our own version of what the *Late Night* show should be. And we did. At first there was the old, stale criticism: here comes Pat O'Brien again. I had to say to myself, *Well, I got the job, didn't I?* I mean, really? And when I finally explained to the wretched, envious print people that the *Late Night* show was not about the Olympics, it was about me being at the Olympics, some of them started to understand it.

So there I was in Albertville, France, with my first major Olympic assignment.

I was no stranger to the summer games, as I reported on the 1984 games in Los Angeles and went to the Seoul summer games in 1988 for CBS News. In Seoul, I covered everything surrounding the games from the influence of Samsung, to a memorable visit to what President William Clinton once called "the scariest place on earth," the village of Panmunjom, located in the middle of the demilitarized zone separating North and South Korea. The US army arranged for me to see firsthand what the area was like. *Intense* is not a strong enough word. Even so many years after the Korean War, the tension was such I could actually feel it in the pit of my stomach. Martial music from the North Koreans blared across the imaginary line separating the countries, and from the South Korean side you could see soldiers just feet away, staring us down. Still, I asked if I could have the experience of stepping over the line into North Korea, just to say I'd done it. The general showing us around said, "Sure, go ahead." I asked him half kidding, "What if they capture me for some kind of political statement?" He said, "Well, I can tell you this: we're not starting World War Three over Pat O'Brien." He wasn't kidding. As I stepped over, I couldn't wait to step back. It was the only few minutes in my life I never had freedom or some sense of control, and it wasn't comforting.

But I wasn't captured by the North Koreans, and now, four years later, was proudly about to settle into a hosting job at an Olympics in France.

South Dakota house, two blocks from the state penitentiary. We lived on the second floor, and I spent my years there in the attic, daydreaming.

Joseph Vincent O'Brien. I think he had bigger plans. His only advice to me was, "You're an O'Brien, you'll figure it out." That was it.

Vera Opal O'Brien. She was an insanely talented piano player to the very end. Her face lit up every time she saw me.

KATHY   AL   DAVID — mom — PAT

My stepdad, Al Moss, Mom, Kathy, and half-brother David. Never had much of a Christmas. I called him "Dad."

Me, Pat Garvey, Ken Cloud, Roger Opheim, and Greg Blomberg. We're still close friends after fifty years. We wanted to be the Beatles. Didn't happen.

On that weekend in February 1964 after the Beatles were on Ed Sullivan, I left school on Friday as Elvis and came back on Monday as John Lennon. I was kicked out of school for that.

Linda and I were the "it" couple at the University of South Dakota. Taken in front of the Delta Tau Delta House in Vermillion. My son's favorite picture.

The '70s. Chicago
newsman. Mayor
Daley, fires, cold
weather, and a
bunch of Emmys.

The first Iditarod. My pilot, Tony Oney, and me in the Yukon. We survived -100 temps,
crashes, and a hundred gallons of Jack Daniels.

Pat, Larry, Magic. NBA, the '80s. (*Courtesy of Steve Lipofsky*)

Mike and me. I send him this every year on his birthday. His response is always, "Ha Ha!"

Magic Johnson.
We've always treated
each other as family.

Not one kid, ever,
will have this photo.
Period. Magic and
Michael always
watched over Sean.

The late, great Chuck Daly gets his championship with Detroit. I wore
Jim Gray's sports coat and handed it back soaked in champagne.

No greater joy.

Not the first ear Tyson went after. Mike and I cried together over our demons and laughed together when we knocked them out.

At the Robert F. Kennedy compound at Hickory Hill with Muhammad Ali. I said, "Champ, we still look good." He said, "What do you mean, 'we?'"

Maria said we were two of the vainest men she had ever seen. We took this picture three times to get it right. Arnold said, "No man but you would have the balls to take this photo."

First Lady Laura Bush at the White House. "Are you hitting on me, Pat." She was funny, a great sport, smart, and gracious. The President stopped by to check on us.

At President Clinton's sixtieth-birthday party, in Nantucket. "Now there's a couple," laughed Hillary.

Linda Bell Blue. "Les is not the boss, I am."

There's all kinds of publicity photos of Lara Spencer and me.
This isn't one of them. I love this woman.

Striking the pose
with Madonna...
in London after
her British Rock
and Roll Hall of
Fame induction.

In the Bahamas two weeks before Anna Nicole Smith died.
Drugs, broken heart, and murder by the media.

Brad and George during *Ocean's Eleven* release. One of us was never named
"Sexiest Person in the World."

Michael J. Fox's advice to me during my first rehab. Mine hangs above my door, his hangs in front of his treadmill.

The First Lady at the All England Club for the London Olympics.
"We love you at the White House."

Two sober guys. Honest. We tried to take the picture that every
paparazzo would pay money for. Any takers?

I told Bono my son was a musician, and he called him on his cell phone
for encouragement. It worked.

Two skinny guys and proud of it.
The energy of a cheetah.

Keith Richards. We chain-smoked Marlboros
inside his suite at the Waldorf. I asked him how
he is still alive and he said, "I really don't know."

The Godfather of Soul. "I taught
them everything they know, but
not everything I know."

Richard has played a major role in my recovery. He even let me play in his band, which was a trip of its own. A caring human being and the beat behind the Beatles.

I kept saying to myself, "Wake up, Pat, you're hanging out with Paul McCartney!"

Gregory Hines and me jammin' in Hollywood.
I still wear the shoes he gave me and I still dance.

Unconditional love. The great Sean O'Brien

This picture was staged, but it's a pretty damn good metaphor.

The Olympics had always belonged to ABC and to Jim McKay. Their approach was always storytelling and inventing and executing the "up close and personal" approach to sports. It worked. While McKay was the gold-standard host, Jim Lampley was the gold-standard late-night host. Perched in front of a fireplace night after night, he waxed poetically, as only Lamps could, on the day's activities. My goal was to at least come close. CBS left the heavy lifting to McCarver and Zahn and to Jim Nantz. Nantz was everything I wasn't, and I was everything he didn't want to be. We got along fine and still do, but he was obviously the next torchbearer of everything CBS. I remember the first day we came in to look at the elaborate set they had built. Jim said out loud in his broadcast voice, "Which seat is the power position?" I said, "Whatever one I'm sitting in." And so it began.

Covering something as massive and global as the Olympics is the frame that every broadcaster wants around his résumé. It's an honor and certifies you as an all-around sportscaster. Those few of us who have Olympics on our résumés read a little bolder because of the experience.

While Albertville was my first serious hosting experience at the Olympics, CBS seemed lost in the assignment. There just never seemed to be a direction, but still we had time to fill and were high in the Alps to present the games to a waiting American audience. Because of the time differences and because of the enormity of covering multiple sports most people had never heard of, the undertaking was, to say the least, a huge challenge. To me, it was a huge party from beginning to end . . . and a way to fill up my passport with the stamps of all kinds of exotic countries leading up to the games.

We were given carte blanche to go anywhere and everywhere in the name of getting the story. Because figure skating was always the centerpiece of the winter games, we did a lot of ice time all over the world.

Before Albertville, we got the assignment of covering the World Figure Skating Championships in Paris. This meant eighteen glorious days in the most romantic city in the world with an unlimited expense account.

So there I was in Paris, 1989, with the world at my feet. I checked into my suite at the George V in central Paris, and after surveying the bedroom, living room, sitting room, and balcony overlooking the Eiffel Tower I did what most budding alcoholics do: I ordered a couple bottles of French wine and walked to the nearest pharmacy and bought some Ambien, which you could get without a prescription in France. My intent was to have a glass of wine and an Ambien and sleep all day and night and wake up fresh the next day, ready to go. Well, I did wake up the next day, alone in my bed with my clothes on. Mission accomplished.

When I arrived at the broadcast center, one of our translators, a beautiful brunette who spoke seven languages, said, "Hey, Pat, thanks for the great night! Wow, you know how to party!" What night? I thought she was joking, so I let it go. Later in the day, she came up to me again and said, "And, boy, you can really play the piano!" Then somebody else came up to me and said, "Way to take over Paris last night, O'Brien!" So I ran down my brunette translator again and said, seriously, what happened last night?

According to her . . . and she was telling me this in English . . . I called her and said, "You have to see my view." She came up and we had a friendly glass of wine. Then we hit a nearby restaurant for a friendly dinner, and then when we came back to the hotel bar everybody at CBS was in there drinking. She explained that I went right to the piano and entertained everybody for about an hour. I was panicked. I didn't remember any of this! "What was I playing?" I asked, now terrified. "Well, you played a lot of Broadway songs. And everybody had a great time singing 'New York, New York.'" I told her I didn't know how to play "New York, New York," and she assured me it was grand. I remembered none of it. When my performance in the bar was finished, she walked me to my room, and I apparently passed out on the bed without incident. I laughed it off as a stupid mistake, but in reality it was a red flag that I chose to ignore and I went on with my life as if nothing had happened. But something was telling me I saw a Pat O'Brien I didn't like.

Meanwhile, this was a golden age of figure skating all over the world with marquee names such as Katarina Witt, Kristi Yamaguchi, Nancy Kerrigan . . . uh, Tonya Harding, Midori Ito, and Surya Bonaly. On the men's side there were Victor Petrenko, Paul Wylie, Kurt Browning, Elvis Stojko, Todd Eldredge, Alexei Urmanov, Christopher Bowman, and Brian Boitano.

Like every other red-blooded American male, I fell in love with Katarina Witt, and she was the most interesting woman on and off the ice. She was ratings gold and she knew it, and we knew it, so we followed her wherever she went. And to get this out of the way right now, the answer is no.

But we became close friends. *Time* called her the "most beautiful face of socialism." She was on the downside of her career, but she remained a crowd favorite with her performances of *Carmen* and her *Playboy*-cover image. She was so important to East Germany at the time, they, too, followed her everywhere, even bugging her apartment and famously computing that her average sex escapades lasted roughly seven minutes. I joked with her that this drama had some serendipity, since seven minutes came out to the combined times of her short and long programs. Not the funniest joke she'd ever heard, but she did laugh. I had an enormous crush on her, so much so that when we taped a long interview with Katarina for the '92 *Late Night* show my director came in after and said, "Will your wife be watching this?" I said of course, and he said, "Then I suggest we do it again without the flirting." We had a lot of laughs and a lot of good times, and her life turned out happy and grand and I'm thrilled for her. We keep in touch.

Speaking of sexual tension, one of my favorite moments at the Paris World Figure Skating Championships was when some basically unknown French couple performed what can only be described as "sex on ice." It was so erotic that when they came off the ice to what we called the "kiss and cry" interview area, the first question I asked them was "Can I offer either of you a cigarette?"

Ironically, our favorite men's skater was Christopher Bowman. We called him Bowman the Showman because of his flair for the dramatic and his habit of not winning a lot of medals and championships, but surviving on his personality. Chris would show up at events without a costume and just tear up a T-shirt for a top and go out there and wow the audience. Brian Boitano, who had a flair of his own, once said that he picked Christopher as one of the most talented skaters of all time because of his showmanship: "He could turn a crowd on in a matter of seconds and he always seemed so relaxed about it."

Turns out, Bowman the Showman was a great actor. In the face of terrible demons and addictions that balanced out his grandiosity, he ran into personal problems he couldn't skate or laugh his way out of.

He died alone in a cheap hotel room in the middle of the night on January 10, 2008. Overweight, bloated, out of sight, and out of mind, he left behind a wife and a daughter. They had long departed and left him sad and single with nowhere to go. He was forty.

In Albertville, France, the highlight of the Olympics was Magic Johnson's return to the NBA. Despite his retirement Magic had been allowed to come back and play in the All-Star Game, in what would be his final great athletic moment. We watched from thousands of miles away in the middle of the night as he shone and took home the MVP trophy. It was a bittersweet moment for all of us who had been at his side from the very beginning, but he was lighting it up on NBC in what used to be a CBS event, and we were covering on CBS what was clearly an NBC franchise.

Speaking of grandiosity, I was feeling pretty good about myself and had these pins made for my team in the Olympics. They read, simply, TEAM O'BRIEN. I handed a few out here and there . . . limited supply, of course . . . and suddenly people were coming back saying the TEAM O'BRIEN pin had become quite the currency on the Olympic pin market. Olympic pins and the collecting and the trading of them has always been like an Olympic sport of its own. So now, in my mind, I had the pin of the '92 games. I wandered down to the village of Albertville and found the pin-trading marketplace, and right in the middle was a booth run by a man described as the "pin expert" at the games. I watched as people brought him pins to trade and evaluate and couldn't wait to wow him with my TEAM O'BRIEN pin. After all, some of my staff had just traded one pin for a pair of skis, an Olympic training suit, and other prizes from the games. I waited in line, and finally when it came my turn I confidently walked over to him and with a smirk on my face presented the TEAM O'BRIEN pin. He looked at the pin. He looked at me. The crowd hushed. Then he said in English loud enough for everyone to hear, "This is a piece of shit."

Despite this turn of events, Team O'Brien put on a terrific live *Late Night* show for half an hour each and every night.

In my mind, I could never match what Jim Lampley had done, so we did it our way with live interviews, remotes from back in the States, including a long interview with Donald Trump, who, at the time, was somebody people wanted to hear from, and, perhaps our signature feature, "Rock and Roll Highlights." All we did was take some of the action-packed thrills of victory and put them with current pop music and it became a hit. Who knew?

So while McCarver and Paula ached and suffered and tried to survive brutal and unfair criticisms of their coverage, we got away with a snappy little show that we were proud of. At the end of each workday, which was in reality the dawn of another snowy day in the Alps, we celebrated with wine and cheese around seven every morning and then staggered into bed to get ready for another Olympic day. Our wrap party involved roughly forty-five bottles of French wine and an epic night of drunkenness and celebration, and then

we came home. I'm not sure we moved the journalistic curve anywhere, but I added another line to my résumé: Olympic host.

That résumé was getting long and impressive and I was far from
done. The best and the worst was yet to come. I was on the move
once again.

12

Citius, Altius, Fortius

Faster, Higher, Stronger

As the nineties rolled in, the separation of powers in the media had clearly taken a dramatic shift. There was no separation anymore. Once there was news, there was sports, there was entertainment, and there was weather. Now, the lines between all these genres were disappearing faster than you could say, "Breaking news." Someone once said that the good news about television is that it gives people what they want; the problem is what they want! Now, it seemed, athletes had become big celebrities on and off the field. Newsmakers and politicians were making headlines in the tabloids, and it was all being mixed together and served shaken and stirred right there in your living room.

If anybody benefited from this situation at the time, it was yours truly. I had spent a decade covering hard-core news, another fifteen years covering every sporting event on the planet, and now the public wanted a little of both, mixed in with the growing world of entertainment news. The wide, wide world of sports became the wild, wild world of everything.

So it made sense that I crossed that line myself, formally, as a host of the number one entertainment show in the world, *Entertainment Tonight*. I was no longer doing double duty, I was doing triple duty, and it was all working for everybody, especially Hollywood. As I made this transition, I discovered that all the A-listers in Hollywood were tremendous and loyal sports fans, so there was no need to introduce myself. This paid off in a big way on the red carpet. Hard to believe now that the "red carpet" used to be only about fifteen feet long and was the path leading to the door of Irving "Swifty" Lazar's Oscar party, held annually at Wolfgang Puck's first restaurant in the hills right on the edge of Hollywood.

Spago eventually became a legendary way of life in Hollywood, but Swifty Lazar was already a legend as one of the most influential agents in Tinseltown. His clients included Humphrey Bogart (who gave him the name Swifty after Lazar, on a bet, secured five deals in one day for Bogie), Walter Matthau, Lauren Bacall, Truman Capote, Ira Gershwin, Cary Grant, Ernest Hemingway, Gene Kelly, Madonna, Cole Porter, Cher, Tennessee Williams, and even President Richard Nixon. He had also represented my old boss David Brinkley.

When the annual party finally moved from Romanoff's to Spago, there was no more coveted Oscar-night invitation. If you were a somebody in Hollywood, you got invited. No nobodies were in sight. At the time, *Entertainment Tonight,* under a different, smarter producing team, made a deal with Spago and Swifty to cover the party exclusively every year. Basically the deal was, we'll cover your party if you don't let anybody else cover it. Done. And there I was, right smack in the middle of it all. In the early nineties I became the doorkeeper of Swifty's party, interviewing everybody who walked in. For some reason that to this day escapes me, Lazar had taken a liking to me and gave me carte blanche at this gala every year.

So there I was every Oscar night, black tie and all, chatting with the legends of Hollywood. No need to make a list because the list was as all-star as it got. I quickly discovered that all these stars would stop and ask me about their favorite football team or baseball team or "How the Lakers gonna be this year, Pat?" It was golden. We owned Oscar night. Eventually, Swifty would put me at a great table, making me part of the evening. Unheard of now. One night after everybody was in, Lazar came outside and said, "Pat, I've got a really nice table for you tonight." It was. From left to right it was me, Madonna, Giorgio Armani, Michael Jackson, Michael Douglas, Al Pacino, and Jodie Foster. At one point, I turned to Jodie (on my left) and said, "No offense to you, but I'm telling my friends I had dinner with Madonna." She was on my right.

I was working seven days a week, shuttling from New York to Los Angeles and back doing sports on the weekend and entertainment during the week. I was also doing special reports for the *CBS Evening News*. I was drinking and partying and high-fiving my way through life.

By the time the 1994 Olympics rolled around, it only made sense that I would cover it from the the sports perspective and certainly from the entertainment perspective. This Winter Olympics was in Lillehammer, Norway, and I was once again assigned to the *Late Night* show, which had now been expanded to an hour. *Entertainment Tonight*, meantime, was mostly on CBS-owned and CBS-operated stations and affiliates, so the confluence of my doing both was perfect. *ET* hired the international supermodel Vendela, of Norwegian descent, to be my cohost during the games. She had a side job, too, as the cover girl for Revlon and Victoria's Secret, among other high-profile modeling gigs. In 1994, nobody was hotter. What made it even better was that she was smart and funny and personable . . . and more important, she could almost drink me under the table, which was saying something at the time. If you thought this part was going to get more interesting, you guessed wrong again. We became great, great friends, and she was a perfect selection for the country we were in. Everywhere she went, she was mobbed.

But the games did not need Vendela or me or even CBS because right before them two of the world's top figure skaters were involved in one of the most bizarre sports stories ever. Enter Nancy Kerrigan and Tonya Harding.

About a month before the Olympics as the two were training for the US Figure Skating Championships, Kerrigan was brutally attacked out of nowhere and suffered a bad leg injury. She had been ambushed in a hallway and hit with a metal baton. She was unable to compete; Tonya went on to victory. In the next few days it was discovered that Harding's ex-husband, Jeff Gillooly, and a gang of other idiots were behind the assault. With all this going on leading up to the Olympics, there was a frenzy in the media. Oprah Winfrey described the story as one "that had it all: drama, scandal, heartbreak, controversy, and competition." As I arrived in Lillehammer, the Tonya and Nancy scandal was front page on every magazine, lead story on every newscast, and suddenly the entire world was circling figure skating as the must-see Olympic event.

What most people did not know was that Nancy and Tonya would not actually be competing face-to-face, like prizefighters, but in separate groups. Still, 120 million people tuned in to watch the "showdown on ice" in Lillehammer. The night of the competition, Tonya had a breakdown of massive proportions. First, during warm-ups, she broke a shoelace and then couldn't find a replacement. Then she went missing.

On this typically freezing night in Lillehammer, I decided to take in the skating in person before my *Late Night* show, and as I snuck in the back door of the venue, there was Tonya Harding—hysterical, crying, red faced, and confused. I said, "Hey, Tonya, what's up?" Through her sobbing all I could make out was "Pat! Do you have a cigarette?" So while everbody was looking for Tonya Harding, there we were sharing a cigarette at a lonely exit in the building. Finally she went out to skate and came in eighth, which means horrible. Nancy, meantime, skated the program of a lifetime and had pretty much secured the gold medal until a relative unknown named Oksana Baiul from Ukraine skated even better and won the gold, leaving the silver and more controversy to Nancy. Kerrigan was so upset she allowed the bitch side of her personality to be introduced to the world and smirked and sighed her way through the medal ceremony. Afterward, we sat down for an interview for my show, and I said to her privately, "Nancy, you can go out now and maybe make five to ten million dollars, or you can take that money and go out and buy a new personality and make five times that much." She wasn't amused. But in the end, she won the life game, while Tonya plunged into the depths of white trash and bad reality shows and Oksana struggled with alcohol and drug addictions. Not too long after the Olympics, I saw Oksana on a street outside of Detroit and mistook her for a homeless person until she said, "Pat? Is that you?" She finally found herself and calmed her demons and is leading a respectable life now, beautiful and personable as ever. Nancy went on to have a family and did develop a great personality and she's doing well, too. Tonya never quite got herself together, becoming a lifelong joke and the sad story of the 1994 Winter Olympics.

The heartwarming story of the games, one that brought a tear to the eyes of many—including mine—was that of Dan Jansen, the American speed skater who won gold in the 1,000 meters at his final Olympics. His sister Jane, who'd coached him, had died during the 1988 Olympics, in which he bravely continued to race but fell in his events. Four years later at the 1992 Olympics he was outskated and seemed destined never to win a medal. When he came home in Lillehammer in a world-record time, the crowd went into raptures. Jansen capped his emotional win with one of the Olympics' most famous victory laps, cradling his daughter, Jane, whom he'd named after his sister, in his arms as he went round the circuit. My producer Rob Silverstein, the best booker in the business, watched this drama being played out on live TV and quickly snagged Jansen and his wife, Robin, for the show. Before they came on, we played Peter Gabriel's "In Your Eyes" as we showed a film montage of the Olympian hugging his wife and daughter. It was a genuine feel-good moment; Dan and Robin were a pleasure to talk to. Rob covered the Vancouver Olympics in 2010 and reminded Dan of that night. Not only did he remember it, but the Peter Gabriel song had become one of his favorites. Dan and his daughter brought to life one of my favorite Olympic phrases. I used to say words to the effect of "One day some little boy will say, 'My daddy won an Olympic gold medal!'"

Another speed skater who caught our attention in 1994 was Norway's own Johann Olav Koss, who is generally held as the best speed skater in history. In Norway, he was Michael Jordan. I sat down with Olav to talk about this, his final, Olympics. He obviously wanted to win since he was competing in his homeland. Big Boss Koss, as he was called, and I hit it off fabulously, and we did a wonderful feature on him before he went on that year to win three gold medals in the longer races. When he came by to visit me the next day, the local tabloid newspaper grabbed a picture of us and for some reason put it on the front page with the headline "Friend of Koss." With that headline, my life completely changed in Lillehammer and all across Norway. Vendela was one thing, but being "friend of Koss" was like winning my own gold medal. Meantime, each and every day of these winter games, I continued my resolve to drink as much as possible when I got off work, no matter what time . . . but I always (and religiously) made it to the local gym, about a two-mile run from my hotel in the freezing cold. The day of the "Friend of Koss" article, I walked in and the place stopped. Norwegians of all shapes and sizes began yelling, "Friend of Koss, friend of Koss," and just like that I became an immediate part of their family. It was amusing . . . and I loved it. So did Koss, who went on to live a life of service as a UNICEF ambassador.

But the biggest coup of the 1994 Olympics, to me, was getting the president of the United States to make his only Olympic appearance on my *Late Night* show.

I first met William Jefferson Clinton in the spring of 1991 when the then governor of Arkansas was on a campaign swing through New York City. I was in the CBS studios hosting all of our basketball coverage when I got a call from my boss saying that Democratic presidential candidate Clinton was in the building for an interview and wanted to stop by and say hi. It wasn't a request, so about ten minutes later, in walks the next president of the United States, who on this day was an avid Arkansas Razorbacks fan. He was a big sports fan, and I was and still am a faithful Democrat, so we hit it off immediately. He demonstrated a remarkable knowledge of the game as we watched his team play, and then he went back to the campaign. So now, three years later, I figured I'd give it a shot, and to my surprise the White House said, "Yes, he'd love that." I later learned that Clinton was a regular viewer of the *Late Night* show, and as Hilary told me, he would roll a television into the Oval Office to catch up on the Olympics. We were told that he was a particular fan of the "Rock and Roll Highlights" segment, so we asked for a picture of the president doing something athletic. They sent us a photo of him skiing, and we added that to the segment, then came out with him live from the White House. It was pretty cool.

Later, in June of 1996, the president would return the favor and invite me to his home the night the president of Ireland, Mary Robinson, was honored at the White House. Linda's and my first impression was how many silver forks and spoons and knives, and plates, there were for each setting on the tables—six or seven by my count . . . but as I sat there under the stars on the South Lawn with the president, I was feeling grateful to be an American and an Irishman. We raised our glasses to my late father, Joe O'Brien, who might have wondered at one time in his life what the hell his son was doing hanging out with the president. And it wouldn't be my only time. Bill and Hillary to this day are loyal friends.

As the Olympic Games wound down, I was feeling rather presidential myself. The ratings were good, the shows had worked well, and my team had performed Herculean labors in producing an hour-long broadcast every night. I was pretty pleased with myself—until I saw *The Boston Globe* and read culture critic Ed Siegel's withering attack. Here is a taste:

"You amaze me, Pat O'Brien. I sit mesmerized by your late-night Olympics show as you go through this nightly posturing as the coolest dude to hit television since David Letterman. Once again,

CBS has brought you back as the host of this bizarre program that runs the length of the Olympics and then, mercifully, disappears into the CBS ozone. But for these two weeks we are transfixed. You are so very cool, Pat O'Brien, promising to take us to technologically enhanced venues at Lillehammer that aren't ready for prime time."

What a dick, right? I guess Ed didn't get the memo that the show was not about the Olympics but about me being at the Olympics, and the ratings were never higher. The only way I found out about the article was from a reporter at *The New York Times* who wondered what I had done to Ed Siegel to attract such a vicious article. My answer was "I don't know, succeed?" My response at the time to Eddie was simply "Fuck you." Not long after that I was offered and gladly accepted a job as a columnist for the New York *Daily News,* which to my detractors in the print media was about the biggest "fuck you" I could offer, proving that I could do their job and they couldn't do mine if they tried. And believe me, many tried. The column, called "Standing Pat," was a success and paid well. I made sure at the time that I was paid more than my print colleague at the *Globe.*

This was all the classic definition of grandiosity at a high level, but I was having the time of my life.

And, lo and behold, I was not about to disappear into the ozone at CBS. I had already had my summer-replacement, late-night show called *Overtime . . . with Pat O'Brien,* and they had me host one of the most successful syndicated shows at the time, *How'd They Do That?* And then another prime-time show, *Beyond Belief,* which reached the top ten. I was also doing syndicated sports commentaries on just under three hundred CBS radio affiliates called "Sports Time with Pat O'Brien," which ran in drive time pretty much everywhere. So whatever it was, it was working.

To reward myself, Linda and I bought a two-story beach house at our favorite getaway, Nantucket. This is where the rich and famous people summered, and now this kid from South Dakota was in the Nantucket phone book. We spent every August there, and every now and then I would borrow somebody's *Boston Globe* and read Ed Siegel's column, which was getting smaller and smaller. No longer at the *Globe,* he now writes for a website. Apparently not ready for prime time. Despite his hallucinations, I was living a dream life, and much, much more was to come, but eventually with a price tag that I didn't count on.

13

Mr. McCartney Is Expecting You

I get asked all the time about the people I have met and what they are like. I'm asked who is the best and who is the worst. But the recurring question from strangers usually is "Does anybody drop more names than you?" I'd have to say I'm up there with Donald Trump, Tom Brokaw, Larry King, everybody on *SportsCenter,* Stephen A. Smith, and Dan Patrick. I could actually top that list. When you are on television at marquee sporting and entertainment events and hosting most of them, you're going to meet some people. And it goes both ways; there's a reason people want to talk with us. We are the link to the fans. So, it's not me, folks; it's the profession. If I didn't get to know people, I wouldn't be around long. So there's the short explanation for the name-dropping. The long explanation gets into grandiosity, the desire to be loved by strangers, insecurity, and, as they used to say in high school, conceit. But let's go with the short answer for now. I'm a name-dropper, and because I am, the audience gets to go behind the curtains of the lives of people who interest them. Can we move on now?

I could fill another book with "encounters" with people who only know me from television and, thus, think they know me. Such as the time I was walking through a Four Seasons outside of Detroit and here comes Arnold Palmer. I said, "Hello, Mr. Palmer," and he followed up with, "Hi ya, Pat." He had his left arm around a good-looking woman's shoulder and was holding a drink. "Say hello to Victoria," he said. She said, "My name is Barbara."

I was walking down a long hallway at the NBC *Tonight Show* set, and walking toward me, backlit by the sun coming from a big studio door, was one of my musical heroes, Neil Young. As we walked past each other, I said, "Neil Young," and he said, "Pat O'Brien." That was my first and last encounter with Neil Young.

Speaking of *The Tonight Show,* my onetime agent, the late, great Ed Hookstratten used to manage Johnny Carson, and one day Hook invited me to lunch at the Grill in Beverly Hills, and Carson was at our table. It was pretty amazing, and we hit it off immediately, especially when we both ordered the same Midwestern meal (I'm from South Dakota and he was from Nebraska): meat loaf with mashed potatoes. As our entrées came, we simultaneously grabbed our spoons and each made a small hole in the mound of potatoes, then poured our gravy inside. As Hookstratten looked on in horror, Johnny said, "It's a gravy lake. It's what we do."

Henry Kissinger. I had met him at David Brinkley's home in Washington, D.C., and spoke to him many times on the phone when he called David, but at the 1994 World Cup soccer match between Brazil and Italy, my son, Sean, and I were guests of Coca-Cola CEO Douglas Ivester, and we sat between Kissinger and Pelé. Good seats. Kissinger, an avid soccer fan, told me that when he was President Nixon's national security adviser, he walked into the Oval Office one time and said, "Mr. President, we have a problem in Cuba." Nixon didn't understand. Kissinger rolled out some aerial photos of Cuba and said, "These are soccer fields." Nixon didn't understand. Dr. Kissinger said, "Cubans play baseball. Russians play soccer." That's how they confirmed that the Soviets had increased their presence in Cuba. Then, Kissinger stood up and his pants fell right to his ankles. He pulled them up as if nothing had happened and went on to the next conversation.

I sat on a plane next to General William Westmoreland, who commanded our noble attempt in Vietnam in the midsixties. The first thing he said was "Hello, Pat, a pleasure to meet you. Now, did you serve in the armed forces?" I said, "Yes," not giving him the details of lying my way out to escape his war. I was in the army three days: one to get in, one to figure out how to get out, and one to get out. He said, "Thank you for your service." I said, "My honor." Even without serving, today I help raise money for Disabled Veterans of America, and on Memorial Day I help put the little flags near each lonely white tombstone at the Los Angeles Cemetery.

On an airplane, one of New York governor Mario Cuomo's aides came up to me and said, "Excuse me, Mr. O'Brien, the governor would like to have a word with you." This was right after he'd made an impassioned keynote speech at the 1984 Democratic National Convention. An empty seat was next to him and I sat down. He began, "I enjoy your work and mine is challenging right now . . . so can we just talk baseball the entire trip?" We did.

So that's how it works, a grand perk of working on television. By the way, everybody has a TV set.

Perhaps the best and most fitting personal perks were getting to know the three surviving Beatles. The Beatles, more than just about anything except my son and some things that go on later, defined my life in so many ways. I've discussed my encounters with George Harrison in an earlier chapter, and we'll get to Ringo in a bit, but I gained the most Beatle access with Paul McCartney.

The first time I met Paul was in London in the fall of 1990.

I was working as a fill-in host for my old friend John Tesh at *Entertainment Tonight,* and for some reason Paul had decided to grant a rare interview. I was vetted and chosen, much to my giddy delight. As I've written here, my fascination with the Beatles went all the way back to their first album and the genesis of Beatlemania in the early 1960s. So I thought I could rest easy having interviewed George Harrison a couple of times during my news career, but this was Paul McCartney! Our meeting place was his office in a village on the edge of London. I walked into his three-story office compound, and except for a receptionist, it was empty. As I walked in, she said,

"Mr. McCartney is expecting you." I waited nervously; then all of a sudden I heard his familiar voice from upstairs: "Is that you, Pat?" I'm thinking to myself, *Holy shit,* and down the stairs he came. We settled into an outer-office area and all went great. We hit it off immediately . . . even though I nervously started the interview with "You know, that's some pretty good stuff the Beatles gave us." He smiled and jokingly retorted, "Pretty good stuff? Stuff? I'll have you know, Pat, that's a pretty good 374 songs we wrote." Point taken and the word *stuff* was removed from my interviewing vocabulary.

As we chatted comfortably, we got into the whole Beatles thing, and when I asked him when he knew he and John Lennon were going to click, he said, "I wrote this lyric that went 'Well, she was just seventeen, she was a beauty queen,' and John pointed to it and said, 'Change that last part to "you know what I mean."'" And from there, Paul and I went through pretty much the whole Beatles thing, and I honestly think he hadn't talked about it so openly in public and enjoyed the banter. So much so that he invited me to dinner with him and the love of his life, Linda, that night. And here comes gaffe number two. I ordered a steak. Just about the entire world knew that Linda was a vegetarian and Paul followed close behind. The minute I ordered the steak they both went after me. "Do you know how long that dead animal lives inside your stomach?" And so on. I learned quickly . . . and throughout the evening, I also observed how madly in love they were. They almost finished each other's sentences. It was beautiful.

Two years later, in April of 1993, Paul was playing in Anaheim Stadium with his wildly successful band Wings. By now, I was the certified "Beatle" correspondent, so I was assigned to sit down with him again. This time, no introductions were needed and he greeted me with a hug. The band had just finished its sound check and the stage emptied. Suddenly it was just Paul and I in an empty arena. So he said to me, "As I recall, you are quite the Beatles fan, so let me show you some things." He walked me over to his guitar closet, and there they all were: guitars and basses that I had memorized my whole life, including the iconic Höfner left-handed bass: the most famous bass guitar in history. He gingerly pulled it off the rack and said, "Here, go ahead, put it on if you fancy." Where was Twitter when I really needed it? So I put the bass on, and as I'm holding it, I'm thinking of all the times from *The Ed Sullivan Show* to the live performance I'd seen in Minneapolis when I had scoped out that very instrument around his neck. I turned it over and on the back was what appeared to be a hastily handwritten list of songs: "Twist and Shout," "She's a Woman," "I Feel Fine," "Dizzy Miss Lizzy," "Ticket to Ride," "Everybody's Tryin' to Be My Baby," "Can't Buy Me Love," "Baby's in Black," "Act Naturally," "A Hard Day's Night," "Help!," and "I'm Down."

As I'm wrapping my mind around this, Paul says, "That's our set list from Shea Stadium; it's still there. And that's John's handwriting." To me, it was like holding the Declaration of Independence.

Then we sat on the edge of the stage and, like two teenagers, started talking rock and roll in the sixties. He knew that I was in a garage band and asked me all kinds of questions about it. Yes, I told him, we grew our hair long. Yes, I admitted, we wore Beatle boots. He seemed generally fascinated by the culture that he helped create and wondered out loud if it was, indeed, the Beatles who led all these kids to go out and buy instruments and perform. Then he sighed and said, "I don't even know where my boots are. In fact, I don't have anything, really, from that time." I said, "Well, Paul, guess what? You have the billion dollars. You can buy it all back." And a side note: all four Beatles wore the same-size shoe and they had to write their names on the inside to determine which pair belonged to which Beatle.

Later that night, backstage about an hour before Wings took the stage, Paul asked if I wanted to come up and join him in playing the opening of "Lady Madonna," perhaps one of the most familiar Beatles piano riffs. "I mean you are a keyboard guy, right?" I thought he was kidding; then Linda chimed in with "Come on, Pat, do it. Fun!" Well, to me, it wouldn't have been fun if I'd messed it up in front of sixty-five thousand people, and it was pretty much out of the question. On the other hand, I had played with B.B. King, Herbie Hancock, John Lee Hooker (who gave me his guitar and scratched his name on it with a nail), Booker T. & the M.G.'s (yes, I played "Green Onions"), Ringo Starr & His All Starr Band, Wilson Pickett, and whoever else allowed me to join them, but this was a little different. Paul McCartney! It was a humble and realistic no. After a wonderful concert, as Paul and Linda were racing to their SUV, she yelled out, "Pat! You shoulda done it. You shoulda done it." Then they were gone. I'm glad I didn't do it. Some things just aren't meant to be and should be left alone. Period.

At this point I was certified bicoastal, dividing my time between our beautiful home in Studio City, California, and a suite at the Four Seasons in New York City, where the CBS studios were walking distance right down West Fifty-Seventh Street. Mostly all of my downtime was spent at the end of the bar at the Four Seasons, where I drank $15 glasses of red wine and held court. It was a lonely life, but I drank away the emptiness. I thought of myself as just a guy who drank a lot. Never did it affect my job, nor did I ever drink while working. But after work, it was a green light. Nobody ever brought it up. Nobody complained. I had the money and the expense account, and CBS provided me a first-class lifestyle that alcoholics dream about. I was loving New York City more and more. I had more friends on the road than I did back at home. The Four Seasons bar was always packed half a dozen deep at the bar with people who ran up ridiculous bills and wandered alone back up to their rooms. But it never got old. One night, late, I looked over, and all the Rolling Stones and various women were drinking, smoking, and having just a great time. I saluted and they waved me over, but I said, "No thanks, the view of you guys from here is really good entertainment."

If I did leave the confines of the Four Seasons, I was over at Il Vagabondo on Sixty-Second Street, where I would regularly have a quiet dinner with famed jockey Eddie Arcaro . . . who would take me back into his past with a gleam in his eye. In New York, there was always somebody else out and about to hang with.

One night I wandered into one of my favorite places, Ferrier, on Sixty-Fifth between Park and Madison Avenues . . . and ended up at a dinner for three with New York Rangers legend Mark Messier, who brought a Stanley Cup to his city . . . and O. J. Simpson, who was, at the time, the toast of America. O.J. was wearing this huge "pimp" hat, as we described it. His explanation was strange: "I think Nicole is following me." We ignored it and laughed it off. Meantime, during dinner these four beautiful African-American women stopped by to say hello. They were pleased to meet Mark and equally pleased to chat with me, but not O.J. When they left, Mark and I jokingly mentioned to O.J. that they had completely ignored him. His response was quick: "If they're not cleaning my house or cooking my meals, I want nothing to do with them."

It was June 1994. A few days later, I was in Atlanta speaking to a large group of marketers at the Coca-Cola headquarters in Atlanta. The next morning my phone rang early and it was a good friend who began with "Did you hear about O.J.?" I hadn't. My friend's next words were "He killed Nicole last night." Now I had known O.J. pretty well for about a decade. We had played golf together, dined in fine restaurants, and, as fellow sportscasters, run into each other a lot over the years. In all that time, and all his friends will tell you this, nothing pointed to future murderer. Nothing. This is not in defense of him; it is to make a point. And that is, if somebody called you and said one of your friends just killed his wife, you might say, "No, can't be" or "You're fucking kidding me!" or a hundred other ways of saying, "What? Say that again." With O.J. pretty much everybody said, "What a tragedy, but we knew it all along." But the fact is, nobody knew it all along. A lot of people who knew O.J. well couldn't put their finger on it, but we all pretty much gave him up the minute we heard the news.

Here was arguably one of the nicest, most genuine guys to be around, and now he was charged with murdering the woman he was literally crazy over. Maybe, it turned out, a little too crazy.

I went back to LA, and within hours the O.J. news was 24-7 on television and radio and in everybody's conversation.

A few days later, Linda and I were hosting a big summer barbecue for about forty people, originally to watch Game 5 of the NBA Finals between the Knicks and Houston. This was the night of the famed O.J. Bronco chase that had been under way all day long . . . and by the time the game came on O.J. was still in the backseat of the white Bronco and Al Cowlings was still driving. Reports were that O.J. had a gun to his head. He was calling everybody he knew, including the NBC studios, where he once worked. Friends were calling each other with "Has he called you yet?" I didn't answer my phone. Poor Bob Costas had to come on the air and say, "Obviously, there's another story going on tonight." It was surreal. Up to now, we had kept the whole O.J. thing away from seven-year-old Sean O'Brien, but as our backyard party went on and the chase went on and the game went on, Sean asked, "Daddy, can you tell me what's going on with your friend?"

They finally rounded up O.J., and so began one of the most gripping murder trials in history. Early on, I called my old friend Robert Shapiro, who was representing Simpson, to ask if I could pay a visit to the Heisman Trophy winner and Hall of Famer. Shapiro said, "Here's the routine: As you arrive at the court, you'll have to spend forty-five minutes getting questions from all the media. When you leave, that will take an hour. Then afterwards, the tabloids will find out everything you've ever done, and whether you've done it or not, you will be in those pages for a couple weeks." I said, "Say hi to the Juice for me."

Many years later, as O.J. was out of jail for a brief time, I was at one of those crazy South Beach parties in Miami, standing in the roped-off VIP section. All of a sudden, O.J. appears and starts screaming at me, "You phony fucking cocksucker. You're not a friend. You didn't have my back! You didn't give a fuck." As he started to lunge at me, somebody behind me picked me up and carried me backward out of the room and into an empty hallway. The person set me down, and I turned around and it was Shaquille O'Neal, who said, "You owe me one; I got your ass out of there."

At summer's end in 1994, it was great to get back to US Open tennis and see old friends and meet new ones. I was hosting the CBS Sports studio show again with tennis legend Vitas Gerulaitis.

Patrick McEnroe was enlisted to be my studio partner, and he filled Vitas's shoes with style and grace. The day before our big first weekend show, we were in a small dressing room and I said, "You know, Patrick, why don't we say a little prayer and have a moment of silence for Vitas." While we prayed, I said, "And, Vitas, if you're out there, give us a signal that you are with us." Neither one of us believed that would actually happen, but about two minutes later there was a knock on the door. I opened it and there stood a beautiful young woman who began, "Mr. O'Brien? Mr. McEnroe? I was one of Vitas's last students at a tennis camp in Florida, and he talked about you guys all the time and I just wanted to meet you and say hi."

Patrick and I looked at each other and didn't know whether to laugh or cry. But neither one of us will ever forget that moment, courtesy of Vitas.

As for tennis, I had my favorites, and it was no challenge to choose in the eighties and nineties when tennis players wore their games on their sleeves and played with passion and grace and grit and style. John McEnroe, in the years I have known him, has assumed every personality available to humankind. In his early playing days he was quite simply a prick. But he was a passionate prick and that's why I loved him. Nobody said no to me more than John McEnroe. But when he went into broadcasting and was able to look back and look ahead, he turned into a gentle soul and an engaging broadcaster.

I think he's the best analyst in any sport. Billie Jean King was always and will always be the grand lady of the game, to me. But I didn't have any problems with any of them, men or ladies.

Oh, maybe Pete Sampras, who was always a little too stoic for me, and I was always a little too loud and grandiose for him. He always approached me with a raised eyebrow. When he first appeared at the US Open in 1993 after just winning his first Wimbledon title, I was courtside, chatting with Martina Navratilova. As Pete walked by, she said, "Hey, it's Mr. Summer," meaning he had dominated the entire summer with his tennis. Not quite getting the compliment, he returned with "Actually, it's Mr. Sampras. Pete Sampras." Well, we all called him Mr. Sampras after a five-hour, grueling five setter with the gritty Spaniard Àlex Corretja. In this night match, Louis Armstrong Stadium was rocking under the lights. Mr. Sampras had arrived with a bad stomach flu and, throughout the match, doubled up in pain and actually threw up at the end, before he aced for the win. Crowd went wild and Pete was carried off the court. He was dating a longtime girlfriend, who cheered him on from his personal box seats. After the match, I sent her a bottle of wine to their hotel with a note: "While HE sleeps." I thought it was funny; nothing was meant but a kind offer and an admiring gesture. Mr. Sampras didn't think of it the same way.

Two days later while he was warming up for his next match, I went over to see how my joke went over with his girlfriend, and as we were laughing, I felt this rocket ship fly by the back of my neck, missing me by about an inch. I turned around and there was Pete with a fuck-you smile on his face. Awkward, but we both lived through it. Let's say this: he didn't have the comedic adventure of Andre Agassi. I covered Andre's first US Open match in 1988 and his last match in 2006 and cried with the rest of the stadium when he gallantly said good-bye to tennis and to his fans.

Andre had his demons, but went through life with a gleam in his eye and a wry sense of humor not normally associated with the upper class made up of tennis professionals. At a tournament at UCLA he won, among other things, a nice watch that he probably wouldn't wear. When they gave him the watch, the tournament chairman said over the loudspeaker, "Now, Andre, where would anybody ever see a watch like that?" Andre didn't miss a beat: "On eBay tonight."

One night Andre gathered some of his crew and me at our favorite New York Italian stop, Elio's, and we laughed and talked and drank about eight bottles of terrific wine. At the end of the meal, Andre graciously picked up the check, which had to be in the five figures.

Two days later, I was there with a couple buddies and said to the manager, "Give us a couple bottles of that wine Andre was drinking the other night." He did. We drank. Turned out, the wine was $900 a bottle. Mr. Rockefeller here learned his lesson. Don't be somebody you're not, and if you try to be, it's costly.

What I admired in Andre was his complete devotion to his Andre Agassi Foundation, and he honored me by having me host it a couple times in Las Vegas. Since 1994 he has raised nearly $200 million for local schools, and the money actually went to local schools and changed kids' lives. Admirable.

The summer of 1996 had been quite something. Leading up to the Atlanta Olympics, I hosted a syndicated show with gymnastics legend Mary Lou Retton, called *The Road to Olympic Gold*, then arrived in Atlanta to survey the games for CBS Sports and for *Entertainment Tonight*.

This Olympics was terribly and tragically interrupted by a pipe bomb that exploded in the Olympic Park, killing 2 people and injuring 111 others. At the time of the bombing, I was drinking heavily at the House of Blues, where my friend James Brown was performing. I idolized James Brown. While playing in my high school band, the Shouters, I had mastered his splits and the screaming and the dancing, and if not for the color of my skin, my character was the Godfather. The first time I met him was at the Grammys, and I walked into the pressroom where he was showing off his award, and in front of five hundred media people he yelled out, "Now we know it's a big event; there's Pat O'Brien." I loved it. That night at the Olympics he spotted me and said, "Hey, Pat, get on up here." I did. As I staggered onto the stage there was a huge explosion. I was standing right next to him as windows shattered and people screamed. He turned to me and mouthed, "What the fuck was that?" I said, "That, my friend, was a bomb." His handlers grabbed him and his cape and he was gone. I called home and alerted Linda and Sean that I was okay and then walked outside. Within roughly two minutes there must have been three hundred responding units. I have no idea where they came from, but they came from every direction and they came quickly and with force. As I walked down the street, a police officer approached me and said, "Mr. O'Brien, we're supposed to get any celebrities to cover." Which I thought was odd, because I was not a celebrity and there seemed to be a lot of other people who needed cover, too. I said to him that my cover was going to be in the nearest bar, and that's where I went. When I got back to my room at the Ritz Carlton, *Entertainment Tonight* called to see if I would go out and cover the story for them. I was in no condition to work and I didn't have a habit of working drunk, so I lied and told them I was in bed, sick. This was a first for me because usually no matter how much liquor or cocaine I did, I was able to jump right back in. Not this time. It was an early warning that I foolishly slept off.

Meantime, there were other warnings at the mother network, CBS. By the end of 1996, CBS Sports had lost the NBA and the NFL, and all that was left for me was the US Open and college basketball. The place was in deep transition, and good people, such as my great friend and producer Rob Silverstein, were leaving. Actually, I got Rob a job as producer at a new show in LA called *Access Hollywood* and he was doing great.

In 1997, Linda and I were enjoying our seventeenth summer in Nantucket, and as we were walking down India Street on a warm Sunday night, we strolled by DeMarco's restaurant. From the front window table, I heard a voice yell out, "Is that Pat O'Brien's voice I hear?" It was General Electric's CEO Jack Welch. He was sitting with then NBC CEO and president Robert Wright. They waved me in. No sooner had we said hello when Jack said, "How do I get that voice over to my network?" I said that CBS was losing steam for me and that, in fact, my contract was up. Bob Wright got right down to business: "Well, we have this show called *Access Hollywood* and it's not doing so great. Let's get you over there to anchor that, and if it doesn't go well, we'll move you to sports."

The next day at lunch at the Galley Beach in Nantucket, my lawyer, Ernie Del, put the contract together for me to be the host of the show, with a seven-figure salary and, in effect, to attempt to become the face of pop culture in America. I grabbed it. Linda and I celebrated that night at the local drugstore with milk shakes and bacon, lettuce, and tomato sandwiches.

We tried to keep it quiet, as I had US Open tennis to host in a couple weeks. However, halfway through the tournament, Reuters broke the story, and every CBS executive was grabbing his or her beeper and trying to find me. It was awkward, but there were no hard feelings. They put together a really wonderful good-bye tape, then sat nervously in the next room, wondering if I would say anything controversial going off the air. When signing off, I said, "I have one more thing to say before I say good-bye here." I gave it a long, long, irritating pause, then said those familiar words "*60 Minutes* is next except on the West Coast. Good night."

CBS threw together a party in one of the trailers and I had to leave early because, alas, my first day at *Access Hollywood* was the very next day. I told everybody how much I loved them and walked out the door with a giant glass of red wine to a waiting limo. As I sped off alone into the night, I could still here them applauding a block away.

I had the glass of wine and a cigarette and thought to myself, *Good God, what next? What next?*

I slept the entire plane ride and woke up in Hollywood.

14

Bad Boy for Life

Just before my first day at *Access Hollywood* in 1997, I was having a good-bye dinner with Patrick McEnroe at Elio's on the Upper East Side. He went downstairs to make a phone call at the communal pay phone, and when he came back up, he casually said, "Princess Diana has been in some kind of car accident." Little did we both know where this story was going and how it would affect my new job, not to mention everybody else in the media around the world.

So on my first day at *Access Hollywood*, the show's ratings went through the roof. *The Hollywood Reporter* and *Variety* heralded my arrival with "Pat to the Rescue" headlines, but it had nothing to do with me at all. As horrific and sad as Princess Diana's death was, I was getting an up-close-and-personal look at what drove ratings in the entertainment business: other people's problems. I discovered quickly that people loved hearing about things they thought would never, ever happen to them. Overnight, I became an expert on the British royal family, building on my foundation that we kicked them out in 1783 and that was the end of that. My only true interest was my love for Sir Winston Churchill's journey and writings. I also soon learned that reporting the world of celebrity was to be a walk in the park compared with sports. For beginners, the show was highly scripted and I didn't have to think on my feet all the time. Nor did I have a platoon of people screaming in my ear telling me scores and highlights while I was trying to appear calm and in control all the time.

I also was about to learn that corralling Jennifer Aniston and Tom Hanks on a red carpet was a hell of a lot easier than chasing after hyped-up, sweaty athletes after a big game.

Still, immediately my leaving sports for entertainment left a lot of people dumbfounded. Men would say, "What kind of dumb shit would do this?" And most women would say, "Where'd this guy come from?" But I had reached another goal in following Howard Cosell's footsteps in crossing every line possible. One Boston TV critic described my change in jobs with these kind words:

"For years you knew him as your personal valet on the Road to the Final Four and your late night d.j. on the Rock and Roll Winter Olympics wrap up show on CBS. If there was a big time sporting event on CBS in the 80's and 90's, Pat O'Brien's presence was as etched in stone as the mug shots of the former presidents on Mount Rushmore in his native South Dakota.

"With a delivery as smooth as an A-Rod home run swing, O'Brien showed that a small-town kid from the Midwest can hit the big time in network television sports. And now as he's successfully segued from the sports world to entertainment, as the host of Access Hollywood."

Two things remained constant in my switching from sports to entertainment: ego and attitude. I was now getting paid millions of dollars to have a bigger ego and much, much more attitude. And there was always significant downtime before and after the interviews, unlike in sports, where the athlete would be brought over all sweaty and panting and then leave two minutes later all sweaty and panting.

My first official *Access Hollywood* interview was done, ironically, in New York, where most stars had fled to remove themselves from Tinseltown. When Morgan Freeman came bolting into our interview room, he sat down and wondered why I'd left sports and all that. He was wearing an Alabama sweatshirt, so I asked him if he went to school there. Small talk. He replied, "How the fuck could

I go to Alabama?" While I was doing the math, I was thinking, *Well, you're the one wearing the shirt.* When Freeman was college age, Alabama was an all-white school. When the cameras rolled, I opened with "So, you went to Alabama?" Laughs all around. The entertainment world had suddenly met its match: the art of being a smart-ass now went both ways.

The other difference was that, while athletes were usually pretty one-dimensional (what you see is what you got), red-carpet celebrities had many, many personalities. There were the personalities that you saw on camera and were mostly protected or sculptured by publicists, and then the ones you saw on the screen and stage. It was a heavenly dynamic for a wiseass such as me, who was now traveling with my own driver, an unlimited expense account, and endless invitations to parties and galas. All I really needed was a wardrobe to match, which they also gladly provided.

Ironically, when I joined the show, I had just published my first sports book, *Talkin' Sports: A B.S.-er's Guide.* I quickly learned that bullshit was pretty much the order of the day in covering entertainment. It didn't take much to get everybody's attention. In Hollywood, perception is reality.

Now, to get people's attention you need what is called "the moment"—some sort of moment that establishes that your show and your people were better than their show and their people. The only way that happens is recognition by the celebrity. How am I supposed to be the big shot on the red carpet if the celebrities don't crawl over to me? Right? So the dirty little secret on the entertainment shows is that they all have the exact same stories, but what separates them is how they are packaged and presented. Enter Pat O'Brien. Presentation was my forte. I had built a healthy career on inside information or, better yet, the impression that I had access and inside information, leaving viewers believing that I had just come back from lunch with Jack Nicholson or Michael Jackson. Sometimes, I had, but more often than not, I was nowhere near them. It was that lesson I learned that night I sat with President

Ford as he drank a scotch in his suite so that I could breathlessly tell my Chicago audience that I had just left the most powerful person in the world, and he told me . . .

So, the red carpet preceding a premiere, the Oscars, Grammys, Golden Globes, and so on represented this perfectly. You earn your red-carpet cred by getting as much as possible out of the little time you're granted with each star. I had an advantage going in from my sports career. Grabbing a celeb walking down a carpet was far easier than finding the quarterback in the confusion after a game, or getting an athlete to talk before he or she showered and left. The celebrities were already showered and dressed and ready to go: this was like taking candy from a baby. Almost by default, I became the recognized "king" of the red carpet. Here's my producer, Rob Silverstein: "We would put Pat on the red carpet and celebrities would walk right by *Entertainment Tonight* and go up to him. Pat O'Brien was always the difference on the red carpet. He was the face of popular culture."

Word spread quickly. I was sitting on a plane one morning and my phone rang and on the other end was then Puff Daddy. (Now P. Diddy, Diddy, Sean John, etc.)

He asked if I could do him a big favor by appearing in his new video "Bad Boy for Life." I said, "As what?" He said, "The white guy." As the video plot unfolded, Diddy moved into an upscale neighborhood, and I was his snoopy neighbor on one side, and Ben Stiller was the complaining neighbor on the other. It also featured Shaq and Mike Tyson. It became popular and was, again, good for my street cred. I had done a lot of stories on Diddy, returning to his old neighborhoods, riding around in his SUV in NYC, visiting his old high school, and, of course, his legendary parties. At one gala, behind the doors at Cipriani in New York, there must have been two thousand people waiting for something to happen when Diddy turned to me and said, "This party is boring," and with that, he disappeared. Next thing I know, he's at the DJ station announcing, "I have just bought you all four hundred bottles of Cristal [at $400 a bottle], and let's get this fucking party going!" The party got going. To this day, Diddy is a good friend and one of the most driven people I know. Having a relationship with Diddy meant that other rap stars had to have a relationship with me, and so Jay-Z chose me for the first look behind his soon-to-be multi-multimillionaire life by inviting me to his first video set with private planes, Bentleys, and women; 50 Cent gave me his first TV interview; Eminem gave me his only in-depth interview over on Eight Mile in Detroit; and they all followed, allowing me to jokingly refer to myself as the King of Hip-Hop. That's how it works.

In old Hollywood this one poor sucker would do the entire red carpet by himself. He'd stand outside Grauman's Chinese Theatre and would go from Lucille Ball to Cary Grant to John Wayne to Clark Gable to Marilyn Monroe and somehow get it all done. Today, up to five hundred poor suckers can be on the red carpet hoping to get just a hello. Only the chosen few do. I was one of those chosen.

But today, navigating the red carpet is like being an air traffic controller. Through the years, an order of takeoff has developed for each celebrity. The first position on any red carpet is always *Entertainment Tonight,* the so-called show of record for entertainment gossip. Then would come my show, *Access Hollywood.* Then *Inside Edition,* the *Today* show, CNN, all the way down to a heavyset clown at KTLA Channel 5 in Los Angeles. Nobody ever moved up. *ET* was simply too powerful and could lay out threats to ignore your movie or TV show, and they worked. Mary Hart had her legs insured, but her producers would cut off your legs if you didn't come chat with Mary. In fact, there was something about Mary, but it wasn't her legs. If you didn't talk to Mary, you wouldn't be getting any free publicity. But when I arrived at *Access Hollywood,* the stars would get out of their limos, see me, and walk right past *ET* to say hello. It used to drive the insecure workers at *ET* out of their minds. That group worked out of fear from above, which preached over and over, "Get them first or else." And I always thought to myself, *Does the audience really know that Brad Pitt talked to them first or me first?*

(At a Super Bowl once, *ET*'s reporter was saying, "And when he came off the stage, he came right to me." Over his shoulder was Mick Jagger coming right to me.) This created bitter, bitter wars between the two shows to the point where *Entertainment Tonight* began saying, no matter who spoke to whom first, "And the star came right to us first to talk about . . ." (We'll go deep into the secrets of the shows later in this book, and you'll find out why George Clooney left Hollywood and why all your favorite stars are depressed and suicidal. And that's how we get you to keep watching and this is how I get you to keep reading. All coming up!)

As I said, one of the biggest battles to win on the red carpet is perception.

As in the Mayor Daley days, I made sure that the stars would see me first. If they didn't, I would just go up and walk inside or down the carpet with them, so it looked as if we might have arrived together. A kiss on the cheek to a stranger is always a bonus, as is a hug. As for the hug, what are they going to do, walk away? That would make them look unfriendly. *Entertainment Tonight* host Nancy O'Dell was a real pro at this. She didn't hug them; she nearly handcuffed them to her. When we worked together, she accused the producers of liking me more than her because they showed more tape of me hugging celebrities than her. Next, you give some kind of friendly greeting that could make you appear to be everybody's family here. I liked "Nice to see you again." And they would always respond with "Yes, you, too!" See? They know me! They know me! Then I would move to second base with "You know we were talking the other night about . . ." *Oh! He goes out socially with those people.* Sometimes I had actually been out with some of them doing very un-red-carpet activities, so we would bypass those greetings. And the few I had never met would think to themselves, *Have I been out with Pat somewhere?*

Once you had them, then what? Your entire job and existence depended on what you did next. So you had to create that moment during the allotted few seconds with the star. One of my favorites to play this red-carpet game with was Julia Roberts. I'd walk up to her and, with cameras rolling, start whispering in her ear. In hushed tones, I'd said, "Okay, I'm not even going to say anything, but right now when people see this, they will wonder what the fuck we are talking about." She was crying with laughter, which made it better. She got it. Sure enough, my brief encounter was billed as "What did Pat say to Julia to make her laugh so hard?" Of course, we never answered that question because there was no answer. Julia was always game to play. While on an interview junket for *Ocean's Eleven* ... after she had answered the same "What's George Clooney really like?" question a hundred times from other outlets, I fired this hard-ball: "Can I ask you a different question? Is there any chance of making out with you right now?" She laughed so hard—good-naturedly, I might add—that we had to stop the interview. No harm done and people loved to see Julia with her hair down. Fifteen years later, they are still running that laugh just for the hell of it because it's so genuine.

The celebrities, with their posses of publicists and agents and makeup crews, have tricks of their own. (I, too, had a posse of assistants and publicists and makeup crews.) The big one is timing the arrival to a premiere red carpet at just the right time. It's quite simple arithmetic: The bigger the star, the later the arrival. Period. The rare ones who don't want to talk arrive so late they are rushed in under the guise of "The movie is starting! Gotta go!" Still, in all my years I was never turned down, even if it was just a respectful acknowledgment. So while other shows would get nothing, I, at least, got a "Hello, Pat" or a quick handshake. Even with just that, we could turn it into the entire show: "Only we got Brad Pitt to stop by," etc. As childish as it seems, it made us look good and translated into ratings. My favorite one in this category was my "exclusive interview" with the late and lovable James Gandolfini. The bottom line is that Gandolfini didn't do interviews. Period. The star of *The Sopranos* either wasn't comfortable with them or just hated all of us, but this quirk made his value much, much higher. Everybody tried to get him to stop. Nobody got him.

So well into this routine, here comes James rumbling down a red carpet and saying no to everybody with a microphone. He was nice, but it was no. I was always respectful to him and, for a long time, didn't bother, but this time I figured what the hell. As he hurried by, I yelled out, "Good evening, Mr. Gandolfini," and all of a sudden he stopped, turned, and walked right toward me. This was like getting the queen of England on her way out of Buckingham Palace to stop and chat. So, Gandolfini strolled over, smiled, and shook my hand. Then, in my ear, he said, "Ba da boom, ba da bing," laughed, winked, and walked away. That was on a Monday night. For the next three days, we promoted "Pat O'Brien's Exclusive Interview with James Gandolfi" and showed only him walking up to me with his hand outstretched. The day we aired it, we casually said, "And James Gandolfini stopped by for a hello," and showed my little encounter. A week's worth of ratings gold. I was sad the day he died in June of 2013, and Hollywood recognized that without Tony Soprano there never would have been a Don Draper.

Jennifer Aniston used to never talk either because all anybody ever asked her about was her relationship with Brad Pitt. I knew it got old, and so one day I wore an I ♥ BRAD PITT T-shirt under my tux, and when she walked by, I exposed it. She came rushing up and took a now-famous picture with me.

The gimmick worked and later, as you'll learn here, backfired.

On the red carpet there's always that uncomfortable judgment call on just whom to interview and whom to politely ignore. It's a keen science because, in this town, a nobody could well be a somebody within a week, so a judgment call here and there could mean tomorrow's exclusive. For example, when the Jenner family became the Kardashians with their new show, I pitched it to our executive producer, Linda Bell Blue, who shook her head, as if to say, "That will never last."

Then there are always those former stars who are invited, but are not newsmakers anymore. Mickey Rooney is a prime example. Once, Mickey was the biggest star in the world, but in this Justin Bieber and Miley Cyrus world, there was no room for the old man. As a courtesy, I always interviewed him, knowing it would never make the air, but the guy practically invented Hollywood and deserved to be noticed once again. Besides, Mickey was a friend. But there are always lessons learned on the red carpet. The former star of *Three's Company*, John Ritter, showed up once with nothing to promote, other than that he was John Ritter. On that alone, it would have been worth it, but my producers said pass and we did. A week later, he was dead, leaving the same producers scrambling for the last interview that could have been ours. From that moment on, nobody was ever again ignored on my watch on the red carpet. Ghoulish? you say. But that's Hollywood. In a related story, I must have voiced Bob Hope's obituary ten times so that if he "suddenly died" we'd be ready for an accurate account of his life. I was sad the day he did die, but we were prepared.

In January 2000 I got a phone call in my car that changed my professional life dramatically. It was from Dick Ebersol's office and the message was "Mr. Ebersol is hoping you can meet him tomorrow at the Century Plaza Hotel." Now, in the world of TV sports, Dick Ebersol is a legend. He got his stripes during the iconic era of Roone Arledge at ABC Sports, then dreamed up *Saturday Night Live* before returning to NBC to run its sports operation in 1989. I called my wife, Linda: "Honey, you will not believe who wants to talk to me!"

The next day, nervous as a kid going into his first job interview, I met with Dick as well as a couple of other NBC Sports executives. After a couple of minutes small talk, Dick said, "We'd like you to be one of our Olympic hosts in Sydney this summer." For a sports commentator this is the equivalent to winning a gold medal and I couldn't say yes fast enough.

With the rapidly changing television landscape NBC had decided to branch out and broadcast different Olympic sports on their cable outlets as well as the network. Prime time, hosted as always by Bob Costas, would remain, but Dick and his crew wisely decided that a market existed for all those sports such as women's softball, boxing, and weight lifting that never got covered for lack of time. I was to host CNBC cable, anchoring all the sports that prime time missed as well as acting as a traffic cop between the venues. It meant that I would be live on air every day for about seven hours. My schedule was daunting, grueling, and I have never been so happy.

Right away it was different. Under Ebersol, the NBC people operated like a well-oiled machine. At CBS we covered the Olympics; at NBC they lived it. The preparation began months before the starter's pistol was even loaded. Dick hosted seminars where he went through previous Olympics, pointing out the good, the bad, and the ugly in their coverage. Throughout there was one underlying imperative: to tell the story and emotionally frame the drama behind the lives of these elite athletes.

The other side of Dick's strategy was to mold all those covering the games into an instant family. A week or so before the opening ceremony he chartered a 747 and took all the on-air talent and producers on the seventeen-hour flight to Australia. On the plane it was a party from takeoff to touchdown, with videos complete with gag reels and outtakes. I was an outsider getting on the plane. By the time we reached Sydney I was part of the family.

One of the first things I did was to get to know some of the behind-the-scenes people, particularly my producer, Jim Bell, an NBC veteran who carried himself with confidence and a quiet swagger. Over pizza he explained that at NBC they did it Ebersol's way, and Ebersol was always right. Whatever I had done at CBS for the Winter Olympics, this was going to be the real deal so I had better be on my game.

Most of the "talent" stayed at the luxurious InterContinental— I had a suite with an amazing view of the Sydney Harbour Bridge and the famed Opera House. Awestruck, I called Linda and said, "You guys have got to get over here." We took Sean, then thirteen, out of school, and my family joined me for the duration of the games.

While they were on their way, Jim Bell showed me around the newly built international broadcasting center, dominated by the USA broadcast host, NBC. As daytime CNBC anchor, I took viewers from one event to another, the first time they had been able to watch the Olympics during the daytime. From my small studio, which looked lavish on television, we were breaking new ground, bringing the Olympics to a whole new audience.

Time-zone differences made daytime coverage, shall we say, interesting. At one in the morning I would go for a run around the harbor front while late-night revelers were still partying. Then I would head for the studio, putting in an eleven-hour shift before heading back to the hotel to spend some time with Linda and Sean. As tough as my schedule was, I have never been happier. The weather was perfect, and the games, dominated by Australian swimmer Ian "the Thorpedo" Thorpe, the winner of five gold and two silver medals, the American basketball team, and triple gold-medal winner Marion Jones, were rightly called the "best ever" by IOC president Juan Antonio Samaranch. As a family we saw the sights, Sean kept up with his studies, and I kept off the red wine.

It was wonderful but utterly exhausting. When it was over, I never wanted to hear two things again: "G'day" and "Good morning, Mr. O'Brien, this is your one a.m. wake-up call."

15

We Gotta Go

The word celebrity is even a celebrity on the Web, with its own Wikipedia page, which defines it this way: "A celebrity is a person who has a prominent profile and commands a great degree of public fascination and influence in day-to-day media." I never thought of myself as a celebrity, but when I look back, I certainly fit the definition, but I have always cringed at the description. Ultimately, whatever I was, I had instant credibility with Hollywood simply by my background and job descriptions. Let's just say that my having done news at a high level, every sport on the planet, and now a daily TV show gave me a thimble of influence here and there. As they tend to do when the ego is in charge, things were moving quickly and I couldn't say no. I had a book, a column in the New York *Daily News*, a daily radio show, speaking engagements that paid in the five figures, a presence on television seven days a week, and a Rolodex filled with A-list phone numbers.

As a celebrity you also inherit a bunch of other celebrities to hang out with every now and then. And you get all expenses paid to show up at things. It's nice work if you can get there. Make that, it's hard work, and I got there. As my friend Jay Mohr famously said on his radio show, "Kiss my ass. I'm famous. It didn't just happen." (Historical note: Jay taught my son, Sean, how to give somebody the finger.)

When I was working at *Access Hollywood*, I was still swimming in the heady wine of the sports world. For example, I was one of the lucky guests at a charity event in Miami and ended up at the same table with Sugar Ray Leonard, Wayne Gretzky, and Pat Riley, among others. Oh, there was this kid at our table named Tiger Woods, who Gretzky and I determined wasn't even old enough to drink. He was a mere twenty years old and on the cusp of massive celebrity, and so the "veterans" at the table were giving him (probably unwelcome) advice. As we were all telling him how it worked, suddenly we realized he had disappeared, and when we looked up, he was dancing with two gorgeous blondes. Gretzky and I looked at each other and said together, "Uh-oh!" By the time we waded through the crowd Tiger was gone. We knew the paparazzi were looking for him, too, so like two helicopter dads, we set out to find him. No luck. The next week, Tiger Woods got his first taste of tabloid media after two women apparently sold their story to the *National Enquirer*. Like most of those stories, it came and went. No harm to his career.

Despite this early media bump, the public Tiger Woods was a guy who won a lot of golf tournaments and in his spare time did a massive amount of charity work through the Tiger Woods Foundation. At his annual banquet, Tiger wasn't at a loss for good guests. I was the master of ceremonies for a couple of the early dinners, and as I gazed out into the audience, there was my entire sports career. Every big name in sports would show up to support Tiger's foundation.

One year, Tiger and Charles Barkley and Michael Jordan and I combined for a foursome for the cameras, and it was clearly God's work that they didn't follow us beyond the first hole. Now, read this sentence twice: my golf game is worse than Barkley's. (Read again.) Tiger had so much respect for the game, he turned to me about the third hole and said, "I will honestly never play golf with you again." I laughed. He said, "I'm serious," and didn't. Later, Michael Jordan, who was very serious about his golf game, instructed me to never ride with him in a cart because "I don't want to be seen going into the out-of-bounds area so much searching for balls." Barkley had no complaints.

When the sun set on the golf games and the dinner, Charles and

Michael and I would hit the tables. Charles and Michael were quickly escorted into the private gambling rooms and I tagged along.

Michael, as history tells us, loved his gambling. I never saw him lose, because he had so much money he would just keep playing until the cards were nice to him. One late night or early morning, we were at a table in a private room at the Bellagio, with nobody but bodyguards. Michael was playing blackjack while talking on his phone to his then wife, Juanita. He took a card while he was showing 15 and lost an even $100,000. Behind him I whispered, "Jesus!" He muffled his phone and turned to me and said, "You of all people should know that it's not about the money, it's about the thrill." The stories surrounding Michael's gambling are legendary, but it was none of my business, so we never discussed it. We had a deal: I never brought up his gambling and he never brought up my growing obsession to drink until my mind clicked off. A friendly agreement. I never pried into celebrities' personal lives, and for this they trusted me. I could have, but what would have been the point—a cheap "one day" story? And then what? Meantime, during those late Vegas nights, Tiger was nowhere to be seen after about eleven. We all thought he was in his room, practicing. I'm serious.

I used to always enjoy the "What's it like to be Michael Jordan?" game . . . where I would listen to him tell stories about his life that pulled open the curtain just enough to get a glimpse.

One time he was laughing about being out of the house late with some buddies, smoking cigars and drinking and playing cards, and he looked at his watch and it was 3:00 a.m. The way he told it, he goes home and flips off his own alarm on his mansion so as not to wake anybody up. Then he takes off his shoes and begins to tiptoe up the winding staircase. Halfway up, he says to himself, "I am Michael fucking Jordan and I'm sneaking into my own home." Hilarious. What makes it even better is that in all the years I've known Michael, he has never talked about himself the way the rest of us big mouths do. He's humble to the core. One time he was driving by himself in his Ferrari through the South and he pulled over to the side of the road in a driving rainstorm. When he tried to start his car up again, it wouldn't start. It was a monsoon. He got out of the car and started to wave and hitchhike, and nobody was stopping. He said to himself, "Of all the times I actually want to be recognized!" Finally somebody picked him up and he ended up in this little town in a little garage. The owner said he could go over to the house and wait. Within minutes, the entire town was there to see the great Michael Jordan. He took a deep breath and stayed up and mingled. The king and his court. He was always loyal to me, a good friend, and that's what mattered to me—not that he was Michael Jordan. He knows that.

What mattered to me in my career was moving and expanding the brand. As much as I tell young people today not to be in a hurry, I didn't heed my own advice. I was in a hurry with the only destination being more. Bad idea.

I got invited to the best of the best parties and functions and to the worst of the worst, which I attended as well. At one in Vegas while hosting a Tiger Woods Foundation dinner, I ended up in some giant suite for a party that had no name or purpose, other than it was Vegas. I was holding court, as usual, and suddenly I went head-first into the glass coffee table. Bang! When I woke up, I was bleeding from a massive cut in my face. My longtime driver, Chris, dragged me out and suggested that I was drugged, since I was only on my second drink. I shrugged it off as a possible occupational hazard and promptly went on with my hosting duties, all patched up and telling people I ran into a speaker at full speed backstage at the event. One of the perks of celebrity is that people look past events like that.

Besides my sports and entertainment connections, I was always pretty well wired into the political scene and certainly into what became the celebrity side of politics. This always came down to the Kennedys. I began to meet members of the family during my many, many summers vacationing in Nantucket. On this Massachusetts island, they were everywhere, and if you didn't see them, you felt their presence. If you think they were powerful on the national political scene, multiply that exponentially for their power and influence on Nantucket and the Cape. My two best friends, Frank Smith and Peter Emerson, were close to the family and I was along for the ride. And, oh, what a ride it was.

Years later, Patrick Kennedy said to me, "You used to sail with my dad, didn't you? What was that like?"

I gave him the honest answer. Every year Nantucket hosted the famed Opera House Cup Regatta, which included the finest all-wooden, single-hulled boats in the country. It was named after the Opera House, a bar my friends and I drank dry every summer during the seventies and eighties. The late senator Ted Kennedy, an accomplished sailor, invited me on a couple occasions to race with him. The first time I said, "Senator, what would you like me to do?" With his trained sailor's eye on the ocean ahead and in that Kennedy Boston cadence, he replied, "Uh, Pat, bring me two frozen daiquiris and then just keep bringing them." Eventually, our little Nantucket crowd included pretty much everybody with a Kennedy name or tie.

Not only were they obsessed with making America better; they did their best to make every social occasion a thrill. In 1995 John F. Kennedy Jr. had started *George* magazine and asked me to contribute to its book, *250 Ways to Make America Better*. I responded with a whimsical entry that was placed in the book along with the thoughts of actual prominent Americans: William F. Buckley Jr., Stephen Ambrose, Rob Reiner, Isaac Stern, P. Diddy, as well as other highly regarded executives, educators, politicians, and entertainers. Here's what I came up with to make America a better place: more jukeboxes.

"Jukeboxes. Bring them back with 45-rpm records (big holes) and five selections for a quarter. Put them inside every lonely saloon along every blue highway . . . and have them available to everyone who's in love, and especially those who are not. Jukeboxes are cheaper than therapy. Selection J-3: 'LOUIE LOUIE.' Because hey, 'We gotta go.'"

To me, "We gotta go" was the sound track for my life, as I was always in a hurry, anxious to get to the next job, next city, next bar, next milestone. "Go" was the Pat O'Brien default mode.

There are more great stories, I believe, about the Kennedys than any other family, any rock group, any tribe, and any monarchy. They are story magnets, and I have inherited a few. The tragic stories run through the veins of America. In the early 1970s, Frank and Peter and I were getting high in our Georgetown apartment, and Robert Kennedy's son Joseph was taking a tour of the modest place, which was plastered with posters of Bobby Kennedy and John Kennedy. As Joseph stood in front of the posters smoking a joint, I said to myself, "Holy shit! That's his uncle Jack!" And "Holy shit! That was his dad!"

After I just got to casually know John Jr., all of a sudden I was covering his death in a small-plane crash near "Kennedy Country" in Cape Cod. We were covering it for the "celebrity" side of the story for *Access Hollywood,* and while moving around I ran into Willie Nelson and shared a joint with him in his tour bus. It was surreal. (Actually, if you just walked into his tour bus, you were sharing a joint with him.) I would soon find out what the "celebrity" side of a famous dead person entailed.

On the coattails of another friend, I got to know Maria Shriver quite well, and through the years she has been loyal and loving. We had a lot of friends in common from the Nantucket days, and Maria grew up a lot faster than the rest of us. While all of us wanted to be her boyfriend, she was more like a big sister or young mother to us. She seemed to always know the right path.

My Hollywood world and my political world united when Arnold Schwarzenegger came on the scene and eventually married Maria. I interviewed Arnold many, many times for *Access Hollywood,* and he and I struck up a friendship almost immediately. The reason we liked each other so much was, as Maria put it a thousand times, we were the "two vainest men" she had ever met. She was smart.

Arnold and I played it out while vacationing every year in Maui, taking muscle pictures on the beach and sitting around talking about "what studs" we were. In our minds we may have looked good on the golf course, but by our own admissions we were the worst golfers we'd ever met. Before Maria and Arnold got married in 1986, Linda and I got invited to their exclusive engagement party, and it was one for the ages. All the Kennedys were in one room, with the Schwarzenegger clan in another, including all his weight-lifting buddies from Austria. It was late and now toast time. With Senator Edward Kennedy sitting next to him, Arnold told the assembled throng that he had been warned that it was going to be a tough job joining the Kennedy clan. He paused and, in his thick Austrian accent, then admitted he'd been given one piece of advice: "Never get into a car with Teddy Kennedy." Extremely bad taste never bothered Arnold—in this case a reference to Senator Kennedy's car crash at Chappaquiddick, which resulted in the death of Mary Jo Kopechne and ended the possibility of another Kennedy White House. Still, it got an enormous laugh, even from Ted. That night always reminds me of the television show *ALF*. ALF was an alien dog who ended up on Earth in a suburban home. In one episode, ALF was feeling unwanted because he was an alien. The mom said to him, "But, ALF, you're family here." And ALF replied, "Yah, and Arnold Schwarzenegger is a Kennedy!"

But Arnold did fit in, if even as a novelty for all the Kennedy adults and kids. They loved him. So did the voters, who elected him to two terms as the thirty-eighth governor of California. I got the first interview with him after he announced his candidacy on *The Tonight Show with Jay Leno*. This really pissed off Jay, who technically had him first, but on a tape delay. I got Arnold walking out of the taping and we beat *Tonight*. We beat everybody. It was classic. Just after he was elected, our families were all in Maui again. One afternoon I was getting some serious rays near the pool when Maria came running up to me laughing and out of breath. "You won't believe what just happened to Arnold!" Well, Arnold was way out in the ocean snorkeling when he heard a man screaming for help. Arnold grabbed the guy and navigated him back to shore. Not one to cross friendship lines, I asked Maria if I could call it in to *Access Hollywood,* since Arnold was in every story at this point, anyway. Also, I was the only media outlet near the private and secretive Four Seasons. I said to Arnold, "Okay, we control this story. How deep do you want the water to be? How many sharks were attacking you at the time? Did you use one hand or two?" It was the first action story for him as the Governator.

One year Eunice Shriver, Maria's mother and sister of JFK, was pestering me to emcee a charity fund-raiser in Portland, Oregon. Unfortunately the July event coincided with my annual family holiday in Nantucket. I hesitated, I demurred, and finally I called Arnie for advice. "Did she call you herself?" he asked. "Yes," I replied. Arnold: "How many times did she call you?" The answer was three. Arnold again: "And did she tell you that her brother John F. Kennedy hosted the first event?" "Yes, she did." Long silence, then: "Well, Pat, you are now vacationing in Portland. Have fun."

I dutifully went to Portland and hosted the event; then afterward Eunice cornered me and said, "Pat, you have to run for governor of South Dakota." The subject had come up before about my returning to my home state and running. "All the Kennedys will be there to support you." I said I'd consider. I figured at the time that I was pretty skeleton free.

Sharing the company of the Kennedys and Hollywood stars, I suppose Maria was right: I was getting rather vain. Then again I had every right to be—at least professionally. I prided myself as the guy the celebrities came to share their stories with: the ultimate insider, so to speak. Because of this, *Access Hollywood* was going like gangbusters, beating *Entertainment Tonight* in numerous key markets. Alec Baldwin's theory that every star would eventually come to me was coming true, no more so than when I got a call from Michael J. Fox in January 2000. He wanted to give me an exclusive interview about his decision to retire from *Spin City,* the Emmy Award–winning show that had continued to make him one of the most beloved actors in America. I had known Michael for years and had seen his indomitable will in his battle with Parkinson's disease, which he'd first noticed when his finger started trembling when he was filming *Doc Hollywood* in 1991.

I had firsthand experience with this terrible, debilitating illness, having lost my mother to Parkinson's a year earlier. Ironically and sadly, my mom was watching me joking around with the women of *The View* when she had a stroke. I got the call after the show and rushed back to Sioux Falls. I got to spend precious time with her before she passed away. Rarely does a son get to hold his parents and love them on their deathbeds, and for me this had a special meaning because my little brother, David, got to be there and was, in fact, holding her hand when she died. My last words to my mom had been "I love you, Mom, and I also just put a sticker on your back that says, 'Kick me.'" She laughed and said, "I love you, too, Pat, and there's not an apostrophe in O'Brien." I said, "You're telling me this now?" And that was it for me and my mom. Her funeral was held at the First Lutheran Church, presided over by a Catholic monsignor, James Michael Doyle. I was sitting in the front row about to deliver her eulogy, and Sean, who was not yet a teenager, said to me, "Dad, are you nervous? You seem like you are and I've never seen you nervous." When I got up to speak, I finally looked out over the packed church, and there were all her old band members, whom I had met over the years as they came to pick her up at the house before a gig. It was touching. I had arranged for the song "I'll Be Seeing You" to be played at the end of the ceremony with the haunting words:

> *But when the morning chimes ring sweet again . . .*
> *I'll be seeing you in all the old familiar places . . .*
> *And when the night is new*
> *I'll be looking at the moon*
> *But I'll be seeing you.*

These thoughts were swirling through my mind as I boarded the plane to New York to interview Michael about his decision to quit the top-ranking show and devote his energy to raising awareness about Parkinson's disease. In this interview he explained why he was leaving and assured his fans that he was not going to the hospital (or anywhere else) anytime soon.

"During Christmas break [in his hometown of Burnaby, BC] I was away . . . and it just felt terrific," he told me. "And I just started thinking, 'The more I do [*Spin City*] the more I have to postpone getting involved with Parkinson's advocacy, and I can't do both.'" Fox also stressed that his abrupt departure had nothing to do with worsening health. "I didn't suddenly take a turn. It's not a case where I've hit a wall and said, 'I can't do this anymore.' Certainly it's a progressive disease, so that it changes; it doesn't get better, you know. But at the same time it hasn't debilitated me. I wanted to make the choice while I could. I feel good and I'm happy and I have energy and there's stuff to do. I happen to believe there is a God, and perhaps I'm in this position so I could do something. This is what was in the book for me."

Viewers responded to this courageous and touching interview with hundreds of letters and e-mails wishing Michael good luck on his journey. To nobody's surprise, the ratings for *Access Hollywood* went through the roof.

From then on, Michael and I spent a lot of time together—interviewing and laughing. I traveled to Phoenix with him to watch the making of a public service announcement for Parkinson's with Muhammad Ali. Ali himself was fighting that battle. During some downtime, Michael and I went to Michael's suite for lunch and to watch a basketball game. We were privately gossiping about and tearing Hollywood to shreds, and we laughed so hard we both fell off the couch on the floor like two little kids at a sleepover. I also hosted a couple of Michael's foundation dinners in New York, and he and Heather Locklear and I hosted an event in Napa Valley. At this event Heather and I got so wasted on wine, we could barely walk or talk. When I got back to my hotel, I finally noticed that my tan suit, a good one, was soaked with red wine. Just as Parkinson's had snuck up on Michael, my alcoholism was sneaking up on me. Ironically, it was Michael who taught me the serenity prayer: "God grant me the serenity to accept the things I cannot change, the courage to change the things I can, and the wisdom to know the difference."

I would soon learn to say that prayer several times a day.

The beginning of the new century brought the beginning of another new Hollywood, with Brad Pitt and Jennifer Aniston and Ellen DeGeneres and Ann Heche and Angelina Jolie and Billy Bob Thornton and Matt Damon and Ben Affleck creating all the couples news.

Matt and Ben were just a couple years off their incredible run of awards for their screenplay for *Good Will Hunting*. When they won the Golden Globes in 1998, they came backstage to our *Access Hollywood* set, and as they walked in, I said, "How great is this, huh?" They both responded at once with "About as great as sitting down with Pat O'Brien!"

It was another indication of how much my sports background was paying off in Hollywood. Matt and Ben were huge sports fans, and they seemed to know more about what I had covered than I knew.

My relationship with them would get us a lot of mileage on our show, much to the dismay of *Entertainment Tonight* and the others. I was, indeed, becoming the Hollywood insider.

So, when this label is put on you, other things happen, and they happen quickly. Almost too quickly.

I appeared as a guest on *Everybody Loves Raymond,* as myself, in a now-famous scene where I am calling a finger football game with Ray and his buddies.

I was also on the groundbreaking *Larry Sanders Show,* a spoof of every late-night show ever made, starring comedian Garry Shandling. Shandling played a neurotic, self-obsessed host with an even more nervous and neurotic staff. I appeared in the episode where the crew was celebrating its eighth season. As most of Hollywood was invited to do, I was asked to be myself or even a little more self-absorbed than I already was. The plot crossed the sports and entertainment line: I was only to be a guest because I was getting Larry Final Four tickets. I had a scene with Mandy Patinkin and Noah Wyle where I screamed at both of them, "Shut the fuck up!" The other guests were k. d. lang, George Segal, Farrah Fawcett, Ryan O'Neal, and Rosie O'Donnell . . . all playing themselves.

After the show, I asked Rosie what she was going to do next, and she said, "Actually, I'm going to a meeting right now for a talk show myself." Little did we know she would turn out to be one of the greats and then one of the punch lines. As a result of that appearance, I was one of the few to be invited up to Shandling's Sunday-afternoon basketball games, a weekly ritual during football season for basketball, pizza, and the NFL on television. (Think about this, though: no flat-screen or HD. We were all still primitive.) The regulars included Bill Maher, Jon Stewart, and the sole woman, Sarah Silverman, among others. It was all in good fun, and then when the invitations were suddenly stopped all of us just thought we weren't invited anymore. We soon learned that, no, that wasn't the case, the games had just stopped. The irony being that we'd picked up another neurosis, courtesy of Garry Shandling himself. All of this eventually came full circle when I was a frequent guest on *Jimmy Kimmel Live!* while he was dating the talented Silverman and I was in Silverman's birthday video for Kimmel mistitled "I'm Fucking Matt Damon."

One Hollywood job led to another: I played myself in *Big Fat Liar,* reporting on Paul Giamatti's character screwing over a kid whose script he stole and profited from. It was a huge kids' hit and came back to me in many ways. One late night, Richie Sambora and I were on a private jet from Los Angeles to New York, and when we landed, I dropped him off at Jon Bon Jovi's house. We came in the back door of the mansion, and Jon greeted us with "Oh my God, Pat! You have to come in right now and meet my kids." They were screening *Big Fat Liar* in his massive home theater, and one of my small scenes was just playing. I worked in a couple of Giamatti's projects and also got to high-five Scooby in *Scooby-Doo 2*. After I did a long segment on the *South Park* guys, Trey Parker and Matt Stone, they put me in their spaghetti sports comedy, *BASEketball*. Virtually every sportscaster in America was in this one, and I literally got the final words by describing the BASEketball championship with these immortal words: "Blah, blah, blah, blah, blah."

Because I was getting good at the "blah, blah, blah" part, I was a guest on the *Late Show with David Letterman,* which was more stressful than exciting. When the producers pre-interviewed me, they kept saying, "We hope you're funny. Dave likes it when people are funny." When I got on the plane, I sat next to Cindy Crawford, who said, "I hope you can be funny." When I got to the dressing room, Rosanne Barr, also on that night, said, "Are you funny?" And when Paul Shaffer fired up "the Cat" to bring me out, legendary stage manager Biff Henderson said, "You better be funny!"—then pushed me through the curtains. I sat down and made some forgettable self-effacing joke and the crowd laughed! I was funny! I had heard that if you weren't funny, Dave didn't speak during the commercials. At the first commercial, Dave leaned over to me and said, "I'm stealing money here." It was funny.

Jay Leno's people called and thought it would be a good idea to have me on maybe once a month and do some "Hollywood gossip" stories. They set up a little set, away from the couch, and Jay and I did our first offering before the live audience. It went so well that after the show, while Jay was thanking me, one of his producers came up and said, "Wow, Pat, you were great. For a minute, I couldn't figure out whose show it was." That was my final appearance on Jay Leno's show. But I was no stranger to the talk-show circuit, as I was somewhat a regular on the classic Tom Snyder late, late night show. The last time I was on, I followed Merv Griffin, who was wearing a bright red sports coat. I suggested to Tom that we wouldn't be caught dead wearing a red coat, and we had a good laugh. CBS had me fill up a summer month with my own show, *Overtime . . . with Pat O'Brien,* which debuted against *Nightline* and didn't last long, but it was part of the learning process.

And then there were two prime-time series, *Beyond Belief* and *How'd They Do That?*, which, after a two-year network run, became a long-running syndication show on cable. There was a VH1 show and a game show for Fox (when I came home, I said to Linda, "I think I just found something I can't do." It never aired). I played myself on *Murphy Brown, In the House, Picket Fences,* and *Arli$$.* Two personal highlights: I got to be the voice of a creepy doll with miracle powers on *Twilight Zone* and was drawn up by Matt Groening as an anchorman in Springfield on *The Simpsons,* then spoofed and imitated many times on *Saturday Night Live.* Jimmy Fallon did the "Pat O'Brien" thing with the mustache and nasal voice, and "Pat's" mantra was "I can't breathe with this mustache!" It was funny and obviously flattering, but when I later met Jimmy for the first time, he apologized, to which I responded, "I didn't think it was mean enough. There's a lot of material there." The next week he was on *The Ellen DeGeneres Show* and she asked him to do his "Pat O'Brien." This time he was so mean and condescending, I thought to myself, *Did I ask for this?* And once again the "real" Pat O'Brien inside said, *Be careful what you wish for.*

Meantime, back at the day job, the tabloids were all about Angelina Jolie's exploits and Robert Downey Jr.'s problems with drugs and alcohol and the cops. Downey had a rough couple of years to say the least: fourteen months in prison, and then three months after getting out and attending rehab, he was arrested again after a wild standoff with police in Palm Springs. I had not yet met Robert at the time, but for some reason I asked to be recused from reporting his troubles, either out of compassion or maybe, deep down, I somehow saw my troubles around the corner. The tabloids and the other shows (even ours) had a field day with him, not yet sensitive to covering people with addiction problems. Ignorance, and a constant joy at somebody else's problems, ruled the day. They still do. But soon, even Hollywood was about to forget about its own problems. Something much, much deeper was on the horizon.

On September 9, 2001, I was in the bar of the Four Seasons hotel in New York during a whistle-stop tour of the East Coast to promote the show. When I scanned the room, I noticed Mayor Rudy Giuliani in the corner chatting with a circle of intimates. We had met a few times over the years, and he waved for me to come over and join him. He was in an expansive mood. His term in office was drawing to a close; he was to be replaced at the end of the year by billionaire businessman Michael Bloomberg. Giuliani spread his arms out and said, "Look at me; I'm done!" I said, "You did a great job, Mr. Mayor." He raised his glass of red wine in a toast to himself and remarked, "I can now just coast; I'm done." Two days later while his city was celebrating a beautiful fall day, the planes hit the World Trade Center.

At the time of the terrorist attacks I was on a local morning radio show in Boston talking up *Access Hollywood*. I was jokingly trying to explain, "If you hated me as a Laker homer, you now have to love me as your Hollywood eyes and ears." As soon as the first plane, American Airlines Flight 11 bound for Los Angeles, hit at 8:46, all thoughts of talking about an entertainment show went out the window. At first we thought it was a small tourist plane that hit the tower, but as it started to burn, I said to the radio hosts, "I'm gonna go; I think there's a news story here." I walked into their transmission room, where there was another television monitor, and to my (and everybody else's) horror, we watched as the second plane exploded into the second tower. As I monitored the horrifying events on that blue-skied September morning, I called home and woke Linda in Los Angeles and told her, "I can't believe I'm about to say this, but I think the United States is under attack. Wake up Sean . . . take the car out of the garage and be prepared for anything. Call you later."

Then I phoned Rob Silverstein, our executive producer, just to confirm that we probably were not on that day, as the networks took over to cover what would become the biggest story ever. Then Mike Marson, my field producer, and I got into our limo and headed back to Boston's Four Seasons hotel. On the way we were silent, numbly staring out the car window at an America under threat. Finally I said, "I think our lives have just changed forever."

When we arrived at the hotel, I went to my room, turned on the TV, and jumped on my computer. Even in 2001, there was no such thing as social networking outside of the AOL instant message service. So I logged on to AOL. The first person I saw online was GE CEO Jack Welch's second wife, Janie, a sassy, wonderful woman whom Linda and I had gotten to know during our many summer holidays in Nantucket. She was panicked.

Janie: "Pat! I can't find Jack. He was on a high floor at NBC doing an interview and I haven't heard from him."

Pat: "Oh, no! Well, I've seen nothing outside of the towers."

Janie: "I've got find him, now!!!"

Then the screen went blank.

While Jack was okay, ironically he was to be on the *Today* show (on his network) to be interviewed for his latest book, but he was canceled when the planes hit. It was now eleven in the morning. I opened the minibar, poured the first alcoholic drink I could see, and sat back in my chair staring at the madness on TV. Suddenly, I just broke down and started to cry. Then it began to hit me that I had originally planned to fly home to LA on American Airlines Flight 11 but canceled those plans the previous day because of publicity commitments. I began crying uncontrollably, sobbing as I checked the dozens of messages on my cell phone. Most were the usual shock and awe: "Are you watching this?" or "Hey, Pat, which flight are you on?" The most emotional one was from *Access Hollywood* reporter Shaun Robinson, a woman whom I loathed with a passion. We will get into that. Her message was hysterical, Shaun sobbing and crying as she blurted out her words. "Pat, it's Shaun. I hope you're not on that plane.

I pray you're not on that plane. Call us right now." Given our toxic relationship, I thought, *bad acting,* but at the moment it was kind of endearing.

Like thousands of others I just sat there, staring out the window on a beautiful fall day in Boston. People were rushing out of buildings, which were being evacuated; the sound of hundreds of police sirens filled the air. Eventually I called Rob and we talked about how the hell a show such as *Access Hollywood* was going to handle this story. We decided that chances were good that this happy-go-lucky television format might be over with for everybody. Period. How could we ever go back to red carpets and movie premieres and sycophantic questions like "What are you wearing?" in this atmosphere? In that moment the two of us couldn't imagine people caring about 'N Sync and the Spice Girls anymore. To lighten things up, I joked to Rob, as we always did, about the shallowness of my cohost, Nancy O'Dell: "Is O'Dell in makeup, wondering how we're going to interrupt the network with *Access Hollywood* tonight?" Rob said, "It's doubtful she's even heard of this yet." A brief laugh and back to my empty room and my fast-emptying glass. I needed to calm down, and the medicine was right there in my minibar. And it was free.

A couple of minutes later the Four Seasons Hotel general manager called. In his thick German accent, he said, "Mr. O'Brien, how are you and what are you doing?" I said, "Drinking and crying." He replied, "That's what the entire hotel is doing. Come to the bar. Drinks are free and we have set up TVs there." On the way to the bar I stopped at the concierge desk and asked them to get me out of town any way they could think of. There were no flights, every car was rented, and the westbound train was fully booked. I had an idea: "Can you call Amtrak and hook on an extra car for us? Cost is not a factor!" They laughed. Already thought of. Already done. Somebody beat me to it.

The bar was packed, everyone watching either CNN or NBC. By midnight I, along with the rest of the bar, was absolutely trashed. I mean New Year's Eve trashed. Instead of going to bed, naturally

I went out seeking another bar, and what I found was another bar full of people staring at a television. The president was speaking. Strangers were becoming sudden best drinking buddies, and I hooked up with a group and we went barhopping. There was nothing else to do. Finally, I staggered to my room and called Rob. When and how could we get out? I wanted to go home. I cried myself to sleep.

The next morning America was at a standstill. Schools and businesses were closed, airports and major public buildings were on alert, and plane travel had been shut down indefinitely. "Everybody just stay home" was the request from the president. Finally Rob called and said that Jack Welch himself had arranged a private plane to get me and some others back to Los Angeles. There was one catch—it was leaving from the Westminster, New York, airport. So Mike Marson and I got in a taxi and were driven back to New York, making our way through checkpoints to the small private airport. When we got there, we were told there were no planes. Period. While we waited in the green room of the small airport for news, my old pal celebrity chef Emeril Lagasse, the star of the Food Network, walked in with the actor Robert Urich. After waiting for about five hours we realized we were going nowhere fast, so we checked into a local hotel and Emeril decided to find us a restaurant.

He picked out a family-owned Italian place, and, boy, were they surprised when we walked in. Right away Emeril turned to me and said, "Let's make the best of this. Come with me." We went into the kitchen and he took over. From scratch, he made pastas, pork, and vegetable side dishes, and for a brief time we forgot about why we were trapped here. We prayed for the victims and for America and sat down and ate our food. The next day it was the same routine, praying, cooking, and drinking for five hours or so. Trapped, if you will, in a great restaurant with Emeril and Bob and an expense account. It was either this or sit and worry and mourn. By the third day we were told our plane had arrived.

This beautiful Gulfstream held about nine people with ease. Before we took off, we had an unpleasant altercation with Lilly Tarticoff, the widow of the late Brandon Tarticoff, the brilliant TV producer, who grandly announced that this was her plane and took all the best seats for herself and her rude entourage. When I protested, she clenched her jaw and said, "And just who are you?" I said, "I host the television show your husband created for NBC!" I got the best seat. After we reached cruising altitude, I talked to the pilots and they told me that there had been incredible security around this flight. The pilot showed me the radar map for the United States. We were one of maybe two dozen or so planes in the air. Normally tens of thousands of planes are on the radar every hour. It was so eerie. When I got home, it felt good to hug my family. Sean has never forgotten the moment he woke up, came down the staircase, and the Towers were just then collapsing on live TV. I had called him and he'd said, "Dad, be careful and come home soon."

Like most people, my experience of 9/11 was in watching the shocking events on television. Meantime, Paul McCartney saw the Twin Towers going up in smoke through the window of a jet plane on the tarmac at New York's JFK airport as he waited to return to England. Before long, he was trying to think of how to respond to the attacks, and what he could do to help. The result was the "Concert for New York City," which McCartney helped organize, feeling that music could be an instrument of healing, just as when the Beatles arrived in America a short time after JFK was murdered. A few weeks after the attacks McCartney was joined onstage at Madison Square Garden by David Bowie, Elton John, Billy Joel, and many others. McCartney's people called us at *Access Hollywood* and said that Paul wanted me to come along, interview him, and attend the concert. Over the years Paul and I had developed a great relationship; he knew I loved the Beatles and his music and felt relaxed in my company.

He came to our offices, we grabbed some coffee, and while the crew was putting the finishing touches to the lighting, we started chatting about Beatles memorabilia, of all things. I have a large collection of rare black-and-white Beatles photos and several John Lennon sketches, and I said to Paul, "This whole memorabilia thing is crazy now." But I couldn't get the word *memorabilia* out and neither could he. He said, "Hard to say when you've had a few, eh?" I replied, "Well, you know, Irish." This was all captured on film, which was shown on a Showtime special aired on the tenth anniversary of 9/11. They left that part in.

Then we talked about how this would be a good time to gather the remaining Beatles together: Ringo, George, and Paul. He said, "You never ask me about that, but you know it would be weird to go up there and look to my left and there's someone missing." That would be John Lennon. The way Paul said it was touching. Afterward he signed something for me for Sean and said, "Here you go, I don't know what that's worth." I said somewhat cynically, "Here I come, eBay."

Backstage at the concert, it was a madhouse with everybody trying to get close to Paul. Thanks to him, my crew and I had the run of the place, chatting with Bill Clinton and running into a lot of rock-and-roll folk I had met over the years: Richie Sambora, Jon Bon Jovi, Sheryl Crow, Billy Joel, and James Taylor. I told Sweet Baby James that I had a picture of him from the 1970s sitting in the back of an old pickup truck. 'I don't even remember you taking that picture," he said. Not that my memory was much better. I was telling Elton John the story of my first-ever stereo. I spent every last dime on this monster system, cranked it up, and put Elton's first album, *Empty Sky*, released in 1969, on the turntable.

Before the first song had even really begun, my whole system exploded because it was turned up to ten. Poker-faced, Elton looked at me, put his hand on my arm, and said, "Pat, that's the fourth time you've told me that story."

When the concert was over, McCartney motioned to me to walk out with him, and I got the only interview he gave as we pushed our way through the gaggle of screaming reporters. We didn't stop and they were yelling, in so many words or less, "Thanks a lot, Pat!"

Paul said, "Hey, come on over to this little party we're having afterwards." By now it was about midnight, and the party, at the W

Hotel, was just for his family, band members, and friends. I felt as if I were a member of the world's most exclusive club. We were all dancing, and Paul got up and sang. As things died down, we sat there shooting the breeze over glasses of good red wine. Early the next morning I had to fly to Washington, D.C., to cover Puff Daddy's 9/11 concert, so I began my good-byes. Paul said jokingly, "And I thought you were this big Beatle fan. What Beatle fan wouldn't want to sit here and drink with me?" He was right. We chatted about the old days of the Beatles, Paul confirming for me the famous story of their first meeting with Bob Dylan. This epic tale is well-known to Beatles and Dylan fans, but when you hear it from the man who was there, it has extra resonance.

The British band was staying at the Delmonico Hotel and got a call that Bob Dylan was in the lobby and wanted to drop in and meet the boys. The Beatles were freaked out! "Bob Dylan wants to meet us?!" Dylan was ushered into their suite and asked for cheap red wine and then suggested they have a smoke. The guys looked at each other apprehensively before they admitted that they had never smoked marijuana. The American songwriter was disbelieving. "But what about your song," he said, "the one about getting high?" The Beatles were baffled. "Which song is that?" John Lennon asked. Dylan replied, "You know, the one that goes 'When I touch you, I get high, I get high . . .'"

He was talking about "I Want to Hold Your Hand." Paul admitted, "Those aren't the words. The words are 'And when I touch you, I feel happy inside. It's such a feeling that my love I can't hide, I can't hide . . .'" True story told by the master himself.

Paul and I had a couple more and I left, flying to Washington with a signed photo for Sean and a thick piece of glass given to me by one of the firemen at Ground Zero in my suitcase. The glass, from one of the tower windows, still reeked of airplane fuel and smoke and was so scratched up, you couldn't see through it. A chilling piece of history, and when I show it to people, they can't find the right words. They just stare at it.

As we all know, 9/11 did change everything. A few months later, in February 2002, I was one of the NBC hosts for the Winter Olympics at Salt Lake City. While I had the thrill of running the Olympic torch again, this time through Santa Cruz in California, the games were overshadowed by intense security for competitors, media, and spectators alike. Everything was locked down solid. No chances were taken. I had two bodyguards with me at all times, and it would regularly take an hour just to get into the broadcast center to go to work and another hour to get out. That said, we managed to have fun. This was my first time working an American-time-zoned Olympics, so we actually had what seemed to be normal days. I was also hosting *Access Hollywood,* also an NBC show, so between the two I was all over the place.

At breakfast one morning, I ran into Sting, who was to sing at the opening ceremonies along with LeAnn Rimes, Earth, Wind & Fire, and the Dixie Chicks. As we sat down for breakfast, Sting was telling me how he kept his voice solid in the cold, dry, icy conditions. He would turn his shower on hot and never turn it off, so his room was basically one big steam room. Being a good follower, I did the same thing, and my room was more like a solarium than a place to sleep and, of course, drink.

Every night, on the Olympic *Late Night* show, we hosted the day's Olympic highlights topped with a rock show, interviewing our musical guests, such as Sheryl Crow, 'N Sync, and the Dave Matthews Band. NBC built a fifteen-thousand-seat stadium and moved all the medal ceremonies to our show, so despite freezing temperatures and the security, we had a good time. After we wrapped for the night, we went to the Marriott hotel and ate steaks and drank as much wine as we could find in a Mormon town. Somehow they managed to find it. As heavy as my drinking now was, I felt I was still in control. After all, I told myself, I was in great shape. I was running every morning and getting in an hour at the gym every day. There were no warning signs that I could see, anyway. So what was the problem, right? I was at the height of my career, my broadcasting work straddling the worlds of celebrity and sport. More than that, I was making new friends.

Kevin Costner is the perfect example. I had interviewed him for several of his films—he even took me to see the musical postproduction for his movie *The Postman*—but we became friends through our love of sports. From time to time I traveled on his private plane to big sports events such as the Final Four. He would provide the jet and I would provide the all-access pass. Seemed fair. And on this one, it wasn't about the perks of being part of a Hollywood star's entourage; I genuinely enjoyed his company. He is a loyal, compassionate, and intelligent man with a wicked sense of humor. He always seemed to have had the right tone on everything whether serious or not. One time we were playing a round at the Riviera Country Club in Pacific Palisades, California, when I remarked that Ben Hogan had described the ninth hole as the toughest he'd played. Quick as a flash, Kevin replied, "And I dated the other eight." Speaking of other women, we were in the bar at the Four Seasons in New York one evening with Jerry Seinfeld. After Jerry headed home, Kevin and I decided to go up to his enormous suite for a nightcap because the bar was getting a little much with people, mostly women, dropping by the table to say hi to Kevin. On our way to the elevator two good-looking women got into step and got off with us at Costner's floor. We all went in the room. One of the girls lit up a joint and Kevin grabbed some red wine for the two of us. So we were talking and laughing, and after about forty minutes Kevin took me aside and said, "I really like the girl you are with. She's cute." I whispered, "I'm not with her." He looked puzzled. "What do you mean? I thought she was your girl." It turned out that he thought they were my friends and I thought they were his. They were complete strangers, so we kicked them out and just sat down on the couch laughing.

On another occasion we were at the Seattle Final Four and Kevin hosted a party in his suite at the Four Seasons. Even though he was only five or six, I took Sean along to hang out. Halfway through the evening he went missing, and I was racing around the hotel in a complete panic looking for him. Kevin's bedroom door was shut, so I presumed that he just wanted some privacy. Finally I knocked on the door, and when I went in, Kevin was sitting on the floor playing a game with young Sean. Here was this big Hollywood star hosting a glamorous party taking the time to play with my young son. Impressive. I would say the same of Brad Pitt, too. I've seen him away from the cameras just spending time with Maddox and his other kids. Given my upbringing, my antennae have always focused on how a father, whether or not he is a celebrity, interacts with his children. Brad and Kevin both pass the "dad test."

A big flaw with this kind of access is that you tend to coddle the stars you like or the ones you want to be friends with. I did this, although I can tell you with certainty, nobody in these media jobs is ever, ever a close friend with the stars. Doesn't happen. For the most part, at heart, I was still the kid at the movie house in Sioux Falls staring enviously at the stars. Sometimes I got carried away with the fantasy. When I was talking to Tom Hanks about his movie *Cast Away*, which was released in 2000, I said to him, "When you were in the water after the plane crash and there are flames all around you, weren't you scared?"

He smiled and grabbed my arm. "Pat, it's only a movie."

16

Not Just Anybody

One time Bill O'Reilly had me on *Inside Edition* when he was hosting the show, and he tried to make a name for himself or ruin mine by accusing me of never asking the tough questions. His theory was that I never wanted to bite the hand that feeds me or, as Ray Romano said about the Golden Globe people, "Bite the hand that we feed." In other words, I was too nice to celebs so they would come back on. I tried to explain, first of all, "What tough questions? 'Your outfit doesn't match and why?' 'Hey, Carrot Top! Your thoughts on Syria?'" It's a red carpet, not rocket-science class.

The irony is that these celebrities never watch the shows in the first place, so they don't care half as much about the questions as their highly paid publicists, whose job security relies on shutting down interviews the minute a question or remark strays from whatever their client is promoting. I would always bypass the publicists, as my persona on and off television was such that many Hollywood stars preferred to talk to me rather than one of my rivals. Dozens of times the publicist would scream, "Time's up!" or "We're done here now," and the DiCaprios and Cruises and Madonnas and Costners of the world would say, "Oh, come on now, it's Pat!" Michael J. Fox was a case in point, as was Arnold Schwarzenegger. Remember when he became governor of California in 2003 I snagged the first interview? And I beat the pack when he cut himself in a motorcycle accident. "Make sure you say that I made it to my scheduled public appointments" was his only trade-off for the exclusive. After we did the motorcycle-accident exclusive, he called me on my cell to say, "Did you get a shot of my cut lip?" Arnold knew the deal and knew I knew the deal.

I suppose this was Jon Voight's thinking when the Oscar-winning actor and father of Angelina Jolie called me one morning in July 2002, a few days after Angie and Billy Bob Thornton had ended their brief but tumultuous marriage. Jon called and asked if we could meet privately. I said, "Sure," and suggested we have coffee at the famous Art's Deli in the San Fernando Valley. I arrived early, but he was already sitting in the back booth. He got straight down to business.

"I want to talk to you about my daughter. I'm brokenhearted. That's the reason I'm here. I feel I can trust you as a journalist."

I am enough of a broadcast journalist to know that whatever he wanted to say was best said in front of a TV camera. We arranged to meet at the Four Seasons Hotel, Rob Silverstein organizing a two-camera shoot. When I walked into the hotel suite, I had no idea what I was getting into. My questions were brief, giving Voight the forum.

He was immediately in full flow, explaining that while the public might see a poised, smiling actor who had enjoyed numerous successes, inside he was a broken man. "I've been trying to reach my daughter and get her some help," he said, referring to Angelina's reported well-known battle with drugs. He went on to talk about her "real psychic pain" and "serious mental problems," his comments coming only weeks after she had controversially adopted a Cambodian boy she named Maddox.

While he conceded that Billy Bob Thornton may have had a positive influence on her, he was concerned that, as his daughter was now a goodwill ambassador for the United Nations Refugee Agency, her behavior could have an opposite, negative effect on her many fans. He put his hand over his face and broke down in tears. It was an awkward yet electrifying moment. Here was this huge Hollywood star sobbing like a father who, frankly, had lost his daughter. For a few seconds I didn't quite know what to do. I was no longer a journalist but acting as one father to another. I put my hand on his knee and patted him and said, "It's okay to cry." He was inconsolable, and the sobbing turned into shaking and panic.

When we finished the thirty-minute interview, we had lunch and then he went on his way, feeling that he had accomplished his mission. If Voight felt that he was going to win his daughter back by this TV confessional, he was sadly mistaken.

In fact, sadly, I had more contact with her than her own father, if only to count her appearances on the red carpet. She always struck me as a free soul who did what she wanted and the hell with everybody else. I could relate to that. At the 1999 Golden Globes she made good on her outrageous prediction that if she won she would jump into the fountain at the Beverly Hilton.

Angie always was gracious to me and we had a harmless, playful relationship. One afternoon, for example, at the L'Ermitage Hotel in Beverly Hills I was waiting for an elevator and when the door opened, there was Angelina Jolie. She was on her cell phone. So was I. Hollywood. I said, "What's up, baby?" and she said with a wink, "I'm trying to find this guy I kind of know because I'm really horny right now." I joked that she had my number and we laughed and that was it.

At the time who knew that she would become a world ambassador doing all the right things, and somehow I was never surprised. I love Angelina Jolie. Sorry, Brad.

While interviews such as Voight's cemented the position of *Access Hollywood* as the show the stars called when they had a story to tell, a few months later, in the summer of 2003, our number one status was assured when we snagged an hour-long network-TV special with the most talked about couple in Tinseltown, Jennifer Lopez and her then boyfriend, Ben Affleck. Much of the tabloid talk centered around "will they, won't they" marriage plans. In response, my producer Rob Silverstein pitched a proposal to Team Bennifer—the nickname for Ben and Jennifer—and to Jeff Zucker, the head of NBC Entertainment, about a TV special that would not only feature on *Access Hollywood* but the *Today* show and *Dateline,* as well.

This was just about as big as it gets in the world of celebrity interviews—and I just about let it end up at the bottom of a bottle. Rob, I, and superpublicist Ken Sunshine, who was the go-to guy for Ben and Jennifer, traveled to Vancouver together to prepare for the interview. By now my drinking was about as close as you can get to being unmanageable. I had two bottles of Silver Oak red wine open in the limousine that took us to the airport. On the plane I told the stewardess to keep my glass filled. I was so sideways that I mistook a female passenger for a flight attendant and, much to her annoyance, asked her to bring me more red wine. I was a disaster waiting to happen, falling asleep over dinner in the hotel. After Rob and Ken got me to my room, Ken said, "This guy has a massive drinking problem." Over the years Rob, riding shotgun with me, had become so used to seeing me drinking heavily but being ready for action the following morning that he hadn't noticed the incremental changes in me. When I told Rob that I wanted to hang out at the bar, he ordered me to go to bed—which was just as well.

For a guy preparing for a prime-time special the day began disastrously. I was out running my miles, as usual, when I was attacked and bitten by a rottweiler. Rob discovered me lying bleeding in front of the hotel and took me to the emergency room to be patched up. Once we got back to the hotel, he sat me down and insisted I prepare my questions carefully, emphasizing that I couldn't float through such an important interview. Everyone used to make fun of me because I often began interviews with a joshing "How great is this?" Not this time.

By the time I sat down with Ben and Jennifer the story of my being mauled by a dog had made the news. So Ben brought me a stuffed toy dog as a joke. It broke the ice and we had a great day filming. Ben and I played basketball for the cameras, Jennifer and I cooked for the cameras, we walked, we talked, and we laughed for the cameras. It was about as in-depth for a celebrity interview as this side of a Barbara Walters special. The trade-off (and there always is one) was that we promised to heavily promote arguably the worst movie ever made: *Gigli*. This thing was described by Rotten Tomatoes as "shapeless and without a shred of originality." And that seemed to be the good review. Nevertheless, our show rated well because we focused on what was called the greatest public romance since Taylor and Burton. From that show on, celebrity coverage went from intense to frenzied. The Ben and Jen interview set the bar higher than it had ever before been for celebrity news. This story seemed so good, it had to be on prime time, the *Today* show, and *Dateline*. It was the first real synergy of a single story throughout the network. By controlling Ben and Jen, so to speak, we completely controlled the entertainment media for a couple weeks. Magazines couldn't get enough. The paparazzi couldn't get enough. It was like the first Kennedy-Nixon debate. And we did it with a foundation of a shitty movie. To this day, Ben and I marvel at how it all changed as a result of that couple days in Vancouver. But for me, the moment of my greatest work triumph in this genre also signaled the start of my fall from grace.

At first only those close to me at work or at home noticed that I was no longer a functioning heavy drinker; I was a fully fledged functioning alcoholic. I didn't miss work and I didn't miss family obligations, although those were somehow and sadly first to go. My family had an annual touch-football game every Thanksgiving; we called it Dadball, fathers vs. sons. We played it long enough for the sons to finally grow up and beat the hell out of us. In the fall of 2003 after the game (which was held every Thanksgiving in Palo Alto, California), I went AWOL, physically and mentally. After the dinner I got so hammered one of my nephews took me back to the hotel. When Sean and Linda arrived later, I was passed out on the floor. Efforts to wake me up failed again and again. Later, Linda would tell me that Sean was nearly in tears yelling, "Is he all right? Is he all right?" Ironically I was wearing a T-shirt that said ROLE MODEL! The last thing I ever wanted to do was scare or disappoint my son, and if I had had control of my disease at that time I would not have done so. But I did.

My life was spinning out of control. I wasn't just drinking; I was drinking myself senseless. I was drinking until I automatically clicked off. At one gathering, I fell over and cut my head on a glass table. After Linda got me patched up, she called Rob Silverstein, one of the fathers at the Dadball games, and explained what had happened. The following Monday Rob called me into his office to talk about what had happened. He spoke to me as a father himself and as a longtime and loyal friend. He was begging me to try to get a grip on my drinking and pointed out that when I wanted to, I could switch my addictions on and off. I had done that with cocaine and cigarettes. "Pat, you have to do something," he said to me. "Otherwise you will lose your job and your family."

An alcoholic's path to death more often than not begins with not listening. I was on that path and too grandiose to believe this could happen to me. I was in denial. I was feeding my alcoholic brain with the only medicine I thought would ease my fears and shame and stress. I had never come to grips with myself and had that moment where I saw myself as I really was. I was too busy trying to be somebody else, and getting highly paid for it. It's the road every alcoholic travels and I was definitely in step. I was rapidly losing my edit button. The only thing that made me feel at ease was drinking, and while I was like a tornado whirling through my family and my life, I couldn't stop. The only voice I ever heard was my own, and it kept saying, "More, Pat, more." I thought I had everything, and I used things and people to fill up a spiritual emptiness inside. Even too much was never enough. I went to therapy, I read inspirational books, I prayed every now and then, but my prayers were for me, not for help. Ironic in that one of my favorite Beatles songs was "Help!" Had I really listened to the words, I might have found something deeper and useful.

> *Help, I need somebody*
> *Help, not just anybody*
> *Help, you know I need someone, help*

17

Girls

The first-class section of American Airlines from Los Angeles International to New York Kennedy on a Friday afternoon used to always be an adventure. A lot of people worked in LA and in New York, and we all considered this commute part of the deal. It was six hours each way when you could sleep, catch up on reading, watch a bad movie, or drink. I drank.

So one afternoon, I jump on and quietly move to my seat at the second-row window. As I'm gathering my stuff and as the flight crew brings me the familiar red wine, all of a sudden Alec Baldwin sits down next to me. He didn't waste any time: "I have a great movie idea for you! So, here's the thing: you become a host of a really popular entertainment show, and suddenly everybody wants and needs to be on it. In order to do your job correctly, you start going out with all the celebrities to get to know them. As a result, you're out every night listening to their problems and drinking and doing drugs and it becomes such a burden, you eventually become an alcoholic and drug addict and go crazy. And when you leave, the celebrities have nobody to talk to."

Baldwin's crystal-ball vision was happening in real life, but I had yet to see it. At the time, I had enough on my plate dealing with the personalities I was working with.

During my time at *Access Hollywood* I had watched this parade of female anchors—insecure, usually devoid of any interest other than themselves, but ruthlessly ambitious in pursuit of goals that were always unattainable. It was like working with a stiletto at your throat. As my down-to-earth makeup artist of ten years, Joy Tilk, testifies, these women were the most self-absorbed people on the planet. Of course, so was I, so I just might have to take into consideration that my alcoholic brain, untreated, was based on fear and shame and extreme selfishness. In fact, looking back, I wonder just who had the these character defects: me or them.

My first cohost at *Access* was Giselle Fernandez, a former television anchor, who was a complete diva. Before I started, my old pal, and now executive producer, Rob Silverstein warned me with, "Wait till you meet this one." Giselle was smart with an incredible television skill set, but couldn't handle not being the star of the show. That's kind of a side effect of talent and it's the absolute definition of what I was going through: my life was the show and I wasn't taking any direction. As for Giselle, if there wasn't a drama going on, she would manufacture one. For example, at the start of the day she would be very quiet and I would keep my mouth shut in case she latched on to a stray comment, like, "How ya doin'?" Then from out of nowhere she would say, "You think I'm fat, don't you?" The crew and I would exchange bewildered glances. She would then fly into a rage and then once her fury had subsided she would be utterly sweet and charming. It was like working with a female Jekyll and Hyde. I remember one Christmas I gave her a watch and as we were walking out of the building we got into an argument over something so small I couldn't even remember it that evening and she threw the watch at my head. "Take your fucking watch," she screamed as she stormed off into the night. She wins the award as the most unpredictable person I have ever worked with. There were days when I wished I'd stayed in the army long enough to learn how to navigate minefields. When she finally quit because she believed the show was too tabloid (good for her, by the way), she disappeared and went into broadcast purgatory. Giselle and I ran into each other a couple years later and she looked happy; couldn't have been nicer. But, honestly, I was a little scared to turn my back on her.

There is something about television and fame that messes up the mind. These women start off fine and dandy and all cute and cuddly and then they want more lines, more camera time, more hair and makeup, better interviews—more, more, more. And each time a certain "more" was denied, they got worse until they imploded or committed professional suicide. After Giselle left, she was replaced by Nancy O'Dell, a former Miss South Carolina who spent three to four hours a day in hair and makeup. While most modern day women can get through the hair and makeup transformation process in under forty minutes, Nancy must have thought there was an award for most time spent in the makeup chair. One day after we had been working together for five months, she came into my office, sat down on the couch, and started crying and complaining about her first husband. Her story this day was that he would make her watch the show with him, and then demand that she tell him he was better looking than her. I know. I'm listening to this completely sober by the way (I never drank at work) and for the first few minutes I had no idea who this maniac was. It took me that long to realize this was my cohost sitting there: that's how different she looked without the four hours in hair and makeup. As opposed to others at *Access,* I was actually able to roll with Nancy's approach to work and, make no mistake, I like Nancy O'Dell. She's terminally cute. She could read the teleprompter with the best of them: the problem was she never really knew what she was saying. And she would drawl on in the same tone for a death or for a wedding. There was one note on her piano. One time about five seconds after she read a segment, I grabbed her script and said, "Quick, what were you just talking about?" She couldn't remember. One time she actually said to me that she had "never read a book cover to cover." When I suggested she never say that out loud again, she said that growing up she was too busy with beauty pageants. I couldn't believe this so I rattled off a few of the regulars: *To Kill a Mockingbird, Catcher in the Rye, Lord of the Flies, Grapes of Wrath, The Diary of Anne Frank, The Great Gatsby:* no, no, no, no, and no. She did always remind us she graduated with honors.

She was also terrible designing a white lie. One day she didn't come in because she said she had a flood in her house. The next day when she got out of makeup, I asked her if she had a lot of water damage. She asked, "What are you talking about?" She forgot her own alibi. Rob used to tell me she used the "dead grandmother" a couple times. She might have just been naïve, but even the most clueless person at least has a foundation for their actions. With O'Dell, there was never any context. One time she stormed into Rob's office crying over her belief that Rob liked me better than her because somehow, through the magic of editing, he made it look like all the celebrities liked me better than her. (To this one, I pulled her aside and said, "Nance, there's a chance we are *not* equal.") Oh, the red-carpet stories with this one.

At the Grammys one year we were interviewing all the rock bands and here came Garbage, the "it" alt-band for that year. Their lead singer was Shirley Manson, who was so charismatic on stage you could not take your eyes off her. Anyway, so we're talking to Shirley, who happened to be wearing a gunnysack as a style statement and on the front it said "Garbage." Nancy asked her this: "What is the significance of the word 'garbage' on your dress?"

At the 2000 Grammys, Carlos Santana took home a record eight trophies for his multiplatinum album *Supernatural* in the greatest musical comeback in history. I had known Carlos since the 1960s, and so, while he declined any one-on-one interviews, he did come into our studio the next day to talk to me. I introduced Nancy and she opened with "Congratulations, I am so surprised you didn't win Best New Artist." I pointed out, as Carlos rolled his eyes, that Carlos should have been best new artist after he ripped up the Monterey Pop Festival in 1967.

Now, we all love to look tan and it's documented that I would do anything to be tan; in fact, Rob and I used to go outside to have meetings, put oil on our faces, and point them toward the Hollywood sun. Nancy enjoyed the fake-tan route and we all thought she most often deserved a refund for the results. At one red carpet, she was so orange she looked like the middle of a stoplight. The great actor and comedian John Leguizamo bounced up and said to Nancy, "Wow, where'd you get that tan?" Without a real answer, she said, "Vacation." John snapped back with "Where did you vacation, Mercury?"

Again, to be fair here, that was the same interview where I said, "John, you were great in *Traffic*, man." And he said, "Pat, I wasn't in *Traffic*."

So we all have our moments, but Nancy's were classic.

Nancy and I always managed to have great shows and, quite honestly, great times together. We hosted the St. Patrick's Day Parade in New York City a couple times and there was never any real dustup. Oh, there *was* the time at the Christmas party where I got a little drunk and licked her face, but nothing that couldn't be cleaned up in Human Resources, where I *did* spend a lot of my spare time while at *Access Hollywood*.

A couple of the main reasons were my big mouth and my stupid actions. Up until now, I hadn't learned a thing about decorum or even consequences: I thought I was too big to fail. Naturally, I was wrong about that, too. Nancy and I have laughed together about all of the above and she's a good sport. But she's addicted to fame. Been there. The only way out is to delete character defects. I will make this prediction, though: this is a book she'll read.

The woman Nancy always kept in her sights was the icon Mary Hart, over at *Entertainment Tonight*. Mary was without a doubt the queen of Hollywood TV, and I worked with her and around her longer than anybody else.

Until she retired in 2011, she set the gold standard; an old-school professional, she knew Tinseltown inside out but was as demanding as any queen. On the outside, one of the nicest people you'll ever meet, but behind her back we called her "the velvet claw." You're going to get scratched, but you won't notice till you bleed. She was the silent vampire.

Mary always kept a low profile around the Paramount lot, preferring to have her producers and followers do whatever dirty work there was. Seemingly the nicest person who ever lived, she was not one to toy with. She was rarely seen around the office except when she was strolling to the set with her small entourage, all sugarplums and fairy-tale stuff. Quite often, staffers would be called into Linda Bell Blue's office and the executive producer would begin the always one-sided conversation with the dreaded "Mary's not happy with . . ." That she carried a gun in her car and went nowhere on the lot without a big bodyguard proved to us that behind the sweet smile there might be another person. Mary had every perk available to any talent on a major show, including her own bathroom, which was way off-limits to the rest of us. She also had her personal bottled-water supply, and when a staffer grabbed a couple of waters without asking, it became a big issue—in other words, no one got to use her bathroom or drink her water. Later on, I got my own bathroom and my own water supply.

Mary was an excellent reader, never lost her dynamic energy, but she did lose her battle to age and a changing audience. She went out fighting, but was eventually replaced by, of all people, Nancy O'Dell, who had lost *her* audience at *Access Hollywood* because, in one high-level staffer's words, "Barbie dolls don't sell like they used to."

Let's turn now from the best-known entertainment anchor to the least known: Shaun Robinson. Shaun jumped around as a local reporter in Detroit, Milwaukee, and Miami and somehow got an audition with *Access Hollywood*. I was her coanchor for her audition. She looked great and charmed the day and night out of everybody on the set. When her brief tryout was over, she squeezed my hand, a little too tightly as I recall, and as I said good-bye and good luck, she stared me down and said, "I really want this job." In somewhat of a suprise to the staff, she got it.

From that moment on, our lives became a living hell. Nobody I have ever known in the business was as polarizing as Shaun Robinson was at *Access Hollywood*. Right away, she made it clear that Halle Berry, Oprah, Queen Latifah, Jamie Foxx, Denzel, Eddie Murphy, Samuel L. Jackson, Whoopie Goldberg, and Cuba belonged to her. Rob Silverstein and I tried to explain that it didn't work that way, even though she claimed that as an African American she would relate better. Never mind that I had spent twenty years covering football and the NBA. One time I brought *The New York Times* to the set, as usual, and I casually said to Shaun, "There's this great article in the *Times* today; did you see it?" She fired back in a very different voice, "Are you saying an African American doesn't read *The New York Times*?" Then she took me to HR on that and other allegations and it cost me two hefty paychecks for crimes they could never quite describe to me. There are binders of allegations that are collecting dust at NBC. Nobody wants to touch them. The network puts up with her personality quirks. And why not? She was tremendous when the camera went on. But they did have to hire her separate hair and makeup people because she didn't think the staff crew could do her justice. I saw this crap every day and when I began to see other, golden work opportunities—the kind Alec Baldwin had seen before me—the prospect of never working again with Ms. Robinson was a considerable factor. She was briefly married to Darryl Hamilton, a former major league outfielder in Milwaukee. Every time I have him on my radio show, in closing I would say, "I feel your pain, brother." No explanation needed, but it was a knowing laugh.

Meantime, I was being courted by two other women. In violation of every contract I had signed with NBC, I was privately meeting with producer Linda Bell Blue, syndication executive Terry Wood, and other senior suits at Paramount, who wanted me to host a brand-new show called *The Insider*. It was based on the premise that I had access to the stars that no one else could approach. In some ways this was life imitating, well, life. And in other ways it was perception equals reality. I was great at creating Pat's World.

Paramount, the company that owned *ET* and *The Insider,* was dying to get me over there, sooner than later, but there were some big hurdles to navigate. For starters, I was still under contract with *Access* and NBC and forbidden to negotiate or even talk to a competitor. At the same time, Paramount was prohibited to tamper with a signed talent. They got around all these things by arranging several secret meetings at the Bel Air Hotel, over in Las Vegas in the middle of the night, over coffee in some secret place: all so as not to leave a trail, since I still legally belonged to NBC. I felt like I was in a Jason Bourne movie: "He has no past, he has no future." During these protracted secret negotiations with Paramount, I went under the name Pete Zoria, an alias I borrowed from my good friend Glenn Frey of the Eagles. Paramount syndication executive Terry Wood and I had dozens of secret phone conversations ("Terry, it's Pete Zoria") as I was trying to do everything I could to make sure this new show wouldn't turn into another tabloid affair. Over at *Access,* we would watch *ET* and laugh, as they paraded out 800-pound men and anorexic twins who each weighed eighty pounds, wet. If I was going to make the move, I wanted the new show to show some broadcast class. Linda Bell Blue, the executive producer of *Entertainment Tonight* who carried supreme tabloid credentials, assured me and the media that *The Insider* was going to be classy and different. Meantime, she was telling friends that there was no way she would hire me, that I had "too many skeletons" in my closet. At the same time, *her* bosses were throwing in everything but my own butler. As Linda looked on from the sidelines, the Paramount people came up with $4 million a year, two furnished offices with the finest antiques, nearly unlimited vacation, a personal driver 24/7, as many Armani and Gucci suits as I wished (and there were a lot of them), first-class travel, the best suites in the best hotels, and they made it very clear that I would be the star of the show. So much for "too many skeletons."

So, with all the money and all the assurances and filled with greed and grandiosity, I said, yes. NBC was blindsided. Even Rob didn't know. Indeed, the departure caused shock and consternation inside the Peacock Network, especially as I had been contracted to be a host at my fifth Olympics for them in Athens, Greece, in August 2004. In a bit of a last-minute panic to keep me, Jeff Zucker, then the president of NBC, flew me to New York and sat me down with one of those "how do we keep you here" conversations. I said it was already done. Jeff then said something else I didn't listen to: "Never do anything for the money!" Rob Silverstein, arguably my best friend in the business was conflicted, telling NBC "we can't do this show without him." But privately, he was telling associates that I was going to "crash and burn" in no time because of the alcohol.

There was a halfhearted, front-page breach-of-contract suit brought against me by NBC, but the judge threw it out the moment she was told that NBC was counting on me for the Athens Summer Games. In the end, *Access Hollywood* gave me a nice send off, wishing me well with a giant cake that was decorated with "See You in The Fourth Position," a reference to the red-carpet pecking order. They spared me the mandatory security escort out the door and, as I walked out alone, I could hear people crying. I seem to have that effect on people. Instead of being grateful for the experience there and for an exciting journey moving forward, I went home and isolated myself with wine and my computer. I was obsessed with focusing on the negatives and it wasn't long before Shaun Robinson came to mind. My lingering resentments over Shaun were boiling in a sea of red wine and impulsive behavior. Recently, Betsy Hoyt Stephens and her two lovely daughters had come to the NBC Studios for a tour. A couple days earlier, she had run into Shaun at a Prince concert and remarked at how good her hair looked that night. Shaun fired with, "You musta been lookin' at me real good!" and then stormed off the set. Shaun then demanded I meet her in the hallway, where she did one of those wag your finger and move your head like an Egyptian deals, ordering me to get rid of them. I appealed to the show's African-American lawyer, who said they'd better go. So it seemed natural that night to go home and get drunk and fire off my opinions in a farewell e-mail to Ms. Robinson.

Without going into details here, I set forth a litany of what I believed were her character failures, told her how much I thought she was disliked by her colleagues, mocked what I saw as her efforts to have me fired, and told her how easy she'd made it for me to leave the show. My impulsive wine-soaked rant made sense to me, so I pushed SEND and almost immediately Shaun went public with it, reading it out loud at some poor woman's baby shower; then it leaked into the *New York Post*'s "Page Six," which ran it as a headline. Somehow, the glowing parts of my e-mail about how good she was on camera didn't make it to print. It reminded me of something I heard a director say to his assistant director: "I like your work but it's you I can't stand."

Anyway, I later publicly apologized and warned America to count to ten before pushing SEND. Then again, I was trying to clean up an early headache for my future bosses at Paramount. In fact, as the e-mail hit the Internet, I was on a private jet to Sun Valley, California, to visit a buddy who had amassed a large fortune in the soup business. He also owned a winery, so it was a well-suited destination for my state of mind: unlimited wine. One night, I got so drunk, I fell backward down the stairs, smashed my head against a stone wall, and was knocked unconscious. My hosts patched me up and I slept it off and figured that I got away with another one, but those incidents were mounting up. Somehow, I was in denial that I had become just another drunk, a bad one at that. I didn't realize it at the time but I was slowly killing myself as fast as I could.

The first bullet in my emotional suicide weapon was my affair with Betsy Hoyt Stephens. I had met Betsy at a Lakers game in May of 2004 and from that moment, my life pretty much went downhill. In fact, people who knew her at the time warned me, "This woman will take you down." But I didn't listen. I was deep in an alcohol fog. At the time, I thought it was a good idea, but the shame and trouble it brought me, and the shame and embarrassment it brought Linda and Sean, are a debt that can't be paid off.

So, I'm having this affair with this mother of two from Pasadena and as much as we tried to hide it, her husband, Roger, of course, found out. Betsy shrugged this off a little too quickly, I thought at the time. There might have been another early flag when, just after seeing her for a couple weeks, she checked herself into the Betty Ford Clinic to "get her head together."

There are no excuses for my behavior at this point. I was taking *myself* down. Not only was my drinking unmanageable, now my life was unmanageable, sitting at home alone, drinking two to three bottles of wine at night. When you drink alone you don't have to talk to anyone, you don't have to explain yourself. Our marriage was turning thirty years old and while things were at an explainable thirty-year stale point, we didn't argue much and Sean didn't have a clue there was trouble coming. Again, it was all on me and I kept it all to myself, not knowing what the hell I was doing or where this was leading me.

Linda (who had stopped drinking twenty years earlier) was fed up with my daily drinking and, after discovering an X-rated e-mail exchange with Betsy, told me to get out. The marriage was dead, but our combined efforts in raising Sean never wavered. It would turn out to be the hardest (and dumbest) decision I ever made. I went back and forth in my mind, but my ego and the alcohol were thinking for me. My biggest concern was Sean, who loved me unconditionally and put me on the tallest pedestal he could find.

Still, thinking only of myself, I picked Sean up from a lacrosse game and on the way home, I told him that his mother and I were having problems and that I was going to move out "for a while." I will never forget the look on his face. I had blindsided my precious son with the last news a senior in high school with his whole life ahead of him wants to hear. Later that fateful, awful night I told Linda that I was leaving and wanted a divorce. As Sean sat in his room weeping, the woman who had supported me for three decades said plaintively, "All I ever wanted to do, Pat, was to love you." She was sitting on the floor of our bedroom, sobbing and weeping and begging me to work it out and kept saying, "I just don't understand this. I loved you so much." It was the worst night of my life. They didn't deserve what I did to them. The alcohol-fueled bad decision spawned a soul-crushing guilt that will follow me to my grave. From that very moment, my life began to quickly drift downhill and was totally unmanageable.

After Betsy's husband discovered the affair, he would call me every day, almost pleading me to stop. As the days went by, the calls got angrier. I was getting it from all sides. I had literally created my own personal tornado. Betsy would laugh off Roger, who is a very successful businessman and a great father, and seemed blind to his feelings. So was I blind to everybody's, even though many people who knew Betsy in Pasadena, including her friends, were warning me not to get involved with "this woman." But, as with all foolish affairs, I was hooked on the exciting prospect of a new, different life with a woman I thought I was falling in love with. I clearly was not thinking. This is called alcoholism: a tornado racing through families and innocent human beings and taking them all down. I was that tornado.

I moved into a suite at the Chateau Marmont on Sunset Boulevard, and, after Betsy and her husband separated in July, started seeing her a lot more. Meantime, friends of hers continued to tell me, "This woman will bring you down." Even her husband made one final, sad call and said, "Okay, you can have her. Good luck, asshole, she's your problem now." With all this going on, I then jetted off to Athens for my NBC Olympic duties, my last NBC commitment (for now) until I started at *The Insider* at CBS/Paramount. Betsy joined me a couple of days later. Behind me were my family, my home, legal problems for breach of contract, the collateral damage from the Shaun Robinson episode, and gossip-column reports about all of the above.

After a wine-soaked flight, it felt good to arrive on foreign soil to get away from the minefields I had set and I tried as hard as I could to tell myself I was doing the right thing. I lost that argument every time to the little conscience I had left. I was running away with nowhere to go, really. So, I dove into the the task at hand and the excitement that always accompanied the days before the Olympics. It was anything but a romantic trip for Betsy and me, as I spent most of my afternoons on the roof of our hotel soaking up the local wines with my colleagues from NBC. The day usually ended with me passing out in bed: hardly the reward for two people who left marriages and kids behind for some kind of fantasy life. Being selfish is one thing, but fucking everybody over as I was slamming a door behind me, is certainly nothing to be proud of. Meantime, Betsy loved the celebrity life and the perks it brought her. Then she pointed out that if she was going to be a "celebrity girlfriend" she needed money to upgrade her wardrobe for the future social events and red carpets. She suggested $5,000 a month.

After spending as much of my money as she could get her hands on in Athens, Betsy jetted back to the States and I went to work. Every morning, I would dust myself off and eventually I would arrive at work, sober, and professionally deliver the Olympic news to America. I was anchoring seven hours of daytime coverage for the cable networks and then go back to my hotel, eat, sleep, nap, and return for the network late night show. All without drinking. But the moment I was cleared, I sat on my balcony overlooking the melancholy nights of Athens and drank alone. My life was unraveling but I didn't seem to care. I had everything but a soul. Later I returned to a classic book, *Conversations with God*, by Neale Donald Walsch. What he was saying was now making sense: "Your soul doesn't care what you do for a living—and when your life is over, neither will you. Your soul cares only about what you are being while you are doing whatever you are doing."

Meanwhile 6,000 miles away on *ET* Paramount Studios stage 28, carpenters, electricians, and other craftsmen were carefully building a lavish studio set tailored to my every requirement. On September 13, the launch date for my own nationally syndicated show, I would be king of all I surveyed. Alec Baldwin's crystal ball was right. To which the only response was to open another bottle of red wine, and with the sound of wild dogs barking in the lonely Athens night, I joined in to say to nobody in particular, "Cheers." I retrieved a photo of Sean I traveled with, put it on the pillow next to me, and cried myself to sleep. My new "life" had begun.

18

For Whom the Bell Tolls

I would learn, a little too late, that in this life we are powerless over people, places, and things. I had it wrong. There I was, king of my own world, and enjoying the perks of royalty. As I looked over Los Angeles from my compound in fashionable Los Feliz, I could almost touch and see my face, huge, plastered on municipal buses and billboards all over town. In New York City, buses and billboards featured my face as well, but the ego bonus was in Times Square, where my likeness looked down on the bustling crowds. My divorce was amicable and behind me for now as much as it could be, and in Betsy Stephens, outwardly blond, sexy, and out there, I had the ornament I thought I needed. I was love struck. But already I was missing the compass that was Linda O'Brien.

I was driven to work in my black Maserati, wore $3,000 hand-crafted Armani suits with $500 silk ties, and matched them with an extensive collection of gold and silver cuff links mixed with one of my one hundred or so watches. Things. When I arrived at the Paramount lot, I had an exclusive parking space by the front entrance, the choice of two offices, two dressing rooms, and a full staff at my beck and call—an only-in-the-movies collection of people, places, and things. It was everything I had ever dreamed of. I was blinded by the bright lights and the big city, and they, as Jimmy Reed had warned us, had gone to my head.

Fueling that, *The Insider,* which launched in September 2004, was doing great, giving viewers what we originally promised to give them—my supposed unrivaled insight into the celebrity lifestyle, force-feeding them that I was the "man." A multimillion-dollar marketing strategy made sure of that. One of our early shows set the tone. I went shopping with Paris Hilton along Robertson Boulevard in Beverly Hills, home of designer stores, the Ivy restaurant, and lurking paparazzi. The idea was to show the viewer what it was like to live as a celebrity. Paris was at the height of being Paris Hilton, so we were surrounded by roughly thirty paparazzi tripping over each other to capture every moment. The whole scene was mayhem and it made for great television. That she was plugging her book like crazy was irrelevant because, as the insider, I was walking down the street with Paris Hilton and a mob of photographers: heroin for the addicted masses.

The fun was beginning. In October 2004, a few weeks into the first season, I got a call from the great racing driver Mario Andretti asking if I would emcee a charity Formula One race around the streets of Manhattan. Along with Andretti, Paul Newman was the big draw. It took me about twelve seconds to introduce these two icons, and a few weeks later Andretti sent me a $5,000 watch as a thank-you. Things.

Later that fall I was invited to fly to London to spend time with Madonna, who was signing her children's book at the famed London Selfridges department store. I sat at a table with the icon and watched as one overly excited person after another emerged from behind a curtain, usually with hands over the mouth as in "Oh my God, oh my God." Halfway through, Madonna turned to me and said, "I need a gallon of hand sanitizer." This was the beginning of a great media relationship with Madonna. Later that year, I went to London to watch her be inducted into the UK Music Hall of Fame. On the way to the event she wondered if she could navigate the stairs to the stage in her tight dress. I said I wouldn't put money on it. I was right; she had to sidestep up the stairway to get her award. But she looked great. Afterward, she suggested we do a little pub-crawling and she took me to her favorite, the Punch Bowl, in the fashionable Mayfair district. She brought her friend artist Tracey Emin, who is a legend in London for her writings and art. Emin had won just about every art award available and was notable for saying "fuck" on national television and using the word *cunt* a lot in her work and when discussing her work. A wonderful character. The three of us talked and laughed through the night while getting hammered. It was awesome. When I got back to the States with fresh Madonna material, my British friends were just as impressed that I'd drunk with Tracey Emin. Once again we showed the audience that I was the guy in the know.

A few weeks later I walked into the lobby of the Hôtel Plaza Athénée in New York and bumped into Elizabeth Taylor. Our eyes met and she said, "Why, you are Pat O'Brien." I could only reply, "And you're Elizabeth Taylor," my mind going back to the day I saw her on the screen in *Cat on a Hot Tin Roof,* based on Tennessee Williams's play, conveniently about greed, moral decay, superficiality, and mendacity. Perfect.

"Would you mind taking me for a little walk?" she inquired, and without missing a beat I offered her my arm and off we went over to Madison Avenue. We chatted about this and that, I can't remember what, and after about ten minutes or so I delivered her back to the hotel—with not a paparazzo in sight.

Suddenly, like my experiences with George, Paul, and Ringo, my life, or the vision of my life, was flashing in front of me.

Another time, right before a Michael Jackson concert in New York, Elizabeth was coming through a side entrance with her dear friend. I noticed that Michael's zipper was not fully fastened. I said, "Excuse me, Michael, but I'm man enough to tell you that your zipper is not zipped." Taylor laughed and said, "I am glad somebody keeps track of these things."

As wonderful as it was to meet Elizabeth Taylor, my heart skipped a beat when Yoko Ono, John Lennon's widow, agreed to be interviewed. I had seen Paul McCartney at some social event and mentioned that I was meeting her and was rather scared. "Don't be," he counseled. "John was right about her; there is something spiritual, an aura, about her." The morning she arrived in my office in New York, we clicked right away. Paul was right. She does have a gentle, warm, and spiritual quality. Before the interview she said, "You're a big Beatles fan. Did you hate me, too?"—referring to how many fans felt she broke up the "marriage" of Lennon and McCartney. I said, "I won't lie, yes." She appreciated my candor. After our interview we went for a walk around New York. Before she left, she signed a card that we put up on the wall. It said, "Imagine, Yoko Ono." Somebody at *The Insider* stole it.

To cap things off, I got an exclusive interview with Barbra Streisand, who, up until then, rarely spoke to the press. I was warned that she was difficult, and we waited several hours for them to get her lighting correct, but it was worth the wait. Contrary to all the crap previously written about her in the tabloids, she was engaging and charming.

When she starred with Dustin Hoffman in *Meet the Fockers,* she and Dustin and I did one of the funniest interviews ever, and it got so out of hand, their publicists confiscated some outtakes when Barbra was trying to say "country" and she paused after "count . . . ," and Dustin said, "Did you just say 'cunt'?" The three of us laughed so hard, they had to stop the interview. I gather those tapes were magnetically eliminated from any future YouTube appearance.

Later I gave Barbra the name Mother Focker and it caught on. A few weeks later at Rob Lowe's fortieth birthday party, she walked up to me and playfully slapped me in the face and said, "Mother Focker? You focking kidding me?" She loved it. Barbra Streisand is a jewel that keeps getting brighter with age, and she has always been loyal to me. It might be the solid Democrat inside me.

About the time Christmas rolled around that year, the show was doing great and I was reaping the benefits of television visibility. I was asked to fly to Boston and read "Yes, Virginia, There Is a Santa Claus" with the Boston Pops. But that wasn't the highlight of that night. When I walked offstage, I got a call from the president of NYU to tell me that Sean had been admitted to the prestigious Clive Davis Institute of Recorded Music. I started to cry. This was Sean's dream, and he had done it on his own despite my efforts to make a few calls to everybody I knew in New York. They had, one by one, politely said, "Those days are over"—he gets in on his own merit. And he did.

Meantime, *The Insider* was doing well, especially in the major markets, so Paramount spent a fortune flying everyone to New York for a Christmas party. I was in sync with the show's executive producer, Linda Bell Blue, who had this brilliant ability to make money for the organization by exploiting Hollywood, but with a management and personality default mechanism that always included putting fear into the heads of everybody who worked for her. I arrived at the party, held at the pricey Shun Lee Chinese eatery on the Upper West Side, with Betsy on my arm and an invitation for what was called the wedding of the century—the upcoming nuptials between Donald Trump and model Melania Knauss in January 2005—in my pocket. As we walked into the party, everybody applauded. I felt as if I had arrived as an insider, and that everybody was grateful to be working on the show. This was about the last time, however. The glossy evening turned into a bad comedy with the behavior of our commanding general. We watched, slack jawed, as she publicly took down a tabloid producer named DJ and reduced him to tears. (In an ironic twist of wonderful fate, DJ later replaced her.) Then, with one eye open and one eye closed, she made an incoherent, rambling speech to the assembled throng of executives and producers. None of the "regular" workers were allowed into one of Linda's big events. Normally a good speaker, she was so tipsy she could barely stand. Her speech sounded something like this:

"I handpickedsh eeesh and every one of you. I know all yoursh skillsh and talentsh and thatsh why you are here thish evening. I know the namesesh of your kidsh. I and I alone handpickshed you for thish."

I looked around the room and everybody was trying to pretend nothing was happening because one wrong look at Linda and you were gone. But she was too hammered to notice this time, anyway.

After she put down the microphone, her husband, Steve, grabbed her and took her back to the hotel. I watched her knees buckle as she tried to make it to the door. It was a sign of things to come. Linda Bell Blue was the female Jekyll and Hyde, and there was never a warning as to which one you were talking to. One time I casually said that I had met with my old friend Les Moonves, who was president and CEO of CBS, the parent owner of *Entertainment Tonight* and *The Insider*. She put her face about six inches from mine and said with an anger that seemed to rise up from hell, "Always remember, Les is not the boss. I am."

Actually she was more like a warden, always preferring glass-walled offices to keep an eye on everybody. Some people never left their desks even for lunch for fear Linda would notice. One valued employee suddenly quit out of nowhere and died a couple months later, unrelated to Linda, I'd guess, but they said he died of complications of stress. I had one former employee tell me he believed he got cancer from working for her and would provide a doctor's opinion on that. I passed. But her leadership style was the definition of a hostile environment. At *The Insider* they even had a designated closed-door space called "the cry room." More often than not I'd walk by somebody's desk and the person would be sobbing, and when I asked why, he or she would just shake his or her head and nod toward Linda's guard tower.

I had, I thought, a great, open relationship with her until, one day, feeling comfortable in my own skin as the insider, I made a joke at her expense. She pulled me into a hallway and said, "Patrick, you never make fun of the executive producer. Do you understand that?" Ten bipolar minutes later, she would call me in and hug me and say something like "How would you like a new suit? Mommy will take care of you." I'm thinking to myself, *Maybe I should have asked for ten million.*

She had maybe one friend on the staff, and I'm not even sure if that was two-way. Her idea of morale building was to bring in breakfast and then tell everybody, "Mommy loves you all. Now let's get to work."

At such impromptu affairs she would force Mary Hart and me to make a speech to pump up the crowd. There weren't enough words invented to make everybody like her. Even though she had somehow convinced her bosses that she and only she knew what the audience wanted to watch. She was right just enough to stay in power. I kind of liked her as a crazy genius and never, ever thought she'd turn on me. While everybody around me lived in fear of her, I did not. After all, I was the guy delivering her vision of what Americans wanted to see when they got home. During one of my appearances on Jimmy Kimmel's show, he put it all together and introduced me with "Here he is, the Cronkite of Crap, Pat O'Brien."

As it was my first Christmas away from my family, I tried to keep things as normal for Sean as possible. Sean hated Betsy, so I tried to keep them apart as much as possible. I spent part of Christmas with Betsy and her two kids but made damn sure Sean knew he was more important to me than anything else. We always had a father-son tradition that we would watch *White Christmas* and then I would read him *The Polar Express* by Chris Van Allsburg, complete with sound effects. As in, "See, Sean, here comes the train. Choo, choo, choo." To this day, we do not miss that Christmas tradition.

The holidays went as smoothly as they could, given the revised domestic arrangements, and when it was over, Betsy and I began to look forward to the wedding of the century: the Trump wedding in Palm Beach. Once again I was the real-life insider, on a guest list that included the Clintons, Muhammad Ali, Michael Douglas, Catherine Zeta-Jones, improbably Prince Charles, Prince Albert of Monaco, and Luciano Pavarotti. I had known Donald for years, first encountering him when he bought into the ill-fated US Football

League during the 1980s. He was a great, outspoken guy with a lot of money. I interviewed him a few times, and when he filed for bankruptcy I called him to commiserate. A few months later I was at one of his casinos in Atlantic City, and his casino manager came over and told me, "You're on Donald's short list because you were one of the only people who called him when he was broke and he really valued that." We had him on my late-night Olympic show, and we would chat from time to time, and he would always take my call. Then he suddenly became DONALD TRUMP and we had a useful relationship: he would use me for publicity and I would use him to show people that I could actually get to him. This relationship was made in ratings heaven. One day he called me and said, "You won't believe what I just bought . . . the Empire State Building!" I had tremendous access to one of the most powerful people in New York City. I liked that.

Naturally my show, *The Insider,* milked his wedding for all it was worth. And it was worth a lot: a million-dollar ring (I know, Donald, it was a million and a half), a million-dollar dress, and a million-dollar crowd, which now included everybody Donald could get to say, "Yes, I'll be there."

Betsy and I flew down to Florida on a private jet and at the airport Donald's Rolls-Royce Phantom with a chauffeur was waiting to take us to a swanky Palm Beach hotel. Then the driver just handed me the keys and said, "Here, Donald wants you to have this for the week." We had full access to Donald, Melania, and all the pomp and circumstance that was part of the script. While it was party, party, party, I was still working, so I had to be on my game. That meant staying away from drinking. With an international who's who in the congregation I didn't want to be making a fool of myself. With so much expensive drink available, it was, however, just too tempting. An interview I did with Katie Couric was scrapped as Linda Bell Blue thought Katie was too tipsy for our chat to be aired. It was that kind of occasion. Katie wasn't alone: everybody was fucked-up. It was a kind of a "get out of the public eye free" affair. And we all took advantage of it.

The ceremony was beautiful: just thirty minutes, Melania in a Christian Dior gown with a thirteen-foot train and a sixteen-foot veil. We all gasped. There were thirty seamstresses, a hundred limo drivers, and forty-five chefs. It smelled good, thanks to the ten thousand flowers flown in. And, of course, Donald did his own hair. He looked like, well, Donald Trump.

Leaving the church was like entering an Oscar-night red carpet: more flashbulbs than I've ever seen, and hundreds and hundreds of onlookers, tasting a sense of royalty, even if it was store-bought.

On the wedding day itself, the celebrations went into another gear and I got into the spirit. We were at a table with Frank and Kathie Lee Gifford, Billy Joel and his wife, and other luminaries. I made a complete ass of myself, even stealing a gold fork from the table. Later Donald confirmed to me that just about everybody did. My drunken behavior was so outrageous that the Trump people came over to me and said, "Pat, it's time to go." For the first time I was embarrassed about my behavior, but when Donald was asked about it during a subsequent TV interview he diplomatically shrugged it off, saying that I was just having a good time. Right, and denial is a river in northeastern Africa.

For the next few days I was a wreck, unable to function. My meltdown could not have come at a worse time. For the previous three weeks I had been hyping the Trump wedding on the show. While I managed to fly back to Los Angeles, it was downhill from then on. I remember sitting in my dressing room feeling as sick as I have ever been in my life. Linda Bell Blue walked in and asked, "Can you do this?" I said I could, but before I recorded the voice-over for the wedding show, I was driven to see my doctor in Beverly Hills. I was so dehydrated from drinking that he had to put an IV drip in my arm. Miraculously it stabilized me sufficiently so that I could go back to the studio and record the show . . . but I had missed the first feed. That was not lost on the folks at *Extra* and *Access Hollywood*, who called the tabloids and wondered out loud if I was too drunk or still too hungover to do the show. Little did I know that my old buddies were coming after me.

At work no one said anything. But they knew better and so did I. For the first time, I was getting scared. The demons hadn't caught me yet, but they were getting close. I went home and drank myself to sleep.

19

Let's Go Crazy

Within days I was back in the saddle, covering the awards season and big premieres: king of the red carpet, even if by default. I was doing the job I had always dreamed of and living the lifestyle any man would dream of. Deep down, I was trying to figure out, was I chasing my ego or was it chasing me? In March 2005 I was to take my first vacation in a year, but first Betsy and I were flown to a Paramount party in New York to celebrate the success of *The Insider*. All the important advertisers were there, along with television executives and backslappers happy that their vision of a new entertainment show was working. The Paramount people, led by Terry Wood, made sure I had my own supply of expensive Silver Oak red wine at my beck and call. I drank it like water, and at that moment I didn't feel as if anything could set me back. I was dead wrong. The train hit me and I never saw it coming.

Feeling invincible, my ego suitably massaged, the following morning I took Betsy for brunch in Greenwich Village. We chatted with Bono in the restaurant and then moved on to a big center table where we were joined by some of Bet's friends. About halfway into the Bloody Marys and the wine, a bindle of cocaine appeared and I grabbed it. Out of nowhere. Maybe this was the first real clue that I was, indeed, an addict because my alcoholic and addictive brain didn't think twice. I hadn't done cocaine since 1983, but the voice inside me didn't think there was much harm in this. However, as

F. Scott Fitzgerald once observed, "First you take a drink, then the drink takes a drink, then the drink takes you." When we left, we were mobbed by the paparazzi, who had been there to mob Bono, but who was counting? They took hundreds of pictures as we jumped into our chauffeur-driven, black SUV with tinted windows.

So far so civilized. Big shot in New York City. Check. It was barely noon, but, feeling no pain, we decided to go to the famed Félix in SoHo and have a few more drinks. The mood inside was all party and joy. Then the day began to rapidly unravel. We ran into a couple of single women who seemed in a party mood and began chatting and drinking and doing more cocaine. By the time we all got back to the Four Seasons suite we were staying in, I was as high as the space shuttle and ready for anything. The drink and the drugs had completely taken over, and even if I'd wanted to surrender, I was too fucked-up to do anything but go for more. It was now only two o'clock in the afternoon. The last thing I remember was ordering multiple bottles of Cristal champagne. At $350 a bottle, it should be noted that I never, ever drank champagne. As more cocaine mysteriously arrived and the champagne flowed . . . somewhere between the girls and the coke and the party, my brain put the brakes on. I blacked out. My control center had blown a fuse. The last thing I remember was Betsy screaming at me, "Pat! You've got to get sober."

The next thing I know, I'm back in California lying on my bed in the Los Feliz home upstairs bedroom. I was fully dressed, and empty bottles of Silver Oak cabernet were on the nightstand. No Betsy. This was one party she skipped. But there was quite the crowd. It was St. Patrick's Day 2005, and while I was used to being in a crowd on St. Patty's Day with a drink in my hand, this crowd was not celebrating. Standing over me were my agent, Abel Lezcano; Linda Bell Blue, who was wearing a fake "I'm on your side" smile; Terry Wood, head of programming for Paramount; John Nogawski, president of CBS Television Distribution; and my attorney, Ernie Del.

I honestly had no idea what was going on. The first words spoken to me were by Ernie, who jolted me awake with "Pat, there's this tape on the Internet. It sounds like your voice." Then Terry Wood started screaming, "We have to preserve the franchise. Make him listen to it. We have to preserve the franchise. Make him listen to it right now!"

Now, remember, I had just missed two days of my life I'll never get back, and I had absolutely no clue what was going on at this moment. The last thing I remember was having a good time as a single man with money in New York.

I've pieced together that day with the help of some of the people who saw me, Betsy's version, and more than a few tabloid reports. The only hard evidence is the tape itself, and, yes, there was my famous voice calmly planning a long night of sex, drugs, and rock and roll. I also know this: somehow I got the phone number of one of the girls and left a voice-mail message for the ages: "Let's just fucking have sex and drugs and fucking go crazy. You're so fucking sexy, I want to fucking go crazy with you. You're so fucking hot. Let's do it. Let's get some hookers and cocaine."

I think you get the picture. Again, to this day I have no memory of this, and to this day no history of this extreme public display, other than that I made a general fool of myself. I've had fun, but this seems to have been an all-timer. Later I would learn that we all went to Scores, the infamous New York strip club, where (according to my credit card bill) I spent $8,000. Pictures show us going to the famed Elaine's bar, where one tabloid account said I "looked like a zombie." Apparently some altercation occurred between Betsy and another couple in the Four Seasons' bar, where she reportedly threw a drink in someone's face. There were no hookers. There was no sex. Nobody got hurt. Nobody got laid. As scandals go, it now seems pretty lame. Although, as Charlie Sheen later told me, "That was an excellent effort, my man."

But at this very moment, there was nothing funny about it.

So I'm pretending to listen to the tape (I have never heard the entire version), and I look over and Chris, my longtime driver, and my housekeeper were frantically stuffing clothes into a suitcase.

I was so messed up that none of it made any sense. I looked over at Ernie for help, and he calmly said, "Pat, we have a bed for you in rehab."

Rehab? I quickly replied, "I'm not going to rehab." Abel and Ernie, my only friends in the room, both said the same thing: "It's time." Meantime, I'm still trying to figure out how I got home from New York, who these women were, and that, without any details except I was going to rehab, I was fucked. In my mind, I was done. Finished. But I was too confused and sick to sort it out. I would soon have plenty of alone time. As I was led out of my house, the last thing I said to Terry Wood was "That tape, that's not me." It was true. It might have been my voice, but it bore no relationship to the Pat O'Brien I had been living as all these years. But the cruel fact emerged: it was me, the 2005 version. Still bewildered, dazed, and drunk, I got into my SUV and Chris drove me to Las Encinas Hospital in Pasadena. On my way to the hospital all I could think about was my son, Sean. How would I explain all this to a young man who had me on a solid daddy pedestal? I started to cry. I began weeping. I was crying so hard, I couldn't catch my breath. What would I tell my son? The first person I called, however, was the only person I wanted to talk to at that moment: my ex-wife, Linda. All she said when I told her I was being admitted into rehab was "Thank God. Thank God, Pat." With that, we rolled quietly through the streets of Los Angeles to parts unknown. I had taken the first positive step to my new life.

Las Encinas Hospital is a hundred-year-old facility that is more of a mental hospital than an alcohol treatment facility. As we pulled up, my first thought was I might be overdressed for this place. It looked menacingly like a place for crazy people, and there I was, its newest customer. It was not exactly Hotel California, but I was reminded of Glenn Frey's chilling lyric "You can check out anytime you want, but you can never leave."

I was still shaky as they escorted me into the admitting room. All of a sudden I was alone. I still hadn't talked to my son, and all I could think about was how I'd let him down. I had no idea what was in store for me. Nothing in my charmed life had prepared me for this. My body was numb. My mind was racing. Every emotion in every book was taking over: fear, shame, guilt, and anger. I was cut off from the world, and nothing in my life at that moment seemed manageable. I was, for the first time, not in control. The swagger was in a distant past.

After about an hour of this rapid self-evaluation the door opened, and in walked Dr. Drew Pinsky, who was the director of their inpatient detox and rehab. Drew and I were friends. I had been on his popular radio show, *Loveline*, many times, and he was a regular at my annual Christmas bash at my home. He was carrying a thick, white binder with my name on it. My initial feeling was "Oh, great, a friend," but to him I was just another patient. He could certainly see that I was a complete mess, but he methodically put me through all pertinent questions: Were my parents alcoholic? Had I ever considered suicide? Next of kin? And so on. Years later Drew told me that what stood out during that conversation was my description of my childhood. Specifically, riding alone in the backseat of my dad's car, tethered to nothing and bouncing around as he drove drunk, maniacally navigating small, bumpy roads in Iowa. We are our past.

I asked him if I could have my own room, and he said, "No, not here." And that was it. Next stop, the infirmary, where my blood pressure and vitals were recorded. I failed every test. My body was nearly shut down. As I went through this humiliating process, I noticed a homeless-looking guy on a nearby couch, who would stare into space and then suddenly scream out loud. My first thought was *I want my mommy.*

The nurse said they would give me something to calm me down and then send me to my room. What I needed was a drink. She said that I should take one of these and one of those and sit on that couch while they found me a room. I followed orders, and suddenly I was sitting next to the homeless-looking guy on the couch and then I fell into a deep sleep. Suddenly this giant dragon was chasing me and shooting fire from its mouth. As it got close, I screamed as loud as I could. I had apparently been given the same medication as the screaming guy next to me. When I awoke, I was told that I would be here for nine days to allow my body to detox and then be sent to a drug rehabilitation center. Like a prisoner, I started doing the math in my head on when I'd get out. I figured I'd be here nine days and then, like new, sent back to my job and my house and my life.

After a couple of days I was put in a cabin outside the main hospital. Ironically it was the cabin once occupied by W. C. Fields, the most famous drunk in the world. As I put my bag on my bunk, I was reminded of an old bit from another actor who always played a drunk, Henny Youngman. He once said, "You know, there's a romance sometimes of being the town drunk. But, New York City?" Years later, Ray Kelly, the commissioner of the NYPD, told me, "Pat, the day you stopped drinking in my city was the best day of my life."

I was drugged up, dopey, and barely coherent. After picking up my meds later that day, I walked outside to go back to my cabin. By now the drugs were taking effect and I could barely shuffle. I started in a walk, then a shuffle, and now was about to crawl. My body felt like Jell-O. Then, in a terrific cloudburst, the heavens opened right above my head. I grabbed a pole for support but could only slide down it into mud. Dressed in a robe, pajamas, I was soaking wet, lying in the mud, the rain drumming on my head. I thought to myself, *How did this happen to me?* Then I started crying and screaming, eventually crawling my way through the mud back to my room, where I collapsed on the bed and sobbed myself to sleep.

The routine at Las Encinas was wake up, eat, therapy sessions, meds, more meds, eat, and curfew time. I cannot remember eating because the food was about ten notches below the Wednesday menu in high school . . . and I was so emotionally drained and physically sick, the thought of what they passed off as food nauseated me even more. During the first few group therapy sessions, all I could do was whimper and cry. I couldn't handle it. Then one day Bob Forrest, one of the counselors, took me into his office and sat me down. "Who won World War Two?" he asked. I said, "The Allied forces," and he said no: "Japan won because they surrendered. If you don't surrender to your disease, you're fucked. By surrendering, Japan did just fine."

I later realized that my nine days at Las Encinas was simply to stabilize my body before I went into full-scale rehab at Promises in Mar Vista, California, which advertises that it's "halfway between Beverly Hills and the Pacific Ocean." Actually it is halfway between hell and the entrance of hell. It's not exactly the "posh celebrity rehab" you read about. That one is in Malibu. This one is a stone's throw away from bad schools, crack houses, lonely Laundromats, and cheap liquor stores. It consisted of two buildings; one, a stately looking 1940s California house with a comforting porch and hardwood floors. Your rich grandmother would live there. The other building was about an inch away from being in a trailer park where your drunken uncle would live. I was placed in the other building.

Foolishly, I asked for my own room, but I was quickly learning I was no longer in charge. I was put into a dark, lifeless room in the back with a guy who had been accused of multiple sex crimes, money laundering, and so on, and a judge had "sentenced" him here until they figured out what to do with him.

I was desperately trying to wrap my head around my new life with little or no freedom, no cell phone, no television, no computer, and few visitors. We had to be escorted every time we went outside, and if we wanted to walk across the street to "Grandma's house" we needed two approvals and an escort. I couldn't imagine where in that neighborhood they thought we'd escape to, but that was the routine. I was kind of partial to limos and red carpets, so this took some getting used to.

In more ways than one, my experience at Promises was more surreal than promising. My voice mail had gone viral, and it seemed everybody was talking about it. Paparazzi were parked anywhere and everywhere they could get some piece of the story. Since Betsy was mentioned in the voice mail during the "threesome" request, she and her family were hounded every time they walked outside. Somebody at *Access Hollywood* gave the tabloids my home address in hopes they could get a shot of my ex-wife or son leaving the gated community. National newscasts were leading with the news with my arrival in rehab. Once I walked by a television and on the screen they were showing pictures of the war in Iraq and the crawl below said, "Pat O'Brien enters a California rehab." I walked by someone on the single pay phone in the facility and heard the patient say, "You're not going to believe who's in here." Helicopters flew overhead. Black SUVs with tinted windows parked outside the place and inside were the photographers hoping for a picture. There were cheers, I was later told, inside my competitors' newsrooms, hoping they had dealt me and especially Linda Bell Blue a blow. The cheers were especially loud at *Extra,* whose executive producer, a Linda Bell Blue wannabe, told confidants she had helped get the voice mail on the Internet. Apparently the woman I called had a friend at *Extra* and it went from there. Then again, I got myself into this with the first call. When that week's tabloids came out, the whispers went to shouting. In the *National Enquirer* (ironically once run by Betsy's father), the headline was "Pat O'Brien's Sex and Coke Scandal." Inside, their story contained seventeen insane allegations and two that were true. The two true ones were that I was Pat O'Brien and that I made that call.

It was all too crazy to even imagine. X-rated e-mails and photos I had sent to Betsy turned up in one tabloid, courtesy of, she said, her husband and a computer-savvy friend, who leaked them and tucked them away in a safe in New York City, for what I don't know. Meantime, some of my "friends" at *Access Hollywood* were offering damaging and horrible quotes attributed to me that were actually said by the people who leaked them. Everybody seemed to have a story, but none of them held up. Yet, they were printed and tossed around as fact. It was fucked-up. I was, ironically, getting an insider's view of a scandal.

Meantime, inside the rehab compound, we could listen to Howard Stern every morning playing the voice mail over and over and over and over, and we would laugh along as he and his crew would break down every aspect of the sordid audiotape I still couldn't remember making. I thought to myself, *This would be really, really funny if it weren't me.* But it was me. I can't blame Howard—it was great radio. The first time I saw Howard on a red carpet when I got out, he shouted, "You are my fucking hero." The whole deal was a perfect tabloid story also for *The Insider,* which it later became.

On the other side of this, I got encouraging, loving notes from old friends Arnold Schwarzenegger and Maria Shriver, wishing me well and offering to come visit. The GE super-CEO, Jack Welch, wrote a note that said, "Be well, your friends are with you all the way and you can count Suzy and I in the front row. You will be better than ever. Love you, Jack."

Matthew Perry dropped by unannounced and brought me lunch. Michael J. Fox, who had once been a favorite of the tabloids, told me to simply "fuck it and breathe." Donald Trump weighed in: "Hold your head up high, pal, you'll be bigger than ever, trust me."

Kevin Costner told me, "It's not what you did that matters, it's how you get back up from it." My friends from South Dakota didn't desert me either. Over the next few months I got calls of encouragement from the state's former senator Tom Daschle. Tom Brokaw called me to say, "Lie low for a year or so."

At some point during my forty-day rehab Linda Bell Blue visited me, bringing e-mails and letters of support from viewers. She couldn't have been nicer, reassuring me that everything was going to be okay. She would hope so—they were still paying me $72,000 a week to get well enough and come back as host of *The Insider.* Nothing would get in the way of Linda's show.

I had been in Promises for about four days when my keepers allowed Sean to visit me. We were directed to go out into the grassy area in the back, where we sat face-to-face. As difficult as it surely was for him, for me it was the saddest thing I've ever had to do as a parent. Sean and I have always been close, and he looked up to me with immeasurable loyalty and love. I could see his world had been taken away, too, if only momentarily. I was gentle, but honest, and told him the truth about what had happened. As for the tabloids, I said, until you read it in *The New York Times* don't believe a word they say. As I spoke, his bottom lip began to quiver, and he just sat there in stunned silence. A single tear came down his cheek, which he wiped away with a shaky hand. I had never before felt so much shame and guilt in my entire life. Watching my son sit there in disbelief and shake, it all began to sink in. I had raised him to love and respect me, and now this. Just as I was trying to explain myself further, a counselor came over and said that our visiting time was over. I pleaded for more time, but the counselor was insistent and Sean had to leave, our conversation unfinished, the reasons behind my behavior swinging in the space between. I went back to my room, which had a narrow view onto the street. I saw Sean get into his car, staring straight ahead. He just sat there, occasionally wiping away the tears rolling down his cheeks. From across the street and through a window, I was looking at the destructive consequence of alcoholism, and it was emotionally killing my own son. The following week Sean and his mother came for family day, where you try to unravel and explain what had happened. When I asked Sean how he felt, he replied, "I feel like you just said, 'Fuck you,' to your entire family."

One night, my counselor came into my room and announced, "There's somebody here to pick you up." Confused, I walked outside, and a weathered-looking guy in a beat-up car was sitting waiting for me. "Hi," he said matter-of-factly, "I'm Bob." Bob was an alcoholics' savior. A former drug addict turned lawyer and biker, Bob was well-known for helping anybody and everybody who needed help. He was a tireless champion for those who suffered. His only payback was that we go to meetings and trust in the program. I got in and we drove to a law office in Beverly Hills. Inside were a lot of familiar faces, men I had covered on the red carpets, musicians who had created the sound tracks of my life, actors, lawyers, Oscar winners, Emmy winners, and so on. But inside this room, every Monday night, we were all alike, with souls in common as alcoholics, discovering the meaning of recovery. Bob Timmons was a gift from God, and as I left that meeting, I wondered to myself why every meeting couldn't be as fulfilling as that one. Despite the level of talent and genius in the room, the atmosphere was not self-centered, but was one of caring and forgiving and learning how to navigate through the disease. I have no idea how I landed there, but this room of focus and honesty would eventually save my life.

As the days ticked by, I started to make a lot of friends at Promises, and we all made the best of our time together. Our main activity was smoking. In between smoking, we attended group sessions, and at night we were bused to local recovery meetings. We were all watched closely as we sat in the back of these meetings looking, no doubt, like the newcomers that we were. One night we drove by a newsstand and somebody pointed out, "Hey, Pat, there you are!" Sure enough, I was on the cover of two tabloids staring back at our white van. As the days turned into weeks, I began to loathe my time at Promises. It was humiliating and embarrassing, especially for a guy with my size of an ego and attitude.

Rehab is a lesson in routine and structure more than anything else. Get up, get meds, eat breakfast, go to group, smoke, lunch, smoke, go to group, speaker, smoke, nightly meetings, smoke, meds, lights out, and worry yourself to sleep. We also had chores. Mine were always to clean up the bathrooms and toilets, which I began to take pride in.

In one afternoon's session, I heard a very inspiring speaker. I called Betsy when I got my "phone time" to talk about what I learned. "That," she said, "is the savvy computer guy who helped Roger hack into my computer."

My good behavior enabled me to graduate to the big house, and I had a pleasant bedroom with a good roommate. Everything we had was searched every day for drugs or alcohol. It was mildly irritating and more amusing, as many of us would figure out more ways to get more meds and trade them like baseball cards.

I had a little drama there as one day I developed a terrible fever. Now, trying to get a doctor in rehab to believe your story is almost impossible, let alone trying to simply get a doctor. As a result of my not having a doctor, my fever went up and up until one night I got out of bed to go to the bathroom and fainted. My head hit the hardwood floor I had cleaned that day. Next thing I knew, I was in the back of an ambulance on the way to a hospital, where they said, yes, you have a fever. I survived.

Meantime, I was getting handwritten notes from Katie Couric and Diane Sawyer asking me to be a guest on *Today* and *Good Morning America* when I got out. Linda Bell Blue would have none of that, and neither would Terry Wood, programming head of Paramount. They had their own ideas. The entire time I was there, they were holding me mentally hostage about whether I'd get my job back. Terry arrived one day with a written list of questions that sounded like Mad Libs as she went through them one by one. Questions like "Are you cured?" I felt sorry for her. She was following orders.

After forty days I was glad to get out. I had been forty days without a drink, so technically I was sober. Did I feel that I had conquered my inner demons? I told myself that I had, but I was deceiving myself— and everyone else. When I left, Betsy picked me up in my red Maserati, and like Bonnie and Clyde we peeled out of there and went directly to the Bel-Air hotel for a nice lunch. At the next table was my great supporter Jack Welch. It felt good to be back in the real world. More important, I felt good about myself and had no interest in drinking again. I thought. Now I realize that all I learned at Promises was how to clean toilets and how to chain-smoke. That's what $40,000 got me.

Back in the free world my life had changed considerably. Every time I turned on the radio I heard some reference to my scandal, everyone delighting in attacking me as some low-life scumbag. Humiliation was now heaped upon humiliation. *The Insider* also hired for me a "sober companion" to live with me and keep an eye on me day and night. The sober-companion business is a cottage industry that was built from the ground up based on other people's fears and weaknesses. These guys make up to $5,000 a week, get to live in big houses, go to premieres, and take first-class flights with rock stars, movie stars, and various celebrities. It is nice work if you can get it. They soon go away, but the problem is, they never take the alcoholism with them.

It was now late April, and Paramount had decided that a condition of my return to air was that I had to pass the Dr. Phil test. *The Insider* was a Paramount show, as was *Dr. Phil,* so it didn't take a rocket scientist to figure out that I was not going to share my scandal and alcoholism with Katie or Matt or Oprah or Diane, but with Dr. Phil. The design all along was to keep this story away from everybody else and keep it "in-house." But, I was told, it was not a "sure thing." I had to go over to Phil's house and let him decide if I was ready and able to go back to work. It was, basically, an audition to determine if I was sober or maybe even ratings worthy.

So I duly drove to Dr Phil's grotesquely palatial Beverly Hills mansion and presented myself for inspection. I was nervous and thinking that if I didn't pass this ridiculous and unnecessary muster, my broadcasting career would be over.

I was shown to his backyard patio, and after about fifteen minutes, Dr. Phil arrived in his tennis whites. He had just come from playing tennis on his private court. He was sweating.

I obviously knew Dr. Phil well, as his studio was right next to mine on the Paramount lot and our sons attended the same school and were on all the sports teams together. Phil and I seemed to be the only parents who attended every game no matter how busy we were. But this was a different kind of game and there we were face-to-face. He looked concerned.

He opened with "How old are you?" I told him that I was fifty-seven.

"Well, fifty-seven," he mused, rubbing his still-sweaty chin. "So if I don't decide to do this, then you'll never work again."

I was speechless, for the first time in my life acutely aware that my destiny was in someone else's hands. I told him that I was scared and remorseful and worried about my son. All true, but he didn't seem to be listening. He seemed to be enjoying being judge and jury, having the power of TV life or death over another guy. He kept saying, "When you leave here, I'm going to pick up the phone and say yes or no to Terry Woods." From that moment, I didn't hear another word he said, although I was smart enough to figure out he knew as much about alcoholism as I did and, as it turned out, less. I was waiting for somebody to come from behind the bushes and say this was all a joke; that's how amateurish and ridiculous it was.

After about forty-five minutes of excruciating agony for me he very deliberately walked into his office, dramatically put his hand on the telephone, and said, "I am going to make a decision right after you walk out of the door, and I am going to tell Terry yes or no. Someone will be in touch with you. Thank you for coming over." I can still hear that fake Texas drawl.

I walked out, numb and needing a drink. About ten minutes later, Terry Wood called and said that, yes, Dr. Phil Medicine Man would put me on his show for a full-hour confessional.

They were certainly going to make me pay for my sins and had programmed my life this way: one hour of a prime-time Dr. Phil special and then an appearance on Dr. Phil's syndicated show. For years I had been reporting on celebrity meltdowns; now the tables were turned and I was not only extremely ill, but, apparently, ratings gold for Paramount.

So now, with Dr. Phil's blessing, I was able to go back on the Paramount lot and to my job. When I got there, I was told that my entire first day back would be taped for the special. So there I was, walking into my own newsroom with everybody staring at me and two or three cameras recording all the drama. Linda Bell Blue had gathered the entire staff of about two hundred people and told me to

make a speech. I did, with yet another sincere apology. I was starting to wonder what the fuck I was apologizing to these people for,
but I played along. Then we went upstairs to my office for a photo
session with Linda and other producers. Every time I spoke, I would
look over and somebody was crying. Others, such as Lisa Summers
Haas, our head of publicity, were rude and treated me like a circus
animal. Lisa was one of the Bell Blue lieutenants who was known
for locking herself in her office and weeping in frustration over her
job of trying to justify the show to the press. Not once did anybody
ask me how I was feeling. Some producers would have nothing to do
with me until they were sure it was okay with Linda.

My loyal hair and makeup staff, Joy and Ing, were stunned by all
this. I was single, with my girlfriend, in all of this, and the worst
thing I could be accused of was doing coke and making a public ass
out of myself. Joy and Ing could see that a different Pat was standing
before them when I made my comeback speech. As Joy said later,
"Pat was zombielike, disorientated just like a guy picking himself
up after falling from the top of a mountain into heavy snow. He
wasn't the Pat we knew and loved. That Pat was showy, fun, intelligent, with a touch of arrogance and unpredictability, but with a big
heart. He had somehow flatlined. I'm not sure if it was the prescription drugs or remorse or both. It was scary to see him so different
from what his personality truly is."

The interview was held at my Los Feliz home. Dr. Phil and Terry
Wood and Linda Bell Blue brought an army. No fewer than fifty
people descended on my property and set up cameras and monitors
and a huge craft-services display. I was upstairs in the same bedroom
where these people intervened on me . . . trying to get my thoughts
together. Before the interview with Phil, they brought in my cohost
from New York, Lara Spencer, to interview me in the same bedroom
where I had my intervention. I have no memory of what we talked
about. Then my loyal makeup crew, Joy and Ing, gave me big hugs
and down I went.

I was just out of rehab and still pumped full of prescription drugs to keep my body stable. I was in no shape to face a national audience. I staggered downstairs and there it all was. They had started a huge fire in my fireplace even though it was a beautiful spring day, and all of Dr. Phil's people were dressed in black. His orders were always for them to be in the dark, wearing dark, so he could not see them or hear them or make eye contact with them. The doctor's office was sacred ground.

The minute I sat down to gather my thoughts, Terry Wood, red faced and dripping of fear, said, "You've got to be strong, you've got to be confident, you've got to save the show."

Meantime, Dr. Phil had yet to even say hello. He was studying his notes, which I laughingly told myself must have had the words *hookers* and *coke* and *fuck me* and *threesome* neatly typed somewhere.

So the cameras rolled and Dr. Phil asked me a question and I started to answer with "Well, everyone who has ever worked with me—" He cut me off sharply, sternly telling me that my response was from the ego. "You can't let your ego answer," said the man who has a camera poised above his parking spot at Paramount so that he can see if anyone dares to leave a car in his place. I tried to finish my answer, but he kept going, and I was thinking, *God, if this is what the first question is like, what is the rest of the hour going to be?* During my confessional I was forced to listen to portions of the tape, and backstage the producer was shouting, "Are his hands shaking? Get a close-up." People later told me that Dr. Phil's son, who was producing this madness, kept screaming at people and was begging out loud for me to break down.

I didn't. Meanwhile back in my living room, Dr. Phil was shouting over and over, "What were you thinking?" I didn't have much of an answer because the premise was wrong. I wasn't thinking.

I did go deep, though, talking about my father's alcoholism, about his leaving the family when I was only three, and my mother's addiction to pills. "I'm an alcoholic; I am an addict," I told the audience. "I have surrendered myself to this program."

Referring to my time in rehab, Dr. Phil asked, "Was it the right thing to do?" I'm now thinking, *And this guy is a fucking doctor? Of course it was the right thing to do!*

"There's a lot of shame involved in this. You lose your dignity," I said. "To go out there and be out there with this is not easy."

Phil paused for the cameras, then asked, "How are you going to stay sober?" My immediate thought was *Well, this isn't helping, Phil.* I told him that "sobriety was not for sissies," and that I had a sobriety companion who was with me twenty-four hours a day ensuring that I kept away from places and people who could tempt me down the wrong path, as well as a support network of family and friends. "I definitely hit a bottom," I told him, all the while wanting to punch this motherfucker in the face. In fairness, at the end of the interview he told the audience that he had seen me with my son, Sean, and that I was a great dad. This was after he beat the shit out of me for an hour.

"I support you. I'm behind you and I know you're going to hold yourself to the highest standard," Dr. Phil said at the end of the marathon inquisition.

"I won't let you down," I said, punch-drunk from the brutal questioning.

My publicist, Ken Sunshine, had warned my agent and my lawyers and even the people at Paramount and CBS that this was a disaster waiting to happen, saying this was the worst thing I could possibly do. He was right. Outside of the Howard Stern world, I think that not many people had known about the voice-mail part of the scandal. Those things usually go away, but Dr. Phil put it out there for everybody to know. It just made things worse.

There were, however, some positives. I received hundreds and hundreds of letters and e-mails from around the country from people who wanted to congratulate me on my courage and to say that my example forced them to look at their own battles.

The night the show aired, Sean and I were home alone together and I asked him if he wanted to watch. He said the best words I had heard in months: "You're my dad. I love you and I know who you are. I don't need anybody to tell me."

Next on my Road to Television Recovery journey was a stop on Dr. Phil's afternoon show on the Paramount lot with a live, pumped-up audience. I was sitting in the greenroom waiting to go on when suddenly Terry Wood came flying in, all scattered and shaky. Paramount had put a hold on anybody else's getting a piece of me: I was to do no interviews, no appearances, no writing. I was theirs. So Terry came in and grabbed me and shouted, "Julie Chen is here. What should I do?" Julie had come from the *CBS Morning News* to get an interview. I was supposed to say no, but Julie Chen was CBS chairman Les Moonves's wife. Since I was on media lockdown and the key belonged to Terry Wood, and Les was her boss and Julie was Les's wife . . . well, you figure it out.

Terry had tears in her eyes. "What should I do? What should I do?"

I said, "I don't know, Terry, but I think I should do the interview. Les and Julie are loyal friends of mine, and I'm not making that call to Les." I did the interview.

When Dr. Phil introduced me to his audience, they went wild. Standing ovation, screaming, prolonged clapping, and all that. I'm thinking to myself, *This is crazy,* and Dr. Phil, who now is taking credit for my sobriety, says on television, "Well, how about that. They love you!" Yes, Phil, they love me, they really do.

A lot of love was out there. My first back-to-work interview was with Renée Zellweger, who couldn't have been nicer. She pulled me away from the crew and hangers-on to ask if I was really okay: "I love you and I want you to take care of yourself, okay?" I dove back into work, and while I had some thoughts that publicists wouldn't want me around . . . turned out they couldn't wait for me to show up. I was now officially one of them: a celebrity with a scandal.

At the Emmy after party in September 2005, Harvey Weinstein, whom I barely knew, came over and said, "You're my hero. You're going to be fine." A number of others slapped me on the back, including Bruce Willis, who was one of the first I spoke to when my scandal broke, and welcomed me back into the fold. Robin Williams winked at me and said, "Welcome home." George Clooney and his publicist summed up my predicament the best: "Nobody goes undefeated."

I was at a private screening of *Into the Wild* in New York when Sean Penn took me to one side. "I've always wanted to talk to you about this thing you went through," he told me. "I really thought that you got a really bad deal on that, but you went through it in a really good way. I felt so bad for you." In many ways the scandal pumped up my street cred with celebrities as they could see that I had experienced the same kind of tabloid attacks that they had gone through. Sportscaster and dear friend Jim Gray weighed in, "Nobody suffered more for less."

Finally, I had a private, one-on-one meeting with Les Moonves. He closed his door, hugged me, and said, "You are really a dumb shit. Pat, you're family and I love you. Let's not go through this again." Leave it to the big boss to be the only one concerned about my health and not my ratings.

One of my first public outings after my rehab was to the celebrity roast of Don King at the Friars Club in New York. At these funny but utterly brutal events a bunch of comedians slice the roastee to pieces. I was nervous about appearing at this arena, but Linda Bell Blue said that it was time and sat with me through the lunch. We were on the dais staring out at the crowd, with them staring back. No movement went unnoticed. While a couple of comedians took some well-deserved cheap shots at me, I was getting through the lunch unscathed until Donald Trump got to his feet. "Hey, Pat"—he looked over at me—"why the fuck did you make those phone calls?" Then he read a verbatim transcript. The room fell silent; people didn't know whether to laugh or to cry for me. At the end I raised my cup of coffee in a mock toast, took a bow, and left. I was just mortified. When I got in my car, my cell phone rang and it was Trump, calling to say that I was a great sport. There was no hint of an apology. It was one thing to hear it on the radio, another for a man I called my friend to read it in front of New York media. I thanked him, and about five minutes later he called again. And then again. I sent his calls to voice mail.

At that moment I decided to follow Winston Churchill's advice: "When you are walking through hell, keep walking."

20

Is George Clooney Dead?

Robert Downey Jr. once told a magazine writer that being an alcoholic was a lot of work for him and for everybody around him. For example, if he missed or was late for a yoga class, he said, a mob of friends and colleagues would show up to see if he was all right. I was now that guy. Executives, crew, and friends alike were watching me with anxious self-interest. Everybody had the eagle eye on me to make sure I was sticking to my program of sobriety. The scandal had changed everything. Each and every part of my day was filled with suspicion and scrutiny. If I ordered an Arnold Palmer (iced tea and lemonade) at a bar, I held on to the receipt long enough to keep me honestly innocent. One time I had an iced tea poolside on the roof in the popular Meatpacking District of New York. Ten minutes later, I got a call from "Page Six" asking me if I had fallen off the wagon.

Meantime, back at the *Insider* ranch, my power and credibility had been compromised to the point where Linda Bell Blue had her company-purchased Christian Louboutin shoes squarely on my neck. No longer could I try to steer the show to what it was supposed to be: an honest look behind the curtains of Hollywood. Instead, my role was being significantly reduced with each week. People in the newsroom who were once my confidants and friends were turning their backs on me. My alcoholism had given Linda Bell Blue and her sycophant "friends" a blank check to do anything they wanted.

The late Steve Jobs used to say, "A lot of people don't know what they want until you give it to them." Linda was giving it to them, like it or not. The show was becoming a video carnival, highlighting seventy-five-pound women and thousand-pound men. Linda Bell Blue really, really believed that what she thought was great was not only great . . . but the only thing that was great. Except when we needed the celebrities for show, the hell with Hollywood.

She lived for this. She picked out the anchors' clothes, jewelry, hairstyles, shoes, monitored the women anchors' weight and even everybody's personalities. We were collectively the dressed-up version of Frankenstein's monster. She also seemed to think she had this magic inner power to know what we were thinking at every minute. "Patrick, what's wrong today? See all those people out there"— she pointed to the newsroom—"they depend on you to be happy, so go out there and smile." For Linda, all the on-air people were hers, inside and out. She controlled our happiness, our sadness, our moods, and our way of life. She was the Wizard, and the Land of Oz was what you watched on television every night. Not only did you have to tell her daily that she was loved . . . you had to love everything she did. In my mind she was insane. I'm serious. She would call everybody back and redo an entire show because my cohost Lara Spencer's outfit didn't "pop," even though Linda had handpicked it. Just as I was horribly addicted to alcohol, Linda was addicted to drama and power, and there is no rehab for that. Her life revolved around arriving for work around 4:30 a.m., leaving alone at the end of a long day, and going home to watch her work with a critic's eye. No kids of her own; by her own admission, we were her kids and most of us wanted Mommy Dearest to go away. Problem was, we all wanted to work on these shows, but these were not the shows we signed up for.

So daily, anything and everything that might make you look away made the airwaves: anorexic, heroin-addicted twins who were dying right before our cameras (we let them), thousand-pound men who were struggling for help (we let them struggle), shark attacks, tornado damage, weddings that had gone bad, little people who married tall people, and every bad face-lift or plastic-surgery procedure we could find. We dug up the Butcher of Beverly Hills, the Cat Woman (who had had so many surgeries she looked like an eighty-year-old cat), a woman with three boobs, the Octomom, and anybody who was spinning out of control or who would possibly command a price at a roadside carnival. We hired this little, short geek who was to scour the Internet looking for freaks. He was good at it and, as a result, was one of Linda's and her assistant DJ's favorite people. While half the staff were being laid off every six months or so to make budget, the other half were traveling around the world to get the exclusive on some horribly scarred person or something, anything, that was disgusting, but could be dressed up for early-night television.

We were no longer covering Hollywood; we were uncovering its every scar. If I went to interview my friend Larry Hagman, for example, we would barely mention that he was once the biggest TV star in the world. Instead we would highlight his alcoholism and resulting failing health: "Larry Hagman's Fight for Life." That kind of thing.

I got the usually unavailable but brilliant comedian George Carlin to sit down for an hour and talk about comedy and the genius that lived inside his head, but that never made the air. Instead, we ran thirty seconds of his talking about his onetime cocaine addiction. He died sober, but that's not what people will remember who watched our show. In fact, we didn't cover his death.

I talked the shy and reclusive Brian Wilson of the Beach Boys into coming to the studio and sitting down for an exclusive. He agreed to sing a couple bars of "California Girls" and talk about the early days of the Beach Boys, but what we headlined were his drug problems and the time he went insane.

I got Yoko Ono to do a rare sit-down, and as she talked about John Lennon's death, one of the editors inserted a single gunshot under her soft voice. It aired. I called Sean Lennon to apologize.

The show brought back Joey Buttafuoco over and over to talk

about his affair with Amy Fisher, then got them to sit face-to-face to talk about the day Amy shot Joey's wife in the face. Who knows what they paid for that one.

My friend Barry Manilow was a regular, and every time we had him on, the tease and headline was "The Time Barry Manilow Lost It All." I think we did this about half a dozen times during my time there. But Barry knew it wasn't my decision; I made sure of that.

The Osmonds were regulars around sweeps time because it was easy to make them cry. I actually got all of them to sit down together: Alan and Wayne and Merrill and Jay and, of course, Donny and Marie. I even had to sweat through an interview with Virl and Tom, who were born deaf. The Osmonds were television gold because, seemingly, each of them had some terrible drama or life-threatening disease. Linda knew that they needed us to revive their careers and that we needed them to exploit. It was a mutual deal. I loved the Osmonds and they loved me back—but nobody in our audience ever heard many details of this amazing family outside of heartache and bankruptcy and death. Donny and Marie would cry over most anything. When Marie Osmond's son committed suicide, *ET* and *The Insider* were in perfect position to get the exclusive. Mary Hart basically became the family spokeswoman during this one, appearing on any show that would have her and sadly telling of how Marie's son Michael struggled with depression. Mary always referred to Marie as "my good friend." And, yes, Mary was at the funeral with cameras and a truckload of lights.

Britney Spears was gold for *ET* and *The Insider,* and when her life went into a tailspin, we were ordered to do a Britney story every day. When Linda and her sycophants got exclusive photos of Britney and her new husband, or Britney with her head shaved, they shed real tears of excitement in the newsroom during massive, childish celebrations over the "scoop." Linda Bell Blue nearly spent us out of business getting to work at 4:00 a.m. and buying the rights to every sleazy picture available from the night before. Nobody on competing shows had a chance. Ninety percent of the time, we didn't even use the pictures, but the game was this: nobody else could get their hands on them because we owned the "licensing" rights. It was a fancy way to perform picture-perfect pocketbook journalism. It got to a point where *Saturday Night Live* did a five-minute cartoon skit of me chasing Britney all around the world, searching for her, saying over and over, "Where's Britney today?" It ended with the Dalai Lama beating me to death with a baseball bat. I deserved it . . . and it was hilarious.

I remember when model Christie Brinkley split from her husband, architect Peter Cook, I traveled to the Hamptons to interview her. Her separation became tabloid fodder after sordid revelations about Cook's affair with an eighteen-year-old and his addiction to Internet porn. So I was under strict instructions to "own the story" and make Christie cry during the interview. Her publicists said that she didn't want to talk about the divorce, so I tap-danced around the subject, but when I brought up her ailing mother, who was dying, Christie burst into tears. I felt for her and hugged her, but when the story aired, the show's headline was something like "Christie in Tears over Split with Peter." Goose bumps all around in the newsroom. That was considered a victory, exploiting her misery to the max and for all the masses to cry along with her. I'm thinking to myself at the time, *Good God, I am going to have to look these people in the face again someday. I'm going to spend the rest of my life tracking them down and making amends to them all.* And I will.

We had the formula down perfect: we could legally make anything up we wanted just by adding a question mark behind our outrageous scoops.

For example, we'd get the opportunity to sit down with a celebrity, any celebrity, and ask them the normal questions first: "What attracted you to this script?" "What was it like working with [fill in the blank]?" Then at the end of the interview we'd hit them with Linda Bell Blue's favorites: weight loss, anorexia, plastic surgery, depression, and suicide. All we had to do, according to the legal staff, was change the intonation of our voices at the end, so it seemed we didn't believe it either.

The game of beat the publicist, whether in politics or show business, is as old as journalism. I never had a problem with any publicist because the celebrities enjoyed my banter. We always had a limited time with the big stars, but when it came to Leonardo DiCaprio and Tom Cruise and Barbra Streisand and Matt Damon and Ben Affleck and pretty much every big-name rock star, the publicist would scream, "Time's up," and the star/artist would say, "It's Pat; we can continue." But the new twist in the dog-eat-dog world of celebrity television was to ask a provocative question that had no relevance or bearing to the star's life but provided the show with a tantalizing headline. Asking the dirty question, the question the producer had circled as a must ask, became the new journalism. As uncomfortable as it was, I duly asked these bogus or hypothetical questions to generate a promo line for the show. I was remarkably good at this, but we were playing a totally sick game with people's lives. It was legal journalistic ambush gone amok. I was not just part of it, but I quickly became the symbol of all that was bogus and hollow about entertainment television. I became a caricature. An Internet skit about *The Insider*'s going inside Regis Philbin's heart surgery was typical of how the show was viewed. We were becoming a freak show. If the ratings were poor one evening, we had to amp up the tabloid fodder for the next night and bring those viewers back. It was a slippery slope. Here's how it worked.

I would brush by whatever a star was promoting, then casually ask, "Did you ever feel like if you gained weight, you might not get the part?" (This was for the women.) They might say, "Well, it crosses my mind." Then I'd say, "Have you ever had a weight problem?" Or one of our favorites if the star was thin: "You're so thin, have you ever been anorexic?" Of course the answer was no. But we would open the show with "Is Eva Longoria anorexic?" (Just using her name as an example.) But we wouldn't answer the question until twenty minutes later. And the answer would be something like, no, she's a workout freak. But we would never run the no—just the question "Have you ever had a weight problem?" It became more and more absurd. If Angelina Jolie was holding a gun on the set of her latest film, we would ask, "Did Angelina bring a gun on a set where children were playing?" Or if George Clooney was going abroad on a charity mission, we would ask, "Is George Clooney leaving Hollywood?" One time Kathie Lee Gifford was in a funny video skit in which she held up a convenience store at gunpoint. We twisted that to be something like "Why did Kathie Lee bring a gun into a store?" Then, twenty minutes later, we'd say, aw, shucks, folks, it was just a funny bit she did.

Anything and everything was turned tabloid. We would go to the red carpet of a movie or event and hardly ever drop the name of the event or charity dinner we were at but use the event to get celebrities to talk about other celebrity scandals, or to react to some national story, or to respond to the death of somebody. Then we'd pass it off like this: "The stars came right to us to say good-bye to a Hollywood legend." I needed a drink and a shower every night when I got home. Meantime, it paid well and the clothes were free.

But much of the time enough celebrities were imploding without any help from us. During the time of my own scandal, Michael Jackson was on trial for child molestation, Martha Stewart was in jail, and Russell Crowe was throwing telephones at hapless hotel staff. No *Insider* spin necessary. They did allow me to stay clear of any of these, and I was able to hold on to my promise not to do stories on my friends. But when I did get to interview a celebrity who had a past we wanted to dig up, I was right there with "You know, I've been through it, too . . . and I'm wondering . . ." Etc.

Slowly everything became grittier, sleazier, and utterly divorced from reality. I always prided myself on asking celebrities cheeky questions that elicited an amused response from the star—and a pained grimace from the attendant publicist. Sample: During the Michael Jackson trial for child molestation and other charges in 2005, his sister La Toya was releasing a new album and agreed to do one interview: with me. Her publicist sent a list of questions that I could and could not ask her. Top of the Do Nots was asking about Michael, the trial, or the Jackson family. So we sat down and the first thing I said was "Let's start with Michael. How's he doing?" While the publicists went crazy, it broke the thick ice surrounding the interview. La Toya started laughing so hard and said, "Michael's going to be fine."

Our favorite topics were always depression and suicide. We were ordered to ask all interviewees if they ever got down-and-out while trying to make it . . . and then hit them with "Did you ever contemplate suicide?" If they said yes, jackpot! But they always said no, and that was still a jackpot because we'd show me asking them, "Did you ever contemplate suicide?" Then cut to their astonished face. Freeze the video and ask, "Did [fill in the blank] want to die?" And all of a sudden you'd see me ask that question and we were on our way. We did the same thing with depression and plastic surgery and bankruptcy and about anything else absurdly tabloid.

In the fall of 2005, Linda Bell Blue called me into her office and announced in an excited whisper that we had "locked up" a Richard Pryor interview. I had a long history with Richard going back to when he lit himself on fire while freebasing cocaine and drinking 152-proof rum in 1980. He was nearly burned to death. Most of his skin had burned away. I was still in local news at Channel 2 in Los Angeles and got a call that Richard would do an interview with me, so I went to the Grossman Burn Center in Sherman Oaks and did a long, thoughtful interview with the man once called the Picasso of comedy. Now, a quarter of a century later, we were to meet again. Pryor's health was as low on the survival scale as you can get: heart attacks, bypass surgeries, and multiple sclerosis had literally paralyzed the guy and reduced him to a wheelchair. I asked Linda, "Can the guy even talk?" She said, "Don't you worry about that; we just need you to be seen with him."

I arrived at his house with an army of cameras and lights and nervous producers and was greeted by his seventh wife, Jennifer Lee. Jennifer was grateful that I had come to visit, as "Richard really, really loves you." In my mind, the only reason Richard was still alive was because of the love and care of Jennifer. She took me into his bedroom, and there was the great comic slumped in his wheelchair, slurring and unable to utter even a word. I walked up to him and said, "What the fuck, man? You still fuckin' alive?" He smiled and laughed while spitting up into a towel. We were on our way. With cameras rolling, I pushed him around his compound and into his living room. The interview was like this: "So, Richard, your fans want to know, how are you feeling?" I think he said, "Thank you," but it came out "Uhakehnkm th th th t han." I looked up at the producers, who made body motions of "Keep going, Pat." Jennifer would help translate some of his answers, but I quickly realized I was interviewing a man on death's doorstep who didn't have the strength to knock or push the doorbell. I did my best to allow the man some dignity, but there wasn't one usable answer from him—just slight facial expressions. I could see his eyes telling me, "I'm in here, Pat. I'm really in here." But he couldn't express anything. It was painful. At the end he was rolled back into his bedroom surrounded by nurses. Then Jennifer came out and said Richard wanted to tell me something privately. I walked in and somehow he got out, "Stay away from the hookers and cocaine." A reference to my voice mail. We both laughed hysterically and I kissed him on his forehead, wiped a tear from his left cheek, and walked out.

A few weeks later, he was dead, and a private funeral was held at Forest Lawn. Only about a hundred people were invited, including me, and of course my cameras and lights and producers and still photographers. I was sitting next to Diana Ross, and all of a sudden, out of nowhere, during a moment of silence, she stood up and sang "Amazing Grace":

> *Amazing grace, how sweet the sound*
> *That saved a wretch like me.*
> *I once was lost, but now am found.*
> *Was blind, but now I see.*

Looking back, those words were my story: "Through many dangers, toils, and snares I have already come. 'Tis grace that brought me safe thus far and grace will lead me home." I wasn't quite home yet. I returned to the office to report to Linda, and she wanted to figure out if we should promote it for the next day to get the maximum exposure.

A part of Hollywood was dead, and in the meantime we were metaphorically trying to kill the rest of them. As I walked out of her office, I saw another one of her trophies: a shot of her with Charles Manson.

21

Helter-Skelter

I was coming up to almost a year of sobriety when, driving home from a recovery meeting, I drove into a liquor store and loaded up. I didn't even think twice. My recovery was a sham. I drank away my month at Promises because I hadn't been honest with myself. The first and most important step of the 12-step program of recovery is "We admitted that we were powerless over alcohol and that our lives had become unmanageable." If you don't get the first step, you don't get sober. Period. I was struggling with not only the alcohol but the ism. The alcohol part is a disease, but the ism part is the fuse and a fuckin' bitch to conquer. My fuse was lit twenty-four hours a day—waking up and going to bed with all the liabilities and character defects of a hopeless alcoholic: fear, worry, selfishness, false pride, arrogance, passiveness, criticism, self-pity, grandiosity, gluttony, irreverence, shame, and guilt. That's a problematic list if you don't follow a strict program. I wasn't even close. And I had the perfect job to trigger every single one of those defects every given moment. The bigger problem was that I was functioning, and so life went on in a controlled zombie state. I dressed up, showed up, and put on the best face possible, all the while destroying myself physically and emotionally. I did not have the humility to admit that I, Pat O'Brien, was powerless over anything. My futile journey to find happiness was making me even more sick, and the only medicine that calmed me down was alcohol. I was lost and I knew it.

So it was good to get back to some sense of normality as Betsy and I went back to South Dakota for a remarkable reunion of my high school band. Dale Gregory and the Shouters had been elected into the South Dakota Rock and Roll Hall of Fame, and now, we decided, it was a summer to gloat. It had been forty years since we were tearing up dance halls and arenas, and here we were at our high school reunion ready to be the entertainment once again. Going back to South Dakota, for me, was always healing, and this proved to be no different. It was normal. Nothing in my life in the past forty years had been normal in a South Dakota way, so I welcomed the change of pace. We decided to play in a downtown Sioux Falls bar called Skelly's, where, ironically, my dad used to drink. Greg, Ted, Dale, Gary, and I spent about a week seeing if we could still put together a set, and by the end of the week we rolled out all the old standbys: "Gloria," "Little Latin Lupe Lu," "Time Is on My Side," "She's About a Mover," and my favorite, "Boys," by the Beatles. It was the first song I had ever performed with the Shouters, and I actually sang the song along with Ringo at his Toronto gig. We expected about thirty people and were giddy that nearly six hundred showed up for one more Shouter Shindig. Betsy, who had never been anyplace close to South Dakota, had a great time, and for a laugh I sat her at a table with all my old girlfriends from high school. We were pretty good for a bunch of guys on the AARP mailing list, and Greg Blomberg, my best boyhood friend (to this day), and I looked at each other once onstage with glowing admiration and pride that we were, once again, making music. The crowd loved it and pleaded for more after our fifteen-song set, but we made a good decision: quit while we were ahead. It was a night to remember.

But my recent past and ensuing scandal were always right around the corner. *Esquire* magazine had published the greatest quotes from 2005, and number one was from George W. Bush about his FEMA director, Michael Brown, after he completely botched the response to Hurricane Katrina: "Brownie, you're doing a heck of a job." Number two was from me: "Let's get some hookers and coke." Well, at least I made *Esquire,* right?

Another part of my past resurfaced while I was in my Los Feliz home one night drinking alone again and the phone rang. "Is this Pat O'Brien?" It was a detective from Ottumwa, Iowa, who said she had been trying to find me for six months. I explained that as I was on television twice a day pretty much everywhere, she couldn't have been much of a detective, and that didn't get a laugh. She was calling about one of my long-lost aunts, whom I had forgotten about, who had passed away and left all her money to her brother, my father, Joe O'Brien. I racked my brain and remembered that I had an aunt who worked at Ma Bell (now AT&T) and made about $40 a week and then drank it away at the local bars. Turns out that Ma Bell was buying stocks for her, and they had grown exponentially into several hundred thousand dollars to go to Joe's surviving kids, which I'd thought was just my sister, Kathleen, and me. During a long probate, we found out that Joe had been married five times and that there were six half brothers and sisters I didn't even know about. One of them, named Marie, who I thought was my other aunt, was actually my half sister. Apparently, Joe's life was equally unmanageable as mine. No wonder he drank. The money was divided, and I was happy for my sis to get a big check. Betsy helped me spend mine. I always said that Betsy made me a millionaire: I used to be a multimillionaire. The girl could spend without guilt as long as it wasn't her money, and it never was. But we had a lot of fun together, even though I later found out that everybody I knew who'd initially told me they liked her later told me, with the freedom of the breakup, that they actually hated her.

I took her to the House of Blues in Hollywood to see my old friend James Brown, and we hung out with Bruce Willis and Bill Murray, and afterward we all went backstage at the invitation of the Godfather himself. He was still sweating profusely when we went into his dressing room and was still wearing his signature red velvet coat with the wide lapels and frills. "Betsy, honey, you watch my outfit while the Godfather changes into a robe." Typically, Betsy grabbed the coat and promptly put it on and was prancing around the room. Brown loved it. He pulled me close and said, "Pat, this is a wild one." I said, yes, I knew that.

I also took her to see another of my idols, the great and incomparable Jimmy Smith: the master of the B3 Hammond organ. A liner note on his first album proclaimed, "Jimmy Smith is so far ahead of everybody, he's lonely." Since I was an organ player and owned a $25,000 Hammond B3 myself, I wanted to meet him. I walked past his dressing room, and he was sitting on the couch with about half a dozen drinks in front of him. I walked in without a knock and unannounced, and all the band guys were freaking out: "Man, it's Pat O'Brien," and so on. I moved to Jimmy and stuck out my hand and said, "It's my pleasure to meet you, Mr. Smith." He responded, "I don't give a fuck who the fuck you are. Get the fuck out of my fucking dressing room." I wasn't used to that, but to this day I feel it is some kind of badge of honor. Two weeks later, the Great One died. I was happy to be able to see him one more time.

Meantime, I was smitten with Betsy Hoyt Stephens, and despite my suspicions about her, I dropped down my American Express Black Card and bought her a huge, seven-carat diamond ring, and about a week before Christmas 2006 I took her to the Bel-Air hotel and asked her to marry me. She said yes. I cried. She cried. We called Jack Welch and Donald Trump and LAPD chief Bill Bratton and showered them with the news. Then we bounced off to the *Insider* Christmas party to show off our gluttony. Eyes rolled, but I was still the star of the show, so we got fake smiles and meaningless hugs to show they cared. The engagement, the ring, Betsy, and her new fiancé made all the magazines and tabloids. I guess technically we were famous, something Betsy's ex-husband warned me about long ago: "She likes attention." She was getting it, and everywhere we went, the paparazzi wanted to see us and the ring and the clothes and, I'm assuming, took enough pictures to last through another disaster, if that should happen. It would.

By now, *The Insider* had become a national ambulance-chaser-television destination. We were no longer covering Hollywood. We were covering the self-destruction of anybody with a name from A-list to Z-list. But as drama and disaster and destruction and ratings and death go, Linda Bell Blue found the perfect victim: Anna Nicole Smith.

There was never a reason for Anna to be famous or attract much attention, but the former *Playboy* model became a tabloid favorite after she married eighty-nine-year-old billionaire oil tycoon Howard Marshall. Anna was twenty-six. I know what you're thinking. We thought the same thing, too. Marshall died a lucky thirteen months later, and then the sparks flew over who would get the money. But Anna caught our attention when she attempted a reality show about what was left of her life. It was a complete disaster, exposing her every defect, and made for tantalizing television. The Jayne Mansfield look-alike became nothing more than an overweight, washed-up national joke.

But she cleaned herself up, got an endorsement for a weight-loss product, and looked Hollywood-red-carpet ready for the courtroom appearances over her late husband's money. She was becoming Paris Hilton/Kim Kardashian famous—famous for doing nothing. We bit. For us, she was impossible not to cover. Her brief walk into the courtroom with her attorney, Howard K. Stern, was must-see TV for us, but it eventually died down.

In June of 2006 she posted a video on her Web site to announce that the rumors were true: she was pregnant, and "really, really happy." The announcement was made while she floated on an inflatable raft in a swimming pool. Sure enough, little Dannielynn was born on September 7, 2006. Last name to be announced at a later date because of the massive confusion over who the father was: Anna's attorney and spokesman, Howard K. Stern, or this boyfriend who came out of nowhere—another nobody, named Larry Birkhead. And that's when we assigned an army to cover her, because just three days after she gave birth her twenty-year-old son, Daniel Wayne Smith, died of a drug overdose while visiting Anna and his new half sister. Anna was inconsolable. Her life, now tragic beyond belief, was there for everybody to watch unfold, and even before she hit bottom, we were already there to pick up the pieces. Linda Bell Blue traveled to the Bahamas and stood alone at dawn in Anna's driveway until somebody eventually came out and she talked the person into making a deal with the devil: let us, and only us, tell her story.

That's how I found myself on a private jet along with Linda Bell Blue, Howard Stern's family, and sundry others on my way to the Bahamas where Nicole lived. At the Ocean Club in Nassau, Bahamas, Linda Bell Blue set up an Anna Nicole Smith war room, suite after suite taken up with lights, computers, teleprompters, phone banks, and the rest. Effectively the whole *Insider* and *Entertainment Tonight* operations decamped to the Bahamas. (Minus the continuing number of people getting laid off back home.) We had presidential-sized suites and catered meals and butlers and whatever else we wanted or needed to cover this growing drama for a waiting nation.

What no one knew was that I had not so gracefully slid off the wagon after that night when I pulled into a liquor store and bought a couple of bottles of red wine. Now my life was consumed not only by the unfolding drama of Anna Nicole's tragic life, but how I could get my hands on wine without being caught. I would order wine on room service and then immediately go down and pay the bill in cash and have the wine voided off the bill. Then I would have to hide the wine in my room in case anyone walked in. I lived on mouthwash and gum to cover the smell. It was hard work consuming a couple of bottles of wine in the dead of night. Somehow I managed. Alcoholics always figure out a way. That's why we refer to the drink as "cunning and baffling." In my brief "recovery," I did no such thing as learn a lesson.

Again, the crazy genius of Linda Bell Blue was that she had somehow "locked up" the Anna story exclusively. If anybody else wanted in, they would have to buy in. I'm not saying we spent millions of dollars to get the exclusive because I don't know . . . but I do know that Linda spent a lot of time in Anna Nicole's Bahamian driveway waiting each day to talk with her and make some kind of deal. Whatever happened between these two blondes, it was our story and a fucking good one. Advantage, Linda Bell Blue. Nobody could get close to Anna but us. And nobody in Hollywood who is down-and-out and has a tear-jerking story does anything for free. Trust me.

We pulled out all the stops for Anna Nicole with no fewer than five cameras, and we recorded everything. When I arrived, I went into Anna's bedroom and she was lying under a huge down duvet, comforted by about thirty pillows. I said, "Where's the baby?" One of her nannies walked over with little Dannielynn and Anna excitedly said, "Let Pat hold her." I cradled this poor child in my arms for the cameras. As Linda Bell Blue's husband later said, "From that moment, you owned the story." Anna and I went to her private tennis court and hit some balls back and forth, and we giggled at how poorly we looked playing tennis in street clothes. The story was a huge ratings success, and Anna was from now on a constant feature of the show. She quickly became the whole show. I had so many back-and-forth trips to the Bahamas that my passport looked like a drug dealer's.

During one trip, Anna took me to see the house she was building for her new life. It had all the Anna things: a pool, a disco, and a dance pole. She was proud of it. She seemed happy with all the cash and prizes, and, of course, being a new mom at that. But everybody saw clearly that she had lost any appetite she ever had for survival. It seemed all she ever said was "I'm tired."

In early February 2007 we were there to catch what proved to be the end of her death march. We flew down to the Bahamas again, though this time with a much-reduced TV entourage. Our interview was painful, almost mournful, as we discussed her son, who had so tragically passed away. She looked so sad and out of it that at the end of our conversation I grabbed her hand firmly and said,

"Honey, I don't think you're going to make it." Her response was star-
tlingly honest: "I don't think I will either." As she said it, her mind
and body seemed to go to some faraway place, so I suggested we get
out of the house and tour the island. We stopped off at a local vegetable and fruit stand and shared some coconut milk in front of two
Insider cameras. We got back into our van and suddenly she said,
"Pat, I don't feel so good." I put my arm around her and she laid her
head on my shoulder and passed out. Once back at her house she
went straight to bed. *Entertainment Tonight,* our sister show, would
wait around to speak to Anna Nicole should she make a recovery,
and I was ordered to return to New York, where *The Insider* was
now based.

I arrived back feeling depressed and empty after my time with
Anna Nicole. I knew for certain that I needed a drink, badly. At the
time I was staying at a suite in the Waldorf Towers hotel. On the
way there I had my driver stop off at a liquor store, and I bought two
bottles of red wine. I was nervous about buying booze openly, knowing that if the media got wind of my drinking, I would be fired. As
I didn't have a bottle opener, I used a pen and my shoe to shove the
cork into the bottle. I was exhausted and my hands were shaking so
much I could barely pour myself a glass. I sat cross-legged on the
floor and drank as much wine as I could as fast as I could.

Betsy, who had a football fashion-accessories business that I was
financing, was flying to Miami to schmooze potential clients at the
Super Bowl. I was left on my own. After drinking the best part of
two bottles of red wine, I stood up to go to another room, felt faint,
and then my knees buckled under me and my head smashed on the
marble floor. For some time I was unconscious. I awoke in a pool of
blood barely remembering where I was. I had the presence of mind
to call Betsy and left a message on her answering service telling her
that I needed help. Then I lapsed into unconsciousness. I later found
out from my friend Michael Klein, who once owned the San Diego
Chargers, that Betsy had found enough trouble to make a public
fool of herself, but she eventually got my message and called the

hotel manager, my friend Ron Oz, and asked him to look in on me to make sure I was okay.

They found me in my underwear lying in a pool of blood on the floor of the marble entrance hall. Ron Oz initially thought it was a crime scene and believes that I could have bled to death if Betsy hadn't called. My clothes were so soaked with blood, they had to toss them.

By now it was around eleven at night and I needed stitching up. Secrecy, too, was essential, so I was smuggled out of the hotel in a service elevator, helped into a waiting security van, and taken to a plastic surgeon that Betsy's dad, Tony, had arranged. He also showed up to hold my hand while they put a dozen stitches in my forehead. They later told me I was cut so deeply, they could see my skull. The next morning I was due to fly to Miami to cover the Super Bowl game, but I couldn't appear in public so soon after my fall. Betsy called Donald Trump, who gladly offered me his private jet but was saddened to hear that I was, in his words, "back on the sauce." Even going Trump, I was in no shape to fly to Miami. I made up some half-assed story about slipping on the marble floor and stayed home until Betsy arrived. She had scalped the tickets I gave her for $7,000. When I went to work, the makeup girls did a fabulous job of covering up the scar, and just to make sure, I wore a beanie when Betsy and I went to watch the Knicks game the night after the incident.

On February 8, 2007, Lara Spencer and I were hosting the show from Times Square when news came that Anna Nicole had been taken to a hospital in Florida. We quickly redid the show, and I raced to the airport to fly to Miami to cover the story. On the way I learned that Anna Nicole was dead, and to prove that nothing remains secret, the *New York Post* called to ask about my "fall." Only two people knew about the fall. As I sat on a crowded flight in the last row, I started to cry. Too much was going on and I wasn't handling it great.

Outside the Hollywood, Florida, hospital where Anna was pronounced dead on arrival, the photographers tried to get a shot of my scar, but thanks to the makeup girls, they went away empty-handed.

My predicament was completely overshadowed by the drama of Anna Nicole's tragic life and death. Things had moved so quickly that I didn't have time to absorb the whole circus or even figure out that, by putting her life out there in front of millions, we were, in part, responsible for her death. Later we would learn she had died of a massive drug overdose, but on the air, I added, "But what she really died of was a broken heart."

Back in New York, as Betsy and I were hunting for an apartment, my heart was broken. I got a call from the president of the University of South Dakota that my mentor and surrogate father, Dr. Farber, was on his death bed. I got through to him and he sounded weak, but glad I called. He said he was worried about me. I changed the subject and reminded him of our world travels and the time we tried to buy tickets to the Bolshoi in Moscow without speaking a word of Russian. He laughed, and that's the last sound I heard from the man who had pushed and poked me into success and given me the self-esteem and the lectures to make a go of it. I traveled back to Vermillion, South Dakota, for his funeral and sat next to Tom Brokaw. As the casket passed by us, we both reached out and knocked on the mahogany box. Doc had made it possible for Tom and me to be rich and famous, and we wanted to somehow say one more thank-you.

For his obituary I called Doc "the closest thing we have to a philosopher-king. He taught us that we do four things: we learn, we explore, we question, and we donate." Both Tom and I gave $50,000 each to his memorial fund, and as Tom and I and other Farber Boys took our places for his funeral service in Vermillion, I reflected on whether Doc would describe my professional life as having the "higher purpose" he hoped all his students would aspire to. I was now a closet alcoholic specializing in describing those who had fallen when touched by the fickle flame of celebrity.

He may, though, have approved of my interview with Bill Clinton later that year.

I visited him in his office in Harlem, and while the crew was setting up in his library, I was glancing through his collection of rare books. As a collector myself, I was intrigued by the books on the White House adorning the shelves. I picked one out called *The White House Cookbook* by former First Lady Mrs. Calvin Coolidge, which dealt with how to set up a state dinner, with the correct protocol for conversation as well as favorite recipes. I was looking at the book when the former president walked into the room. "Give me that book," he said. Worried that I had transgressed, I quickly handed him the book. He took it off me and then formally presented it to me: "I saw the look in your eyes when you picked it up. You will get better use out of it than me. Enjoy it; it's a White House heirloom." The book now has pride of place in my library at home. He signed it, "Happy Holidays, Bill." A naturally generous man, President Clinton, who experienced a couple of scandals of his own, was concerned about my well-being when I was going through the mill. He and Hillary sent me messages of support through our mutual friend Ken Sunshine.

In this business there are car crashes and there are car crashes. Keith Richards is the car-crash king—he has lived large and lived to tell the story. I once asked Mick Jagger how Keith was still alive, and Mick said simply, "Keith is alive because he is Keith. He's cheated death more times than any of us." It's funny, but though I have interviewed Mick Jagger as often as Paul McCartney, Mick always refers to me as "the Beatles' guy," acknowledging that they were my first musical love. The first time I had anything to do with Mick was in the lobby of the St. Regis Hotel when I was covering a football game with football legend and analyst John Madden. This guy came over and talked sports with John for about forty minutes. After he left, Madden's producer said, "Hey, that was really cool." John was taken aback: "Huh, what? Who was that guy?" With a shake of his head, Madden's producer said to him, "That, my friend, was Mick Jagger."

Fast-forward twenty years later to the time I was talking to Keith

Richards about all our yesterdays when I noticed that he was wearing a weathered pair of boots. (I am a great shoe lover—one of the reasons why Sarah Jessica Parker and I got along so well during the *Sex and the City* days. I knew my shoes and she admired that.) I asked Keith where he got them, and he proudly said, "I stole them from Johnny Depp." He was working with Depp on the set of *Pirates of the Caribbean,* took a liking to the boots, and simply stole them. Knowing that the latest *Pirates* movie was due out in the summer of 2007, I took a picture of the boots so that I could show them to Johnny Depp when I spoke with him. When I showed him the picture of the boots on Keith Richards's feet, Johnny said, "So that's where those went." Taking a page out of his Jack Sparrow character, I famously said, "Leave it to *The Insiderrrrrrrrrrrrr* to solve that mystery." Johnny liked that.

He was a fun guy to chat with, but like all of the A-list names, he was only available on his schedule if he had something to promote. These people don't just say yes to a request. However, in Johnny's case, I almost got him to move off the curve. My wife, Linda, was obsessed with Johnny and his acting skills. We were staying in New York at the Regency, and early one morning I was coming back from a run and ran into him. He was there for an all-day junket for a movie. I said, "Hey, can you do me a favor? My wife is upstairs still in bed, and she's a big fan. Can you walk up with me and let's wake her up?" He laughed for a couple seconds considering it; then his publicist marched in and pulled him away. But he was thinking about it.

Sandra Bullock is another who gets it. She is playful, genuine, knows how to a give good sound bite, and doesn't take herself too seriously. I was stunned when she married Jesse James, thinking there could not have been two more different people. Jesse had given one of his custom motorcycles to Kid Rock, who brought it along for an interview, and I opened my big mouth and said, "Who would ever want to get on something like that?" A TV camera caught the moment and it went out. Jesse was furious with me, I was told, so the next time I saw Sandra, I begged for his number to calm him down. She gave it to me, and I called him and it all ended well, for me anyway.

Jennifer Garner was another sweetheart. She was friendly, fun, and at ease with herself. I remember saying to Ben Affleck before they started dating and while they were working on the movie *Daredevil,* based on the Marvel Comics character, "Is there anyone nicer in Hollywood? There has to be another side to her. It's too good to be true." He agreed, saying that he was always waiting for the other shoe to drop—but it never did. They are now happily married, with three children. Catherine Zeta-Jones, happily married to Michael Douglas, is another absolute darling, and at red-carpet events we would often sneak off and have a cigarette together. Michael Douglas and I go back a long way, and when *The Insider* moved to New York, he was one of the New York–based celebrities who shot promo pieces welcoming me to the city, the two of us filmed chatting in my Trump Tower apartment overlooking Central Park. "Oh, look, you can see our building from here," he said like a little kid. I used to run into his mom and dad, Kirk, around town, and I would always shout out to Kirk Douglas, "I am Spartacus," the iconic cries at the end of the movie. By the way, I am not Spartacus; Kirk is.

Nicole Kidman, too, was always up for something different, for fresh ways to conduct an interview. She loved it when I brought her, the slender screen siren, a box of Krispy Kreme doughnuts, then her favorites, before a TV chat. We would always be connected through Keith Urban, who, like me, was forced to conquer his demons.

At a busy Oscar night the year after *The Queen* came out, Helen Mirren's publicist came up to me and said, "Helen wants to meet you and say hi." I was honored, and after she won her Oscar, she came back to our Oscar set holding two martinis. I said, "I don't drink," to which she said, "Good, they are both for me anyway." We talked about sex and orgasms, and then off into the night she went holding her gold statue and her martinis.

Talking about sleeping with the stars, I remember when I was flying from New York to Los Angeles and in the seat next to me was Liza Minnelli. We chatted for a while and then we both fell asleep. When I woke up, our faces were close together, and for a few seconds I thought to myself, *How did I end up in bed with Liza Minnelli?* Of course nothing happened.

Other stars were not quite so playful. Much as I loved the James Bond movies, I couldn't wait to meet Sean Connery. I excitedly walked up to him at an event I was hosting and introduced myself, quietly thinking that the man who invented the role of James Bond and I would hit it off. Instead, he was boorish and boring. I was crushed. I interviewed Robert De Niro many times, and we always talked about watching the Sugar Ray Leonard–Roberto Durán "No más" fight in the Hollywood Hills home of Robert Walden. (Durán himself told me he never said the words *no más*. Howard Cosell put the words in his mouth in Cosell's legendary staccato fashion: "And Roberto Durán says, '*No más, no más,*' the fight is over.") Anyway, De Niro was a tough interview because he hated the process. His answers were either "Yes" or "No" or "Maybe," and one time I just stopped the interview and said, "Bob, I have a family to raise. Let me show you what it's like . . ." And I told him to be me and ask questions and I would play him. I answered each question with a "Yes" or a "No" and he laughed and said, "Am I really like that?" I said, "Yes."

Not surprisingly, I got along well with Mel Gibson, because we would sneak cigarettes right before an interview. I did think of him as always being uncomfortable in his own skin.

I was trying hard to at least look comfortable in my own skin, but I clearly was not. As former Senate majority leader and South Dakota buddy Tom Daschle would later say, "Pat always maintained a good game face." But the inner turmoil and ensuing loneliness were hidden behind the O'Brien armor of self-confidence and grandiosity. I was now living a horrible life of shame and guilt and in my mind the only cure was to drink. Deep inside, I knew I had built my own prison and couldn't find the key.

Hollywood meltdowns were now becoming epidemic. Shortly

after Anna's death, Britney Spears decided to shave her head in the middle of the night in front of the paparazzi. As I was watching this one, I remembered when I first interviewed her when she was a pimple-faced nineteen-year-old "Genie in a Bottle." Not many days afterward, she, too, checked into Promises for rehab. She went to the "good one" in Malibu. In April 2007, *30 Rock* star Alec Baldwin was all over the show after leaving his eleven-year-old daughter, Ireland, a vitriolic phone message calling her a "thoughtless little pig." I thought, *Oh no!* as everybody played it over and over. I owed it to Alec to try to cut him some slack as, of late, I was the only entertainment reporter to whom he would grant an interview. I reward loyalty. I asked that I not be the one to do this story, but the show couldn't get enough. I ran into Alec at the US Open Tennis Championships that fall, and the first thing I said to him was "Didn't my story teach you anything?" We shared a knowing laugh, two in-the-moment idiots tainted by public humiliation.

A few days after the Baldwin story emerged, another friend, David Hasselhoff, was filmed by his daughter in a drunken stupor on the floor of a Las Vegas hotel trying to eat a hamburger. Painful. I had known David and his wife, Pam, for years. They lived near me in the Valley, and I knew, certainly better than anyone else on *The Insider,* how he struggled with his alcoholism. For the show, the story was gold; for me, it was an unnerving reflection of my own life. I recused myself on that one, too.

My confident exterior was rapidly crumbling. I was a functioning time bomb. Anna Nicole's death was a huge trigger for me, and covering that story and trudging back down to the Bahamas for her funeral preparations made it easier for me to drink away my sadness and confusion. I was drinking every night until I passed out. One night I woke up in my office at home and the room was on fire. I had fallen asleep and a piece of blazing wood had fallen out of the fireplace, setting fire to the wood floor. In my drunken state, I dared not call the fire department, so I put out the fire as best I could and went to bed.

In December 2007, on the anniversary of my engagement to Betsy and on the night of the *Insider* office Christmas party, I made a sickeningly familiar telephone call to Betsy. "I fell. I fell and I'm bleeding," I slurred. I had drunk so much that I had blacked out coming down the stairs at my Los Feliz home, fallen headfirst down two flights of stairs, and smashed headfirst into a solid wall at the bottom. I remember trying to catch my balance and then nothing. Betsy drove over and found me, in my underwear, lying in a pool of blood, a large gash over my eye. I insisted that she not call 911. Instead she phoned our physician, Jay Schapira, who said that if Betsy could get me into a car, he would meet us outside the Cedars-Sinai hospital emergency room and get me checked in without being noticed. Getting a drunk, bleeding, belligerent, barely conscious 165-pound man into a car was no mean feat, but Betsy managed. I was a disaster, crying, scared, and confused—and still drinking on the way to the hospital. Wheels were falling off one by one. Consequences were piling up in serious, life-threatening numbers.

The next morning I woke up in a hospital bed with a brace around my neck, surrounded by half a dozen doctors. It appeared that in this fall, along with my first fall in New York, I had broken a disk in my neck, which was now dangerously close to my spinal cord. They had quickly fused my neck by screwing a plate in there so it wouldn't collapse and cause me further harm. The doctors said I was millimeters away from being paralyzed for life. As I only had to wear the brace for a day, I went back to work without anyone the wiser. The makeup girls fixed up the scar over my eye, after I told them that I had banged my head, which helped explain why I had missed the office party.

My physician knew differently and told me that I had to curb my drinking; otherwise I would be dead in a year. He wasn't kidding around. He brought in a specialist counselor who advised me to return to rehab. "I can't," I told him. "I have to work. I'll lose my job!" I still thought I knew better, terrified of losing my job and desperate that I would lose my fiancée. So I continued the façade and so did Betsy, who was planning a lavish sixtieth birthday party for me on February 14, 2008, which was also to be our wedding day. She designed a beautiful invitation to send, a "save the date" card from her and Sean to the glitterati of New York and Los Angeles. They included Charlie Sheen, Bill and Hillary Clinton, Mayor Bloomberg, Jack Welch, Bruce Willis, and Kevin Costner. Betsy had ordered a white Christian Dior wedding dress and quietly asked Father Peter Jacobs, a colorfully liberal New York priest, to officiate. Father Jake was Pope John XXIII's personal secretary, but was thrown out of the Church after he married Princess Grace to a non-Catholic. He also officiated over her funeral. He also was my drinking buddy and tour guide when I went to Rome, and I had grown close to him spiritually and alcoholically.

Meanwhile I was spending around $2,300 a week on Silver Oak wine, drinking alone but inside crying for help. I had my own voice-over studio in my lavish New York City Trump apartment, so after taping the show in Times Square, I could go home and put the finishing touches on it. I stayed sober until they cleared me, and then I was off to the races.

The death of Heath Ledger on January 22, 2008, was the last straw.

I was at home drinking when I got a frantic e-mail from the office: "Heath Ledger dead. Holy shit, holy shit." This was quickly followed by a call saying that Linda Bell Blue wanted me outside his apartment in SoHo and to get a shot of me when they brought the body out. Now I had interviewed Heath a couple of times on the red carpet. More significant, I had sat next to him on several occasions at 12-step meetings. I felt for the guy. I knew he was uncomfortable with the Hollywood scene and was trying to handle his prescription-drug problem. On this night he was trying to get to sleep and overdosed on pills. I cleaned myself up, and with a heavy heart I made my way to his apartment in SoHo. Hundreds of media were there and I navigated my way to the front, and without seeing my credentials a cop said, "Let him through; that's Pat O'Brien." Suddenly I found myself standing next to the car carrying Heath's body. Quickly trying to think of a stand-up, I cleared my throat; the footage of me spitting found its way onto YouTube. I did an old-fashioned, straight up-and-down news story on Heath's final ride out of SoHo. When that video was transmitted to Los Angeles and came up on the monitors in the office, people were cheering. Linda Bell Blue was hysterical, saying we had to own the story, ordering me to Brooklyn the next day to where his former girlfriend actress Michelle Williams lived with their daughter. I was utterly miserable. Did they expect Michelle to come out all chatty and filled with information? I think they were that delusional. People from the office were calling my cell and telling me how great I was doing when a friend of mine had just died with the same disease I had.

Heath's body was taken to the Frank E. Campbell funeral home on the Upper East Side, the same place that the rich and famous from George Gershwin and Irving Berlin to John Lennon and Judy Garland to Notorious B.I.G. were taken after their deaths. Campbell's was known for secrecy and protecting the families, but that didn't stop us from parking right out front. There my cohost, Lara Spencer, and I stood like well-dressed vultures, waiting for the hearse to take Ledger's body to a then-unknown destination. My mood was not helped when a photographer from the New York *Daily News* started goading me about how many bottles of wine were hidden under my bed and how many bottles of pills were in my medicine chest. He was trying to get a reaction from me so he could get a precious photograph. Lara squeezed my arm and I contained myself. As Lara and I stood there waiting for something to happen, back in Hollywood all the producers were screaming at us on our cell phones, "Follow the hearse, follow the body."

They weren't happy when I announced there was no fucking way I was doing that. I wanted to let at least somebody die with dignity on my watch. Lara and I stood there in utter disbelief as we fielded one call after another to "go inside," "get a shot of the casket inside the hearse," and so on. We held on to each other tightly that day.

Not one ounce of joy was left in my job. From that moment on I knew that my days at *The Insider* were numbered.

So I did what came naturally to me now—and reached for as much alcohol I could drink to soothe my nerves. My drinking was now so bad that I could barely make it to work in the morning. A couple of weeks after Heath Ledger's death I managed to get to the office but could no longer function. I was weak and racked with pain. I called Linda Bell Blue and told her that I was too sick to work and was flying to my house in Los Angeles. She replied that my request was impossible as I had work to do before the Grammys, to be held at the Staples Center in downtown LA on February 10. After a lot of ugly back-and-forth, I hung up on her and headed for the airport—to hell with the consequences. She called me again and asked if I was returning to LA. I said that I was. She said that my coverage of the Grammys—my favorite awards ceremony—would be discussed at a later date. From that moment I knew I was fucked. I hated my job, I hated Linda Bell Blue, but most of all I hated myself.

Somehow I got on to a plane, then drank solidly all the way to Los Angeles. When I arrived, I was so befuddled that I had forgotten that Betsy had agreed to pick me up. Instead I got into a taxi, but I had forgotten where I lived and where I was. The taxi driver dropped me at a gas station on Century Boulevard near the airport, and after a frantic, sobbing, garbled conversation with Betsy, she was able to pinpoint my position. She found me sitting on a curb and immediately took me to Dr. Schapira's office at Cedars-Sinai. After they went into a brief huddle in another room, Dr. Schapira returned and told me that I had to go into rehab, saying, "I don't know if I can keep you alive anymore. Your vital signs are gone and you look like hell." Then Betsy came in, dramatically took off her seven-carat engagement ring, put it on my little finger, and told me that it was her or the alcohol. Then she got up and walked out.

I was shocked and devastated. Here I was all alone, about to turn sixty, totally immersed in the disease of alcoholism, and about to lose my job and my fiancée as a consequence. I was confusing getting help again with failure and was putting what was left of my job over what was left of my life. Finally I walked out of Dr. Schapira's office, promising to do something, then stumbled six blocks drunkenly looking for a taxi—no easy feat in Los Angeles, even sober. By the time I got home I was so sick, so tired, and in so much pain that I wanted to die. It was like having severe poisoning and you're still alive but dead on arrival inside. I was beside myself with agony and shame. Somehow I made it through the night, but not before I had drunk myself into insensibility. In the morning Betsy and her assistant came over. I was still at my desk at home drinking. She packed a bag and told me that she was taking me to rehab. There were no ifs or buts. We got into my BMW 760, and the first stop she made was at Gelson's supermarket, where she bought me a bottle of my favorite Silver Oak. "That is the last bottle of wine you are going to have," she announced, before starting the ninety-minute drive to the Betty Ford Center in Rancho Mirage. Betsy was an excellent nurse, albeit expensive. She was also a loyal enabler. On the way I called Linda, Sean, and Linda Bell Blue and told them that I was going back into rehab. I really dreaded telling my beloved son; I was crying like a baby, punching the dashboard, and later shouting, "What am I going to do? I want to die." I just thought my life was over.

On February 8, 2008, I went into my second rehab when I should have been looking forward to my wedding, my sixtieth birthday, the Grammys, the Emmys, and the Oscars.

I checked in again as Pete Zoria, but that deception lasted for about a day before my cover was blown. It's hard for anybody to keep a rehab secret anymore. On visitors' day all the aunts and uncles take notes and get it out there. It didn't matter—the show announced that I was in rehab again dealing with my problems. The good news for me was that I had at least upgraded my rehab facility. The Betty Ford Center is a beautiful compound with a spa, a swimming pool, a beautiful lake, and a good gift shop. I was also able to sneak in a BlackBerry, which they missed in the initial search of everything I had arrived with, including socks and underwear. I hid the Black-Berry in my back pocket, which they didn't search, no doubt thinking nobody would be stupid enough to hide a BlackBerry on his body. Although I knew more than one person who smuggled in syringes and crushed up their legal meds and vitamins and shot them up in the bathroom. I had a nice room and for the first time a roommate I could relate to, but I was clearly not ready to surrender to my disease, let alone a higher power. I was going through the motions at $40,000 a month. I thought I had outsmarted the process when, in fact, I was only digging myself in deeper. All the help in the world from a hospital to guidance counselors was right there, and I breezed by it every day.

My favorite pastime was eating and smoking and working out with my own trainer in the gym. A typical day at Betty Ford for me began with my 6:00 a.m. wake-up call. I had been assigned to be the human alarm clock for everybody else, so I got up, washed my face, checked my e-mails on my hidden BlackBerry, then went room to room to wake everybody else. My reveille went something like this: loud knock on the door, then open it and scream, "Wake up, cock-suckers; you're in rehab." That refrain became pretty popular, and eventually everybody was saying, "Good morning, cocksucker." Re-hab humor. After being shocked out of bed, we all joined in a morn-ing meditation, then went off to the nurses' office to get meds and blood pressure taken. That, too, became a game, where we would award the guy with the best numbers. Breakfast was always huge and delicious, and then in my one hour of morning free time, I strapped on my headphones and ran around the lake about ten times. Shower and then a big group meeting that usually involved a speaker and slide shows that would show a damaged liver and other pleasantries of being an alcoholic. The lectures were an hour long, and I did learn one thing: I was definitely an alcoholic. Lunch. Nap time. Group meeting again, and then we'd spread out into smaller, more intimate meetings with a counselor where we told all our se-crets. All of them. There were also grief meetings, family meetings, pain meetings . . . and the ever-popular mental-health meetings, in which they would determine if we were actually not alcoholics, but just fucking crazy. I passed the crazy tests. Afternoon spare time, I lay out by the pool, listened to music, and got a fabulous tan. Dinner was always a feast, and then another big group meeting, where we would be told again we were going to die if we didn't stop drinking. As the sun set over the desert, everybody smoked, then you were told to go inside and write about your day and what you learned. At 10:00 p.m. we would make a gratitude list of things we shouldn't take for granted; then lockdown and bedtime. If you left your room after ten, a buzzer would go off and they'd come find you. On weekends, the schedule eased up a bit, and everybody was allowed a couple hours with their visiting wives and kids or girlfriends. Betsy came once.

The whole idea was to give all of us some structure in our lives outside of drinking, and while some struggled without drugs and alcohol, for some God-given reason I never once missed drinking. Remarkably, I had no cravings. It's a strange disease.

I spent the entire thirty days sneaking phone calls to my agent, trying to hold on to my job. My agent and legal team brilliantly succeeded in getting me paid this whole time, so it was more a paid vacation than anything else. The only thing I missed was my son. I cried myself to sleep nearly every night over the guilt and shame of disappointing him.

When I left Betty Ford, I was tan, buffed, and in great physical shape. Emotionally, I was still on death row. Back to work I went, and on the first day Linda Bell Blue took me to breakfast and announced that I was no longer the host of the show and was demoted to special correspondent. She matter-of-factly told me she was lopping a million dollars off my salary. I'm thinking, *So that leaves me two and a half million dollars and I can live with that.* Lara Spencer was now the host of the show, and I showed up to do some brief camera work and still did most of the voice-overs since, ironically, the voice that had gotten me in trouble was still the blueprint for the sound of *The Insider.*

I returned to New York and the comfort of my Trump World Tower apartment with three views of the city from sixty floors up, my car and driver, and all the perks and rewards of success. I stayed sober for about six weeks before I started secretly drinking again. All it took was one glass of red wine on my way home one night and my brain's DNA screamed, "Thank you, Pat, welcome back," and asked for more. One drink is too many for an alcoholic, and a thousand is not enough. I hid the bottles in case Betsy came to town, and I wandered around the quaint park across the street from the United Nations with a huge coffee mug full of red wine and sat there and smoked and drank. I was still working every day, but my lifestyle was peeling at me from the outside in: I was losing so much weight that at a big dinner at the Waldorf Astoria Hotel, Mariah Carey grabbed me, pulled me aside, and loudly said, "Enough, enough. You've had enough, now stop it, know what I mean?!"

I spent hours on the phone to Betsy, drunkenly weeping and saying over and over, "I just don't know what to do!" She took this as a suicidal cry for help and left her kids in Pasadena and flew overnight to New York, only to find me in the apartment at 7:00 a.m. in my bathrobe sobbing and drinking a large coffee mug of red wine. Eventually she managed to stop my sobbing, cleaned me up, and took me outside for breakfast. She took me to a deli on Third and Forty-Fifth Street, and I sat on the curb, crying, vomiting, and about to pass out while she went inside and bought coffee and bagels. Somehow she sobered me up enough to put me in the hands of my driver to take me to the Broadway set.

Not that I was much in demand. With the show relaunched in June, I was now very much the outsider on *The Insider,* reduced to bit-part appearances while Lara Spencer kept the show on the road. My drinking was now so bad that I even alienated my few remaining allies on the show. My best and most loyal and closest friend on the show, Sarah Huber, was a fun, smart girl whose job was to tape voice-overs with me. On several occasions she called me at home to record a voice-over from my makeshift studio with high-tech equipment installed in a closet. However, often when she called, I was too drunk to speak. She covered for me, but then it happened again just as the newly formatted show was due to go on air. When I came to work, I apologized to Sarah, and she told me that she would do anything to protect me, but that if I continued on this path, no one could help me. She was right. I was on a path of utter self-destruction. I was unhappy with the show, unhappy with myself, unhappy with life.

In September, Linda Bell Blue threw me a lifeline, sending me on the road to cover the 2008 presidential elections for the show. She knew I loved politics, and I think she thought my return to my first love would help my self-esteem. I first went to Iowa to interview Joe Biden's wife, Jill, and we had a couple laughs as I used to be the Senate private-elevator operator and took Senator Biden up and down many times. I also had a great time being around Iowans and the familiar solid Midwestern hospitality. All went well and I was starting to feel like Pat O'Brien again; however, I would later learn from one of my field producers that I was acting bizarrely. According to his eyewitness account, we pulled over our stretch limo (in Iowa!) so I could go inside a store to buy some cigarettes. Twenty minutes went by and I didn't come out. The producer went in and I was nowhere to be found. An hour later, he found me wandering in a cornfield. I had no recollection of that one either. He did not turn me in. Instead, they sent me to Alaska to interview some of Republican vice-presidential candidate Sarah Palin's closest friends. That also went well until I returned to my hotel room in Anchorage. I met up with an old friend from my Iditarod days and we promptly got wasted. After he left, I ordered yet another drink and sat down in one of the bar's comfortable lounge chairs. I began to go over the past couple of weeks at work, which started with being warned by Linda and the Human Resources staff that my complaining e-mails to

Lara Spencer would not be tolerated. I said, "What e-mails?" They handed me copies of everything I had sent Lara. There were no copies of what Lara had sent back—similar complaining e-mails about how fucked-up the show was. Lara and I were great friends and remain so, but as I thought about this, all alone and way above the forty-ninth parallel, I did what alcoholics do: I got angry and resentful and then my disease attacked again. I fumbled with my Black-Berry and managed to send the following doozy e-mail to everybody at *The Insider* and *Entertainment Tonight* and all the executives:

"Hi, folks, I just spent a couple of days in Iowa—I'm a little bit of a favorite son there—and I spoke with maybe a thousand people and was very hands-on. Even Joe Biden said, 'You should be running (for president)!' But what I came away with was, these people can't afford gas, books, food, or schools or movies!

"I was approached a hundred times by people asking, 'Can you help us?' I tried to tell them we care, but they didn't buy it. They wanted to, but watching Anya and Lara [Spencer] pick out accessories makes the viewers want to vomit. I'll get killed for this, but I'm actually the one not afraid for my job. I want people to be happy."

The segment I was apparently enraged about was called "Look for Less," which featured Lara and her clothing slave, Anya, telling viewers how they, too, could look like a million bucks, while the two were wearing clothes that no normal person could ever dream of affording. I pushed SEND. (As I read the e-mail now, it makes a lot of sense, but let's get back to Alaska.) In between pushing SEND to basically everybody and waiting for some kind of a response, I passed out in the bar and somehow woke up at six in the morning in my hotel room. I have no idea how I get there. Somebody had emptied the minibar in my room, so at sunrise I walked out into the freezing Alaska morning looking for a liquor store. A taxi driver reluctantly drove me about five miles to some horrific neighborhood and said, "This one opens at seven." It was six thirty. I stood outside the steel-gated entrance with a couple of homeless guys, freezing to death. Suddenly I looked at the sign on the liquor store: 9 A.M.–MIDNIGHT.

I was fucked. I started to walk back to the hotel, hoping to find a bar along the way. As I was walking, my BlackBerry was blowing up. The first e-mail was from Sarah: "Why did you do that?" Then from Lara: "Did you really write that?" Then from another close friend, reporter Victoria Recaño (who also looked after me as much as she could): "You're all over the internet again. The email is on the internet!!!! Call me. Call me!!!!" Another from Sarah: "What is wrong with you? Where are you?" I quickly checked my BlackBerry and there the e-mail was. I had no memory of writing it.

I finally found a gritty Eskimo bar and walked in hoping I wouldn't be recognized. No problem there, I was the only customer. I ordered two glasses of the worst wine I have ever tasted and guzzled them both and called my publicist, Ken Sunshine. I calmly told him everything I had done, and he said, "We'll try to do damage control from here. Good luck." I called one of Linda's soldiers, DJ, and he lied, "I haven't seen it." DJ was a dear friend, but with that answer I knew he was no longer on Team O'Brien. I finally called Linda Bell Blue, and she ordered me to be in the office first thing the following morning for a meeting with her and Terry Wood. I said, "Should I bring a lawyer?"—hoping for something like "Naaaw, what for?" Instead she said these chilling words: "That's your decision. Just be on time."

My life was unraveling again and I was alone and in fucking Alaska! I knew my luck and my chances had run their course. I went back to the hotel and had three quick glasses of wine, quickly packed, and headed to the airport. While in the tunnel to get on the plane, I sat down to rest and passed out, but somebody, I still don't know who, somehow folded me onto the plane and into my seat. No pictures. No leaks.

I landed in Seattle and went to the airport bar to drown my sorrows. At this moment my alcoholism had won the battles and the war and had taken over completely. I started to selfishly feel sorry for myself, when I should have been feeling sorry for what I was doing to Sean and all those people who worked hard to make me look good on television. No, this was about me. As the saying goes, "Poor, poor me. Pour me a drink!" As I'm writing that script, the next thing I know I woke up in the front seat of a police car, nursing a huge bump on my head. The cop said, "Mr. O'Brien, this is your lucky day. I got the call that you fell off the barstool, hit your head hard, and somehow the staff there protected you and called the police. I got the call and I'm a fan and can see you need help. I think we got you out of there without anybody seeing you, so that's a good thing." I'm thinking, *This is a cop?*

He then dropped me off at a local hotel, checked me in, and left me there.

It was now nighttime and I went to the hotel lobby bar and drank until they refused to serve me any more. I went to my room to order drinks through room service, and the manager told me that I was found crying in the bar and disturbing other residents and they were cutting me off. Period. Meantime, I had no idea where I was, so I called my lifeline, Betsy, and she couldn't figure it out either. "What's the area code on the phone?" she yelled, but I couldn't function. She hung up and called our friend LA police chief Bill Bratton to see if he could help, but he said unless I was a missing person, he could not make an exception. Good for him.

The next morning I tried to clean up, nearly overdosed on black coffee, and got on a plane for Los Angeles, knowing that this time there was no leniency, no understanding, no sympathy—just hard-core reality. I was going to be fired.

I got home, took another shower, shaved again, and dressed for what I knew was going to be a career funeral. I put on my best Armani suit and tie, covered up my bruises with makeup, and looked in the mirror. It was frightening to see what was looking back: the shallow, sad eyes of a broken man. I managed to whisper, "I'm sorry, Sean. I'm so sorry." Then I lay facedown on my bed and cried for about forty-five minutes. I got up and buried my face in a sink full of ice, fixed my makeup, and drove my black Maserati to my inevitable date with the hangman at Paramount Studios.

The meeting lasted eleven minutes. During that short time, Terry Wood said she had spent the entire weekend trying to put out fires. Linda Bell Blue just stared at me. Terry was screaming, but everything was in slow motion. Nobody asked me if I was okay or needed help. Terry finished with "You are suspended without pay indefinitely." As I left, Linda grabbed me and hugged me tenderly and said, "Patrick, I will never say anything bad about you. I mean that. We'll make a decision quickly." And that was it.

I got back into my Maserati, which I had parked in Dr. Phil's spot for the fun of it . . . drove home alone, walked into an empty house, loosened my tie, sat in an empty room, and drank myself into oblivion. I remember saying, "God help me." And that's the last thing I remember from that day.

22

Let's Really Go Crazy

Believe it or not, there was some good news to hang on to. First and foremost, I was still alive. Somebody was watching over me. Second, there were no financial issues: I had managed my money well, and for some reason my accountants had had the good sense to insure me for just about anything, including this. I could hang on to the cars and houses and various cash and prizes I had accumulated along the journey. But now, with no place to go every day, I gathered the strength to go into the most important truth in the recovery bible, which guarantees this on page 417:

"And acceptance is the answer to all my problems today. When I am disturbed, it is because I find some person, place, thing or situation—some fact of my life—unacceptable to me, and I can find no serenity until I accept that person, place, thing or situation as being exactly the way it is supposed to be at this moment.

"Nothing, absolutely nothing, happens in God's world by mistake. Until I could accept my alcoholism, I could not stay sober; unless I accept life completely on life's terms, I cannot be happy. I need to concentrate not so much on what needs to be changed in the world as on what needs to be changed in me and in my attitudes."

So I gathered the strength to get up one more time, dust myself off, and give it another go. One thing was certain: I was running out of choices. I wrote another $30,000 check and moved back into the Betty Ford Center. I found somebody to drive me there and, once again, drank all the way, thinking this would also be my last bottle of wine. It was easy checking me in, as I had just checked out a few weeks earlier. Nothing is more lonely than checking into a rehab center alone.

Upon arrival, my alcohol blood level was .36. Overdose and death isn't much further on the blood-alcohol-content scale. The admissions doctor looked at me and said, "Congratulations! A point thirty-six and you're not dead! Welcome back."

Every single number associated with my liver, pancreas, heart, and down the list was off the charts. "You're in good hands again," I was assured.

I checked in again with all the accompanying searches and was assigned another room, this time with a small deck near the pool and with good sunlight for tanning. I also got a roommate who wasn't a complete whack job; but then again, something was clearly wrong with all of us. The familiar surroundings gave me some comfort, but I was hurting deeply inside for what I had put everyone through again, especially Sean. I told myself that maybe this time I would listen and become a human being again. The 12-step program defines my predicament like this: "We admitted we were powerless over alcohol and our lives had become unmanageable."

The key word is *admitted*. I would try. It's the biggest mountain to climb for an alcoholic, and I was never any further than the molehill. I had always been successful at escaping disaster, and the only way to do that this time around was to do the work.

I certainly went through the motions and assured Sean and Linda that I was going to be all right. Meantime, Betsy had pretty much given up on me and was entertaining as many men and women as she could in my absence. Some of them in my New York Trump apartment. And she was still trolling New York lesbian hangouts with one of her friends, a married mother with kids who lived in Connecticut. I still looked to Betsy for support, but this time she didn't visit. She'd had enough and I didn't blame her. Or maybe she was just busy.

At Betty Ford, one of the mandatory assignments is to make a huge time line of your entire life from your first breath to the one you had been granted now. So on a six-foot-long piece of paper, I went through my entire life: a sentence here and there about growing up, my parents, school, death of parents, birth of my son, incredible successes and failures. Then next to them you put your drinking history. Then you put the consequences. Then you tack it on the wall for everybody to see and you go through it with them year by year. As I got to the drinking and the consequences, my schematic looked like the Richter scale for a bad earthquake. After my presentation, which lasted about an hour, another patient said, "It seems to me that this Betsy woman might have been the wrong decision, because you seemed fine up to that point." Bingo.

At the day's end I had to write a report on what I had achieved. Each day my report came back with a white flag from my counselor on it saying, "Surrender or else."

Some days I thought the spiritual side was kicking in, then all the resentments I was foolishly holding on to would kick in and I was back to square one. Meantime, poor Sean was so scared about all this, every time his phone rang he prayed I wasn't dead. One of my counselors, a former alcoholic turned monk, suggested I put all my feelings about Sean on paper. We called this counselor the Drunk Monk, but this was the best sober advice I ever got. My handwritten letter began:

"My Dear son, Sean,

"Well, here I am, your big strong invincible Dad in his third rehab. I painfully remember when you visited my first rehab, you started to cry. I had scared my little boy. I remember when you left you sat in your car and wept. I had divorced your mom, got in a national sex scandal and was reduced to public humiliation. When I got out I said 'Do you want to talk about it?' as we do everything and you said, 'No, you're still my Dad and best friend.' Over the past couple years we have talked a lot about my alcoholism but for the last six months I have been living a lie. Even to you. A couple times you would call and I would just start crying. I know you have been scared to death, in fact you told me that everytime your phone rang you thought I was dead. Son, I know how you look up to me—we are so close— and you put me on that pedestal. I am so sorry I scared you."

Then I quoted from a letter he had written me during my rehab: "Dad, you will always be my first and most important role model. Though you are at a little bump in the road, it shows me how much you care. I'm your biggest supporter."

I finished with "Sean, I did this for me and for you. I love you with all my sober heart, Dad."

I graduated knowing that one thing was certain: I was an alcoholic. Sadly, nobody picked me up, so I hitched a ride back to LA with one of my best friends in the program. A month later, he was found dead, alone in a downtown Los Angeles hotel room. Alcohol.

As for me, for thirty days I had exercised, eaten well, and rested, so I felt great. Before I headed east to see Sean, I went to a Lakers game and met up with Maria Shriver. She had known the devastating impact of alcoholism in her own family, and right there in front of the floor seats, she grabbed me and nearly screaming said, "I'm not kidding, you sort this out. Your time is running out." She was so animated that a couple of the celebs in the front row looked as if they were going to run for the exits. But Maria was right and I didn't listen. Mr. Big Shot here felt sufficiently in control of his life to drink all the way on the flight to New York. When I took Sean to dinner, I didn't drink, but when we walked outside in the New York fall night, he said, "Dad, I know you're drinking; your teeth are black!"

I realized again just how much I was disappointing my son—just as my father had disappointed me. I had also written my dead father a letter from rehab, and as I wrote it, I realized even more that my problems were forever linked to my childhood. The handwritten letter said:

"Dear dad, I will make this letter about as quick as our relationship. You don't know how much I wanted and needed a loving father. It made me so sad to not have an active father, instead I got an empty seat at the dinner table, an empty seat at Father & Son nights and nobody to call when I'd finished a sports night on TV to say 'dad what a great game.' I got no kisses goodnight; no stern talks about my behavior, no help with my homework, no pats on the back when I accomplished something and your alcoholism scared me.

"But even knowing you just a little, I still look up to you because you gave me the gift of life & you gave me enough little memories to pretend when you were sober. I wish you had the gift of sobriety so that we could have shared our lives together & you could have held your grandson but most importantly so that you could have told me that there's not a boogieman when your dad was around. I forgive you dad. Love your son Pat."

Back in New York and so far gone now, I didn't let parental sentiment get between me and my Silver Oak. As soon as Sean left for the evening, I started drinking heavily. I fell off the bed and hit my head on the nightstand. I called Betsy, even though she had told me that she was no longer interested in staying with someone who was intent on killing himself. Even so, she continued to run up incredible bills on my credit cards and drive around in my cars. She was costing me $20,000 a month.

Trump Tower security found me unconscious and bleeding profusely by the side of the bed. They called 911, and the paramedics took me to NewYork-Presbyterian Hospital. I was so belligerent that they warned me the next step would be to strap me down. Such was my mood that once I was stitched up, I decided I wanted to go home. Without asking anybody, and as soon as the coast was clear, I hopped off the gurney I was lying on and walked out of the hospital in just my hospital gown, with no cash, credit cards, or ID. Fortunately a taxi driver recognized me and took me back to Trump Tower. He didn't charge me, but he did say, "Mr. O'Brien, is there somebody you can call?" I said, "Not really," and went sixty floors up to my apartment and collapsed on the couch. I didn't want to alarm Sean.

Once I had sobered enough to open more bottles of wine, I started drinking again. Once more I blacked out, fell over, split my head, and called the long-suffering Betsy in tears. This time she phoned both the Trump concierge and 911 in New York. As luck would have it, the same paramedics attended my second fall and took me, kicking and screaming, back to the same hospital. This time the duty doctor informed me that as I was a danger to myself, I was going to be placed on a seventy-two-hour psychiatric hold. So just a few blocks from where my picture was on every sign in Times Square, they put me in a holding room with only a mattress and a small window and locked the door from the outside. No chair, no blanket, no pillow. I was scared to death and I was cold. No phone calls and no charming the nurses and the doctors for a release. I was now officially a mental patient. I soon discovered that I was treated just like everyone else— the woman down the hall who wouldn't stop screaming, the guy who talked to himself nonstop, and the bearded character who made imaginary phone calls all day to make-believe people. Welcome to my world. Seventy-two hours later, I was moved by dark of night, with a blanket over my head to ward off possible paparazzi, to the Astor psychiatric unit in the town of Beacon about two hours north of the city. No need for the blanket because nobody, including my family and friends, knew where I was. They told me this was not a 5150 but the only hope in stabilizing me. There was no paperwork. They reached Betsy, who flew from LA with a bag of my pajamas, books, reading glasses, and toiletries. By now she had been reduced to a really, really expensive traveling nurse. She always made sure she traveled well—first-class and a car and driver.

She was shocked as much by the place as by the sight of me. I was black-and-blue with stitches in my head and weighed about 130 pounds. Betsy told me later she wouldn't have wished my situation on her worst enemy. My worst enemy at that very moment was me. We are way beyond moral issues here. I was in denial, deceiving myself again and again, as my addiction searched for another way to stay alive. As Sigmund Freud described this process: "There is a general tendency of our mental apparatus . . . it seems to find expression in the tenacity with which we hold on to the sources of pleasure at our disposal, and in the difficulty with which we renounce them."

My self-esteem was as low as my anxiety was high. The only thing that kept me going was that I knew I could keep going. But I was flying solo without my stabilizer: alcohol.

During my stay at Beacon, which is ninety miles north of New York City, I was restricted from doing anything, including going outside without two or three people with me. I finally called Sean and told him I was in a "hospital" and that I'd be out soon. He offered to come and see me, but I didn't know where I was and I was in no shape for my son to see the dad he looked up to. Even the head doctor said, "Look at you. You are no longer Pat O'Brien. You're bruised and beaten and a skeleton of yourself. You are staying until I can get some life in you." I don't know how many rules he broke, but it was the favor I needed.

I was there about ten days until they finally let me out in the care of Sean, who made sure I got settled in my apartment.

Dr. Gerald May, who wrote *Addiction & Grace* and is a noted authority on addictive behavior, writes that the addict keeps finding ways to deny that he is addicted and inevitably "the higher power he is surrendering to is the addiction itself." Within a couple of days I was drinking again. This time, I called Sean. He knocked on my door, and when I saw the look of sheer panic on his face, I tried to apologize, but the poor guy didn't know what to do. Nothing in his upbringing was related to what he was looking at. He did all the right things: first he hid the pills from my medicine cabinet and checked the house for bottles. Then, out of sheer panic and fear that I would die, he decided to sit with me through the night. He started crying and said, "You are my whole life. I don't want to lose you. Please don't do this to yourself. Look at you. You don't weigh anything; your jeans are falling off. Please, please, please don't do this anymore. Please, Dad, don't do this!" As he lay weeping on the couch, I went off to bed. I was shaking so hard I couldn't wait for him to go so that I could have a drink to calm me down. There was no room for any emotional discussion. That only takes up the space where even a son's love and compassion can't satisfy the emotions that alcohol does. About noon he left, as he had to go to class. Imagine being a sophomore at NYU with your whole life ahead of you and this shit pops into your life. Afterward Linda called and said, "When you think of taking another drink, think about the damage you did to your son last night."

That afternoon in early November I decided to fly to my beach house in Nantucket, a holiday home that was stocked only with happy memories. I told myself that I was going to relax and think about my future and how to somehow make amends for my past. Actually I was going there to die. When I left the airport, I drove to the local liquor store thinking I would buy one bottle of wine and watch the election on TV. It was November 4, 2008. The lady behind the counter said, "Honey, I've only got one case of Silver Oak." Without missing a beat I bought the whole case and drank myself into a stupor as I watched Barack Obama, who had campaigned on a platform of hope and new beginnings, storm to victory. As I wandered around the house that held so many memories, a glass of wine in my hand, I drank and drank as if there were no end.

Eventually, after drinking solidly through the night, I called Betsy again. All I could mumble was "Help me, help me, help me." She realized where I was and had the presence of mind to call Don Hahn, a great guy who looked after my home when I was not around. He came over and reported that I was in terrible shape, near death. I had emptied twelve bottles of wine. Linda got ahold of Joe Walsh of the Eagles, a recovering alcoholic and a real friend; then she patched me in to another fellow traveler, Terry Hendrick, from my college days. She then patched me through to good friend Michael Klein, who patched me in to a Betty Ford counselor. Finally Sean was patched in, and God knows who else . . . but they all listened to me scream for about ninety minutes that I wanted to die. The Betty Ford counselor said, "Don't stop drinking because you'll go into a seizure; get to a hospital." My body was in such pain that if I had died there and then, it would have been a relief. Dr. May again: "The fall is tragic in the classical sense, an abject crashing down after the pinnacles of pride have been attained." For example, I was apparently proud of myself that I was at least trying to stop drinking. He continues: "Once this is recognized, it brings guilt, remorse, and shame in bitter proportion to the pride that preceded it. Self-respect disappears. Suicide is considered. Without even the will to resist, the use of the chemical increases, dramatically, further impairing judgment. A critically dangerous situation results." I was at the critical dangerous situation.

Don stayed with me through the night, but realized he wasn't competent to care for a hysterical, crying drunk and wisely took me to the Nantucket Cottage Hospital.

As I walked into the emergency room, the first thing I did was projectile vomit. After taking one look at me, the duty doctor said that no way could I travel until I was stabilized. I spent the night, heavily sedated, in the hospital before being taken by ambulance to the airport. I boarded a private medevac jet, which Betsy charged to my American Express card to the tune of $30,000, and went to Hazelden, my fourth rehab.

Hazelden has a secluded five-hundred-acre campus at Center City about forty minutes outside Minneapolis. They picked me up in an ambulance, and the next thing I knew, I was in freezing-cold weather and in another hospital. It was November 5, 2008.

Even in my numbed sense, I immediately felt at peace and at home there. It might have been the comforting staff, it might have been the feeling of being back in the Midwest, it might have been the realization that this time there was only one solution. Stop drinking, find God, and work at a program that would keep me away from alcohol once and for all (hopefully) and let me move on. My body, my brain, my skin, my bones—all of it was telling me, "The party's over, Pat." I had hit bottom.

From the moment I got settled in, I felt a sense of health and sobriety. As luck would have it, or maybe as God designed it, the counselor assigned to me, Chuck Rice, got me back on the tracks. The first thing he said to me was "You're going to die." He told me that my problem was that I was always thinking about my job, my money, my image, and of course my son. "Pat, you can't do this for Sean. You have to do it for yourself or Sean will be arranging your funeral. Forget about Betsy, Sean, everybody but yourself, and I guarantee you that you will walk out of here sober. All that other stuff will have to wait." Another counselor was particularly keen on eliminating Betsy, saying, "In so many ways, she might be your biggest problem."

It began to snow and the trees were sparkling with beautiful feathers of frost. It all reminded me of South Dakota, and I felt a sense of rebirth and new beginnings. As I walked outside taking inventory of my situation, I listened to the crackle of snow beneath my feet. Suddenly, I felt as if the world had dropped off my shoulders. I was finally getting my "God moment."

I sat down in the snow by the lake and said the serenity prayer: "God grant me the serenity to accept the things I cannot change, the courage to change the things I can, and the wisdom to know the difference." I let the snowflakes melt on my eyelids, and for once it was not just tears running down my cheeks. I felt it was God, washing away my fears.

I jumped headfirst into recovery, embracing every second of the program, attending every lecture, taking notes, and clinging for dear life to the Hazelden program. I organized meditation groups and bonded with a group of great guys who were all in the same predicament. Chuck Rice encouraged me daily: "This is your life now. Or else."

I was hoping to see Sean and he agreed to fly from New York to this little country town for Thanksgiving, forgoing, for the first time, our annual family reunion in San Francisco. Hazelden was strict about letting guests dine with patients, even family and even on holidays, but Chuck arranged for Sean and me to have a private, catered Thanksgiving dinner on the campus. Afterward, Sean and I went for a walk and he made me promise to "just quit lying." His visit, surely not on his schedule, showed me what a treasure he was, and from that moment on, my mind free of alcohol and chemicals, I pledged to never let him down again.

Right there and then, in a forest in Minnesota, the promises of recovery began to take over. After Sean left, I went for a walk through the forest and I found myself skipping through the snow. In the wintery silence I could almost hear an inner voice say "welcome back."

23

The Beginning of the Beginning

After six weeks, on December 12, 2008, I left Hazelden confident and ready to restart my life. Now weighing a healthy 160 pounds, I felt fit and ready to begin again. In many ways it was bittersweet to leave Hazelden, which had become a place of salvation and redemption and comfort for me. As I walked through the Minneapolis airport on my way back to Los Angeles, many people shouted out, "How about those Vikings?" I was never so happy to hear small talk. The airport was full of families on their way to visit relatives, and children already dreaming of Christmas, white or any color. These holidays had always been my favorite time of the year and I soaked up energy with the anticipation of a child. I was feeling really, really good about myself and started to put the holidays into a sober context. I would later hear fellow traveler Father Leo, who likened alcoholics to Rudolph the Red-Nosed Reindeer, who was asked, not told: "'Won't you guide my sleigh tonight?' Then all the reindeer loved him as they shouted out with glee: 'Rudolph the Red-Nosed Reindeer, you'll go down in history!'"

I walked by the packed airport bar and into a Starbucks for my first fresh cup of coffee on the outside. I boarded my plane without incident, ordered a water, and before you could say: "My name is Pat, I'm an alcoholic" I was sound asleep. I woke up to a balmy Los Angeles.

I came home to an empty house and put on some Christmas music and pulled out the one decoration that has given me the greatest pleasure. When Sean was eight we were opening up presents and he began to tear up. "Dad, I don't think you got enough presents," he said before running upstairs. A few minutes later he came down with a gift hidden behind his back. "Here, Dad," he said, and he handed me an empty Paul Mitchell shampoo bottle hastily wrapped in used festive paper. The tag said: "To Dad From Sean. Love you!" It's the only Christmas decoration I never store away. And now I was prepared to give him the one present that he was wishing for: sobriety.

I had no job and I wasn't looking. I wanted to soak it all in, but, inevitably, life got in the way. I had an agonizing back operation and shortly afterward I was diagnosed with prostate cancer. I was diagnosed on Monday and on Thursday had my prostate and the cancer removed. When I came out of the operation, the doctor said, "Pat, your porn career will continue."

Meantime, Betsy showed up one day and said she wanted to break all ties and walked away with the seven-carat diamond ring and other cash and prizes. Then she tried to sue me to take posses-sion of my 1965 Corvette. She also kept most of the furniture and all of the jewelry and sold a grand piano I had given to her daugh-ters. I got a call from her from, of all places, Dubai. She was crying and had been abandoned by her friends and needed advice. I was in Jamaica on a sunny afternoon enjoying my sanity and sobriety in the land of Ganja of all places.

This time around, I had a blank canvas in front of me and on my list were a lot of possible dreams. I had always toyed with returning to South Dakota and doing one of two things: buy the Hamburger Inn, a lone diner that seats about ten people and serves the best burger in the country for under $2.00, or run for political office back home and fulfill one of Dr. Farber's wishes. In fact, as I refer-enced briefly earlier, the late Eunice Kennedy was adamant that I go home and run. She would grab me by the arm and with that look I'm sure every Kennedy has burned within them would say, "You

have to, Pat. We'll all come back and help you." I asked then Governor Schwarzenegger about my scandal and he promptly said, "Fuck
the scandal," and to prove a point, appointed me as a Commissioner
to the California Service Corps.

But for now, it was time for reflection and putting new pieces of
my life together with the promises of recovery that boast a new
freedom and happiness and the ability to go through life without
fear. A new life I learned would materialize if I worked for it. And I
have. Even while going back and forth from New York to Nantucket
to South Dakota and Montego Bay, I have been steadfast about attending AA meetings at least five times a week. Somebody asked me
how long I needed to go to meetings and I politely replied, "The rest
of my fucking life." But through the grace of God, I have learned
that it's better to know I'm an alcoholic sitting in a meeting than to
wonder if I was an alcoholic sitting at home alone drinking. I have a
disease soaked in brain dysfunction, genetics, low self-esteem, fear,
guilt, shame. And if I don't address all of that baggage every day,
things go south quickly. So, I trudge forward. I have, if you will,
fallen in love with a life well lived in recovery, where I listen to
voices other than my own for a massive change of pace. Massive. As
the book of Alcoholics Anonymous says, "it works, it really does."

Here's a headline: I was not anonymous. It seemed like everybody knew my story and if they didn't, it was a Google click away. I
was anxious to test the waters and just like that, when Walter
Cronkite died, the president of CBS News, Sean McManus, proved
his loyalty and sent me a personal invitation to the private service to
be held at Lincoln Center in New York.

Quite frankly, I was surprised and rather apprehensive. While I
had been nearly a year sober at the time since leaving *The Insider*, I
had deliberately kept a low public profile. I wondered how I would
be received by my contemporaries: was I an outsider now attending
a gathering of America's biggest insiders? I bravely tested it. They
were all there: Katie Couric, then the *CBS Evening News* anchor;
Brian Williams, anchor of *NBC Nightly News*; Charlie Gibson; Diane

Sawyer; Barbara Walters; Les Moonves; and the *60 Minutes* crowd. Barbara came over and asked how I was doing, Dan Rather put his arm around me and gave me a big hug. Everyone couldn't have been more welcoming. Buzz Aldrin, the second man on the Moon and a fellow traveler in the world of sobriety, gave me a thumbs-up and President Clinton gave me a beaming smile of recognition. With President Obama sitting a few feet away, it felt good to be back among the movers and shakers, to imbibe "the heady wine" of success, as Tom Brokaw memorably said, if only for an afternoon.

The best speech, as usual, was from Clinton, who related a story about Cronkite during the impeachment scandal surrounding Monica Lewinsky. As Clinton was fending off a hostile House and Senate, the consummate newsman called him and asked if he wanted to go sailing. At the time a picture of him on a sailboat with "the most trusted man in America" would have helped his battered political image. He went on to say that both men knew the value of that picture. What he was really saying, of course, was that Cronkite was being loyal to a friend in trouble. It was a quality I had learned to appreciate. Indeed, when I turned sixty I got a beautiful letter from President Clinton that said, in part: "You've become a fixture in American popular culture, and you can take pride in the affection you've earned from so many people over the course of your remarkable career. I've come to understand, as my own birthdays accumulate, what matters most with each passing year: knowing that you have made a difference in the lives of others, and knowing that you have the friendship and admiration of those around you."

When the Cronkite service was over, groups of media characters stood around reminiscing. I went over to one group that included all the network presidents as well as my first boss at NBC, Dick Wald, a tough Irishman who once ran NBC with an iron will and who David Brinkley and I had once played a trick on, by throwing his shoes off a balcony at the 1972 Democratic Convention in Miami.

Wald was in the middle of a story when he saw me approach. I hadn't seen him in maybe twenty-five years, but his face lit up and he told his well-heeled audience: "Now if you want to meet the guy who *really* ran the show when I was around, there he is, Pat O'Brien." He put his arm around me as he revealed that if he wanted to get David Brinkley to do something he called me first. It was a public endorsement I could not have scripted. It was my Clinton/Cronkite moment.

When I was discussing this book with John Murphy, the head of publicity at St. Martin's Press, we had several wonderful lunches at the Beverly Hills Hotel. In the summer of 2010, as we walked to our table, we ran into former first lady Nancy Reagan. She grabbed me and said, "Pat! Are you okay now? We were *so* worried about you." For a while there, I was starting to lose perspective about myself, wondering if I worried and upset so many people that forgiveness would have to come in subtle remarks like that of the former First Lady. However, when I went to London to cover the Olympics again for NBC, Michelle Obama raced over to me and as I started to say, "Hello, Madame First Lady, I'm—" she quickly said, "I know who you are. We love you at the White House. Barack, as you know, is a big sports fan and he grew up watching you. He sends his good wishes."

Okay, now we're getting there. When I turned sixty-five, I got this note: "So, you are going to be 65! Well, I'm going to be 80 the next day, but I know we will be young forever. Thank you for being you. You have done nothing but make many, many people happy for the last 65 years. Thank you, thank you, thank you! Happy, happy birthday to a lovely man! Yoko."

I've always thought that my journey has been not unlike Dorothy's in *The Wizard of Oz*. Life is good and then suddenly a tornado hits and she lands in some foreign faraway land with witches and scary monkeys and little people. There are trees that want to pull her in, poppy fields, and nothing that reminds her of Kansas. She meets up with three unlikely characters and they go searching for the Wizard of Oz to get them home. Their journey is filled with fear and anticipation. But at the very end she discovers that all this time, through all this drama and fear and uncertainty, she always had the ability to go home again, just by clicking her heels and repeating "there's no place like home." The whole time she could have been home and she didn't know it. The man who wrote the book *The Wonderful Wizard of Oz,* on which the movie is based, was, like me, a South Dakotan. His descriptions of Kansas (based on South Dakota) and the journey to Oz are even closer to me because of our common heritage. But there is a line in the play based on L. Frank Baum's book that didn't find its way into the movie. As Dorothy looked on while the Lion got a medal for courage, the Scarecrow got a diploma for brains, and the Tin Man got a pocket watch the shape of a heart, she looked at the Wizard's huge balloon that would take her back to Kansas and said: "Will that balloon take me all the way back to Kansas?" To which the Wizard replied: "Well, Dorothy, we never know if anything works until afterward."

Mine was indeed a leap of faith and, once again, you can find me in all the familiar and right places. I've had an abundance of second chances and for that I am grateful.

While my life is charmed, there is still work to do. For example, I will probably need Matthew, Mark, Luke, and John to help me write what will be lifelong amends to Sean and Linda, the only two people who really need an apology. Sean likes to write me notes for important milestones and on a recent Father's Day he wrote: "You've taught me everything I know about being a man."

I have tried to teach him that you don't have to go through life with the danger of excitement, fear, anger, worry, self-pity, or foolish decisions.

Thank God for the gift of desperation that allowed me to take a good look at myself. I wish everybody could have that moment . . . perhaps without the drama that accompanied mine . . . but just have that moment where you say maybe, just maybe, this isn't the way to grab onto life. Letting go of a lot of things and people and character defects has given me a life where the music plays loudly each and every day.

Arguably one of the greatest ballerinas ever was Tanaquil Le Clercq, who was the great muse and love of George Balanchine. At the height of her fame in the 1950s she contracted polio and was paralyzed for life. At the time she asked, "If I'm not a dancer, who am I? Who am I?" But she, too discovered herself by realizing it was out of her control and she could only change the things she could change. From a wheelchair she passed on her talents to others.

As I look ahead, I don't want to slam the door on my past, because it was a learning experience so vivid and so terribly wonderful that I will keep it in my back pocket so I never forget how I got this far down the tracks.

As F. Scott Fitzgerald wrote about his favorite character, Gatsby: "So we beat on, boats against the current, borne back ceaselessly into the past."

I had the best seat in the house and I thank you.

Acknowledgments

There was a time when I would roll my eyes every time I heard an athlete winning a game or an actor picking up an award proclaim "I'd like to thank God, who has made all this happen," etc. Now I am one of those people.

So I'd first like to thank God, who has made my life today possible. But I also have a rabbi and many others on my team. Let's start with Marc Resnick, my editor at St. Martin's Press, who guided me through what turned out to be a longer process than he expected, but thanks to him, you are now reading this book. To the indomitable Sally Richardson, who put her iconic literary faith in me, and I'm grateful. And, not enough space to thank Kate Canfield for all she did, but, like everything else, she'll fit it in here. And to all the folks at St. Martin's who are dedicated to the great American pastime: editing and polishing meaningful books. While the Irish might have saved civilization, wouldn't you know that God gave me a good Irishman to help save this book. I thank the great John Murphy at St. Martin's, who seems to be the only person not in the movies who gets fawned over at The Polo Lounge in Beverly Hills.

The easy way to thank everybody and not leave anybody out is to start with the first name I drop in this book, my attorney Ernie Dell, and go all the way to the last name, F. Scott Fitzgerald. In between they all had a part in my journey. There are some great, great people on that list, as well as some real demons . . . but they all had a part in shaping who I am today. Many of them helped remind me that, in more examples than one, it was I who was the demon, not the other person.

In that spirit, I want to thank the people who keep an eye out for me each and every day. That list begins with Jeff McFarland, Joe W, Richard S, and all those gentle souls who pulled up the lifeboat for me.

Those who saw me through my "irrational compulsions," as writer Olivia Laing described the consequences of drinking in her book *The Trip to Echo Spring*, include George Savitsky, who is much more than just a brilliant accountant, and the great producers who shaped my grandiosity and made it a hit in television and radio: Jim Bell, Rob Silverstein, David Michaels, Bob Mansbach, Eric Mann, the late Paul Hogan, and, of course, Dick Ebersol.

To Lara Spencer, who lived this book and survived.

To John Hogan and Sam Betesh, who navigated me through a brief and wonderful radio career. To Bob Pittman, whose loyalty has been show-business grace. And to John Sykes for a rich friendship.

My South Dakota crowd: Blomberg, Garvey, Opheim, Cloud, Tabbert, Kirk, and the late Surfer Joe.

We still remember everybody's home phone numbers from back in 1963. And to Dave Olson and Terry Hendrick who hugged me early and Monsigner James Michael Doyle, my first and favorite spiritual advisor.

And to my Nantucket crowd: Frank Smith and Peter Emerson— we survived literally every possible scenario.

To my media hero, Don Imus, who is as loyal a friend as you can find. And with him come Bo Dietl, Mike Barnicle, Mike Lupica, and all those bartenders in the eighties and nineties. To the late David Brinkley and to Tom Brokaw, who were there at the very beginning to launch my career, and, of course, to my three favorite doctors: Dr. Bill Farber, Dr. J, and Dr. Jay Schapira, who somehow has kept me alive all these years.

To Andrew Morton, who taught me how and how not to write your own book. And to my agent and manager, John Ferriter, who knows how to navigate this crazy business better than anyone.

Thank you to all the sports heroes mentioned in this book who allowed me to report as well as hang out. As Michael Jordan said about all the outsiders, "you think you know all the stories, but you don't." And to the late Vitas Gerulaitis and Arthur Ashe: your passion and love are missed down here.

To Charlie Sheen and Michael J. Fox and Rob Lowe: who taught me about celebrity and how to handle it in your own way. And to Heidi Klum, for no particular reason other than to put her name on this page.

To my loyal and wonderful makeup and hair team, Joy Tilk and Ing. They had their work cut out for them and they delivered.

To all the men and women who still suffer from the disease of alcohol and drug addiction: there is a way out and you don't have to find it on your own. There's a road map that works.

To Chuck Rice, who showed me the way and saved my life. And to my sister, Kathleen, and my little brother, David, who watched and held their breaths. And to the two people I care most about, Sean and Linda.

To the late Godfather, James Brown, who gave me the material to describe many of my colleagues: "I taught them everything they know, but not everything I know."

And of course to the Beatles, who not only wrote the sound track of my life, but who all became part of the long and winding road. And on that note, to quote John Lennon after their final public appearance: "I'd like to thank you on behalf of the group and ourselves and I hope we passed the audition."

Index